UTOPIA
The Perennial Heresy

UTOPIA

The Perennial Heresy

by Thomas Molnar

UNIVERSITY
PRESS OF
AMERICA

Lanham • New York • London

The Intercollegiate
Studies Institute, Inc.

Copyright © 1990 by
University Press of America®, Inc.
4720 Boston Way
Lanham, Maryland 20706

3 Henrietta Street
London WC2E 8LU England

Copyright © 1967 by Sheed and Ward, Inc.

Co-published by arrangement with
The Intercollegiate Studies Institute

Library of Congress Cataloging-in-Publication Data

Molnar, Thomas Steven.
Utopia : the perennial heresy / by Thomas Molnar.
p.   cm.
Reprint. Originally published: New York :
Sheed and Ward, 1967.
Includes bibliographical references.
1. Utopias.   I. Title.
HX806.M56   1990   335'.02—dc20   89–29048 CIP

ISBN 0–8191–7667–2 (alk. paper)
ISBN 0–8191–7668–0 (pbk. : alk. paper)

 The paper used in this publication meets the minimum requirements of
American National Standard for Information Sciences—Permanence
of Paper for Printed Library Materials, ANSI Z39.48–1984.

To the memory of my mother; with love to my wife.

PREFACE

FROM TIME TO TIME the belief spreads among men that it is possible to construct an ideal society. Then the call is sounded for all to gather and build it—the city of God on earth. Despite its attractiveness, this is a delirious ideal stamped with the madness of logic.

The truth is that society is always unfinished, always in motion, and its key problems can never be solved by social engineering. Yet, man must conquer, again and again, the freedom to see this truth. In the intervals he succumbs to the dream of a mankind frozen and final in its planetary pride. The dream—utopia—leads to the denial of God and self-divinization—the heresy.

I wrote this book to show the reader the truth about utopia and heresy, and the link between them. I cannot hope to rid the world of the utopian temptation; this would be itself utopian. But the book may help some of my more lucid contemporaries to undo their commitment to the grotesquerie of the perfect society of imperfect men.

CONTENTS

INTRODUCTION

JEAN-PAUL SARTRE has written that, for men of his generation—those born around the beginning of the present century—the decisive events are not the two world wars, but the rise of communism and the founding of a Communist state in Russia. Sartre's estimate would indicate that such tragic and catastrophic occurrences as modern wars, despite the deep scars left on their contemporaries, count for less in our collective memories than events which embody, or seem to embody, mankind's great hopes and aspirations. Who today, excluding the professional and armchair historian, is interested in the Thirty Years' War or the Napoleonic wars? Yet the French Revolution is considered to be one of the significant dividing lines of history.

Although communism, neither as intellectual doctrine nor as world political movement, has yet exhausted its appeal and power, still it has arrived at such a point of development at this stage of the twentieth century as will enable us to survey its history and draw up its balance sheet. Whatever may have been its achievements or destructiveness, whatever evolutions and transformations may have internally occurred, clearly communism should not be viewed merely as a political, economic and revolutionary trend born

1

in reaction to *laissez-faire* capitalism and nineteenth-century liberalism. Communism, in other words, is not a phenomenon limited in time and space; while coeval with mankind and human history, it is a modern manifestation of a tendency deep in the thinking of man. Contemporary communism of the Marxist variety is revealed as purely illustrative of a mental attitude which transcends it and which has taken concrete form in many historical periods under different names and in various garbs.

It may be better to abandon the term "communism" altogether since it denotes only one aspect of the larger tendency we wish to examine. We shall, indeed, be interested in communism, but only insofar as it has common features with other movements. Our study should provide some interesting insights into our comprehension of communism as a twentieth-century reality. With the endless succession of utopian movements as background, contemporary Communist ideology may appear both as more and as less menacing than we generally believe: more menacing, because, as we shall find, it represents an invincible penchant of our reflection upon God, men, society and the world; less menacing because utopian thought and utopian projects must forever fail to overthrow history and capture man's mind.

The object of our study will be utopian thought, its roots and ramifications. At once we encounter a major difficulty: utopia and utopian thinking are not necessarily objective, scientific terms on whose meaning everybody agrees. Those whom we shall call utopian thinkers or their followers, in most cases, do not consider themselves "utopian" at all; in their own estimation, they are the only realists. A precise definition of "utopia" and "anti-utopia" is the first project in this study.

A second and decidedly related difficulty arises when we choose to examine utopianism in our own day. Because of unwelcome notes associated with the word "utopian," proponents of modern forms of utopianism will both resist and resent any such label attached to their work.

This book professedly sets out to denounce utopianism as far more than a harmless imaginative and intellectual exercise regarding political systems. In fact, we shall find that the utopian mentality is not limited to the field of political planning; it forms an autonomous category of thought. Just as philosophers have been classified as realists and idealists or as rationalists and empiricists, so shall we observe that even deeper commitments allow philosophers to be classified as utopian and non-utopian.

In the course of our investigation we shall use various terms to describe the utopian type: we shall speak of *historicists* who assign to the historical process the task of establishing the perfect and just society; of *enthusiasts* who discard the institutional part of their Church and its mediating function to place themselves directly under God's commands.[1] We shall speak, too, of *heretics* of various sorts who have, in the course of the last two thousand years, held the belief that internal light is sufficient guidance for salvation, because only the spirit is of divine origin, whereas the body and all external forms of the Church and religion are Satan's snare. Here and there, too, we shall use the term "Platonist," but in that usage which Karl Popper adopts when he speaks of efforts by Plato, Hegel and Marx to arrest change and impose a "closed society." Finally, we shall refer to the *Manicheist,* the believer in complete separation of spirit and matter, of good and evil.

The utopian tendency in man's mind is very strong and appears in almost every age. If we seem to prefer to use the term "utopian" instead of the others mentioned, it is because we wish to focus attention on the political constructs germinating in this type of mind; and the reason for this, in turn, is that political concerns have superseded the religious and metaphysical. During the Middle

[1] Cf. Ronald Knox, *Enthusiasm,* Clarendon Press, Oxford, 1950.

Ages, for example, the great issues confronting men were debated in a theological framework. While basically the issues have remained the same, our age prefers to couch its central debate in a political terminology.[2] By concentrating this study on utopianism, our efforts will not only deal with the central preoccupation of the age, but, through it, with one of the few real essentially speculative problems of all time.

Finally, mention must be made of an important built-in corrective in what we are about to undertake. While students of utopia have endeavored to distinguish among types of utopias—and generally according to the intention of the utopian writers themselves —we shall establish that the basic motivation of all utopian writers is the same. We shall emphasize, for our part, a much more useful distinction. Past utopian predictions about the airplane, the submarine or about the social-security system, among others, may no longer be called "utopian" in the twentieth century, even if they were so considered in earlier times. Fairness and caution must characterize our efforts to distinguish between what is realizable in a given utopian proposal and what is not.

Conditions and Nature of Utopian Thinking

A few remarks on the general nature of utopian thinking will help to outline our later discussion. First, in what circumstances does the utopian imagination best thrive? In generally unsettled conditions, in insecurity and suffering. However, it is not merely insecurity and suffering which have such an effect on popular imagination; the very presence of evil in the world constitutes the most general incentive for contemplating new systems from which evil would be excluded. The utopian argues that it is not enough

2 In his *Tractatus Theologico-politicus* Spinoza indicates the indissoluble relationship between theology and politics, that man builds his kingdoms in accord with his concept of God. Our thesis here is that utopia is to the political realm what heresy is to the theological.

to envisage reforms or even to initiate a series of reforms. Evil has a dramatic character, so that the more dramatically evil—scandal of creation—is exposed, the more violently will utopian passion denounce the scandal. In this connection, Norman Cohn observes about medieval chiliastic movements:

> Each case [chiliastic outburst] occurred under similar circumstances—when population was increasing, industrialization was getting under way, traditional social bonds were weakened or shattered, and the gap between rich and poor was becoming a chasm. Then . . . a collective sense of impotence and anxiety suddenly discharged itself in a frantic urge to smite the ungodly . . . and bring into being that final Kingdom where the saints, clustered around the great sheltering figure of their Messiah, were to enjoy ease and riches, security and power for all eternity.[3]

Utopian thinking is no mere exercise in wish-fulfillment; it is a constitutive element of our mental attitude, and, as such, it possesses its own structure. Because evil is present in the world as inseparable from the good and allied with it most of the time, utopian thinking is something which is reasonably to be expected as reaction. But utopian thinking is itself evil (as we shall see in the chapter on theocracy), and it leads people to commit evil. The one intolerable fact to the utopian is the scandal that evil exists in an otherwise perfect or potentially perfect world.

Why this great sensitivity about evil? Obviously the utopian is a religious man (the term "religious" is taken here in its widest sense) who believes either that something has spoiled an initially flawless situation, in which case matters ought to be rectified, or else that out of a fundamentally imperfect situation a perfect one may be

[3] Norman Cohn, *The Pursuit of the Millennium,* Harper & Bros.. New York, 1961, p. 32.

brought forth, provided the vision of perfection can be made to prevail.

Caution must be exercised regarding such words as *evil, good, perfection* and *imperfection*. What the utopian denounces is not so much evil in the moral sense, but the impudence of a world which is content to exist full of flaws and defects—an ontological condemnation rather than moral. Some utopian systems tried to explain this situation and, simultaneously, to purify it by introducing the dualistic principle: there is a good god and a good world, and a bad god and a bad world. Hans Jonas, writing about the Iranian branch of Gnostic doctrine, speaks of the King of Light who rules over a world of splendor and of light, of mildness without rebellion, of righteousness without turbulence, of eternal life without decay and death, of goodness without evil—a pure world unmixed with evil. The world opposed is the world of darkness, utterly full of evil, of devouring fire, falsehood and deceit, a world of turbulence, of darkness, of death, a world in which the good things perish and plans come to naught.[4]

Other utopian systems do not juxtapose the two worlds, good and evil, but consider them as consecutive in time. Original purity was followed by the creation of an imperfect world whose aspiration to regain its lost perfection is founded not on goodness as such, but on knowledge capable of effecting salvation.[5]

Consequently, we may describe utopian thought as a belief in an unspoiled beginning and attainable perfection. It is to be noted in study of the utopian mentality that advances from the hypothetical, or postulated, state of perfection to the state of restored perfection is always accompanied by pessimism and optimism to an exagger-

---

[4] Hans Jonas, *The Gnostic Religion* (second edition), Beacon Press, Boston, 1963, pp. 56–57.

[5] "In its unredeemed state the pneuma immersed in soul and flesh is unconscious of itself, benumbed, asleep, or intoxicated by the poison of the world: in brief, it is ignorant. Its awakening and liberation is effected through knowledge." Jonas, *op. cit.,* p. 44.

ated degree and in bewildering mixtures. Very often the pessimistic conception of the universe, as found in thoroughgoing materialism and its belief that chance so created everything that even man himself is a fortuitous aggregate of atoms, leads to an irrational optimism regarding the possibility of establishing a happy community. In such a case, pessimism and optimism do not really stand in contradiction; each has its appointed role: the utopian may be pessimistic about individual human nature, but optimistic about the ability of man's social nature, as embodied in society, to overcome the recalcitrance of the individual. To overcome individual resistance will mean force, but the utopian holds that, if the goal is goodness and perfection, then the use of force is justified. It is even justifiable to establish a special government of the elect as repositories of the doctrine of the perfect society; these elect have the supreme right to oblige every individual to shed his selfishness and to don the garments of a candidate for perfection.

Candidacy for perfection may be of indefinite duration. The very notion of government of the elect, or theocracy, implies that it is forever threatened by the forces of unregenerate evil or, at best, by its surviving vestiges. Theocracy, then, may never relent,[6] for, as long as danger exists—and the very absence of enthusiasm for theocratic rule is interpreted as danger—the repressive force may not relax. Wielders of such force must be shown proof that their subjects, candidates for perfection, live in a permanent state of enthusiasm.

Naturally, because danger to such a theocracy will always exist, the elect will insist on regular enthusiastic demonstrations of consensus. Under Communist regimes, for example, the individual may not simply retire into silence; he must enthusiastically speak, write, approve and proclaim louder than the next fellow.

[6] Cf. Part I of Karl R. Popper's *The Open Society and Its Enemies*, Harper & Bros., New York, 1962. Popper interprets Plato's ideal State as an attempt to perpetuate theocratic rule by arresting change (degeneration).

Pessimism about the individual, optimism about the collectivity, and enforced enthusiasm—these are not the only contradictions in the utopian mind. There is a remarkable contradiction to be noted between Rousseau's *Discourse on the Sciences and the Arts* and his *Discourse on Inequality*. In one work, Rousseau shows preference for a closed society in which the completely socialized individual is but a molecule of the social body; in the other work, he has unreserved praise for a state of nature in which its asocial individuals fear a society bent on their destruction. Although Michel Collinet[7] explains that Rousseau wrote both tracts in protest against the society of his time, which permitted neither freedom nor civic integration, nevertheless the same paradox characterizes all utopian thinkers: they believe in unrestrained human freedom; at the same time, they want so thoroughly to organize freedom that they turn it into slavery. Clearly, then, the utopian has certain philosophical presuppositions about the past of the human race, its nature and potentialities. He uses his assumptions toward constructing an imaginary community and world order. In other words, in speaking of the utopian mentality, we are in another world of special data systematically organized by a logic which is determined by a specified ideal.

The Need for a Radical Transformation of Man and Society

Some have maintained that these utopian constructions are a game played with rearranged elements of reality. But, as Raymond Ruyer has noted in his *L'Utopie et les Utopies,* the most obvious element in utopian literature is its social and political criticism, its dissatisfaction with society, with the political regime and with the obstacles to happiness. Further, as indicated earlier, these

[7] Cf. "L'Homme de la Nature ou la Nature de l'homme" in *Le Contrat Social,* May-June, 1962, p. 148.

utopians evidence no desire for reforms; their criticism goes much deeper than simple advocacy of change; in fact, the very foundations of the human situation are precisely what utopians would like to uproot and reconstruct. In this sense, utopian thinkers fully deserve to be called "radical" because their reconstruction of society and man demand total re-thinking about God and creation. The utopian, as thinker, is irrational and logical at the same time. Once he constructs his imaginary commonwealth (sometimes even an imaginary world with laws of physics different from ours), once he takes the big leap into another system of thought, he proceeds with strict logic, leaving nothing to chance. His human beings behave, or are made to behave, like automata; the organization of their lives never changes as they perform with clocklike precision the tasks assigned by the central authority. Precisely because he has established his own fundamental thought-system, the utopian thinker's people are no longer bound by human nature and its rich variations as we know human nature; the utopian has authorized himself to deal with his *dramatis personae* much more freely than a novelist or a playwright. His characters, their umbilical cord with mother earth and ordinary humanity severed, are puppets, quasi-zombies, lacking historical dimension, bereft of freedom and choice.

Whence do utopian thinkers derive justification to deal with human beings as if they were objects subordinated to the laws of natural science? Many of them model their society after the simplistic concept they have of physical nature and its laws. Philosophers have often shown a strange penchant for regarding the human body and the social body as mechanisms constructed in imitation of the laws of astronomical, physical or biological sciences. Some medieval thinkers believed that the political structure and hierarchy should copy the structure and hierarchy of celestial bodies and should function accordingly. In our day, many believe that the human community will grow, develop and restructure itself according to the laws of evolution which are supposed to point in the direction of increasing unity and perfection. Generally speaking, then, the utopian speaks of mankind's need to be "integrated" with the universe, that is, ruled by knowable and immutable laws. When asked why, if there is such a concordance between nature and man, history has not been "orderly" before, the utopian usually answers that inadequate enlightenment and the conspiracy of the clergy (the explanation of the Encyclopedists), the corruption of magistrates (the explanation of Rousseau), exploitative economic systems (the explanation of Marx) and the like have stood in the way.

The Enthusiast

In his desire to start from the "unspoiled beginning," the utopian feels he must clear away what has gone before, that is, everything from the customary meaning of words to traditionally accepted authority. He feels that he possesses a light not given to others, one not subject to the scrutiny of reason. "For the enthusiast," writes Msgr. Ronald Knox, "the speculative intellect is dethroned, and all impressions may pass, authorized by [his] 'light.' "[8] The utopian "enthusiast" distrusts human thought and reasoning, despises words which conform to reality and exalts that vagueness of abstractions which gives him the feeling of communion with a super-reality.

> The Platonist . . . will divorce reason from religion; it is a faculty concerned with the life of the senses, and nothing assures us that it can penetrate upwards; he is loath to theologize. . . . The God who reveals himself interiorly claims a wholly interior worship as his right. Nor will this directness of access be merely one-sided; the soul's immediate approach to God finds its counterpart in an immediate approach of God

[8] Knox, *op. cit.*, pp. 585–586.

to the soul; he issues his commands to it, reveals his truth to it, without any apparatus of hierarchies or doctrinal confessions to do his work for him. Finally, since God, not man, is his point of departure, the Platonist will have God served for himself alone, not in any degree for the sake of man's well-being. In a word, he is theocratic; he quarrels with the theologian for supposing that God can be known derivatively; he quarrels with the liturgist for offering outward worship; he quarrels with Church authorities for issuing divine commands at second hand; he quarrels with the missionary for urging men to save their souls, when nothing really matters except the divine will.[9]

The enthusiast strips God of all the attributes by which He may be known and worshiped, that is, by which a multiplicity of relationships may be established with Him. But by exalting God, the enthusiast intends to be sole interpreter of his will and his essence, and ordinary norms of thought and language are inadequate for his interpretation. The enthusiast's language does not conform to normally experienced reality since it is intended to express a super-reality. In this way the enthusiast separates himself from his fellow men and from the canons of intelligibility, and he contradicts what F. C. Copleston, S.J., writes about the scope and intention of the philosopher's language:

Ordinary language reflects the common experience of men. . . . What the philosopher does is not to invent a gratuitous theory or even to make a discovery of which the ordinary man has no inkling, but rather to express explicitly and in abstract terms a distinction which is implicitly recognized by the ordinary man in concrete instances.[10]

[9] *Ibid.,* p. 579.
[10] F. C. Copleston, *Aquinas,* Penguin Books Inc., Baltimore, Md., 1955, p. 81.

The Cyclical Concept of Time

Man has always faced the problem of the "unspoiled beginning." Birth and death have given him clear notions of beginning and end, and he has formed strong beliefs and devised meaningful ceremonies surrounding both. Too, during his lifetime man experiences the need of new beginnings in the face of such great turning points and undertakings as adolescence and marriage or when changes take place in himself. For example, man has always wanted to be rid of guilt, to "make a clean breast" of things. To do so, he has instituted ceremonies of cleansing and forgiveness. In this respect, societies are no different from individuals. History attests that in primitive societies annual ceremonies announced the cleansing of the whole community and that such celebrations were even more elaborate and awe-inspiring when they occurred only once in the nation's history, as when Romulus laid the foundations of Rome. Such events leave a deep imprint on the soul of the collectivities and to insure that succeeding generations might duly commemorate them, they were accompanied by outright cruelty, bloodshed and the sacrifice of victims. Romulus cut down his brother Remus and sacrificed a hecatomb; at year's end, the Jews charged a goat with all their sins and drove it out into the wilderness.

Mircea Eliade notes that the primitive mentality is so preoccupied with archetypes which are considered as sole reality that it believes that every accident is the result of a spell, a fault or a sin. The important things in life are so regulated that the unexpected is regarded as intervention by some evil spirit, evil eye or the envy of the neighbor, and its effects must be neutralized and abolished. C. G. Jung once saw a crocodile in an African village attack and kill one of three women who had gone to fetch water from the river. Instead of attributing this to the woman's carelessness or to chance, the natives saw in the accident the effect of a spell cast on that particular woman.

Now the "accidental," or that element which does not conform
to the archetypal, may be called in our modern frame of reference
the "historical" element, and it occurs as the result of unpredictable
interactions among men as free agents. Mircea Eliade[11] notes
further that in primitive societies "history was refused, ignored, or
abolished by the periodic repetition of the Creation and by the
periodic regeneration of time," and that the individual and collective curse, or sin, could be restored to archetypal innocence by
immersion in Being through, for example, regenerative rites in
the Spring or other purifying rites. Nor was this so only in primitive,
pagan societies, for, again according to Eliade,

> in the Messianic (Judaic) conception, history must be toler-
> ated because it has an eschatological function [in other words,
> because it leads to the end of time], but it can be tolerated
> only because it is known that, one day or another, it will
> cease. History is thus abolished, not through the conscious-
> ness of living an eternal present, nor by means of a periodi-
> cally repeated ritual—it is abolished in the future. Periodic
> regeneration of the Creation is replaced by a single regenera-
> tion that will take place in an *in illo tempore* to come. But the
> will to put a final and definitive end to history is itself an
> anti-historical attitude.[12]

At the height of the Middle Ages, writes Eliade,

> cyclical and astral theories begin to dominate historiological
> and eschatological speculation. . . . Increasingly precise cor-
> relations are attempted between the cosmic and the geographi-
> cal factors involved and the respective periodicities. . . . The
> Middle Ages are dominated by the eschatological conception

[11] *The Myth of the Eternal Return,* translated from the French by Willard
R. Trask. Bollingen Series XLVI, Pantheon Books, New York, 1954, p. 111.
[12] *Ibid.,* pp. 111–112.

(in its two essential moments: the creation and the end of
the world), complemented by the theory of cyclic modulation
that explains the periodic return of events.[13]

These examples show that, in order for "new beginnings" to be
possible, men had to postulate a cyclical theory of time which
allowed for regeneration. We shall see in another chapter how
Indian philosophy and Buddhism managed to escape from the iron
ring of endlessly succeeding existences (cycles), only to find self-
annihilation in the Nibbana. It is evident that the western utopian,
unable by his cultural conditioning to adopt the primitive view of repeated cycles and living in the Judaeo-Christian conceptual universe,
must adopt the view that one single regeneration will take place,
putting an end to history (that is, to the rule of chance and of the unpredictable) and ushering in a kind of timeless time, the last
chapter in the Book of Man when everything will be settled,
predictable, scientifically planned, and happy.[14]

The Linear Concept of Time

The foregoing, of course, clearly contradicts the concept of
time and history which Christianity introduced into Western thinking. By teaching that God assumed human nature for man's
salvation and that this was the central event of history, Christianity
shifted the emphasis from collective guilt and salvation to the
individual as a person and to his conscience through which he
enters into a unique relationship with God. The human person

13 *Ibid.,* p. 144.
14 Cf. Raymond Ruyer, *L'Utopie et les Utopies,* Presses Universitaires
de France, 1950. Ruyer quotes A. Döblin (p. 70) as holding that utopia is
anti-historical by its very essence, that it is a human project for interrupting
history, for leaping out of history to reach a state of stable perfection.
Ruyer himself notes that Hegel and Marx set a halt to their dialectical movements: Hegel saw the end of philosophy in the Prussian State; Marx saw the
end of philosophy in the Communist State after the proletarian revolution.

becomes, then, the focal point of historical events. As a free agent with responsibilities, he can no longer avoid or abolish the consequences of his actions. (It is something else that he may be forgiven.) Furthermore, while men individually may repent and so achieve salvation, the community as such cannot by that fact be wholly and permanently purged. At best, it can learn from past mistakes, but both the individual and the community will continue to carry the marks of all their deeds. In St. Augustine's views, for example, time is linear, not cyclical, and the "two cities" which provide the historical framework for man's earthly destiny run their course through all the changes of time from the beginning of the human race, and they will so move on together until the end of the world.

Western thought has made repeated attempts in the past two thousand years to discard the linear concept of time and history because, as Mircea Eliade points out, man is afraid of the concept of irreversible time which does not grant him another chance. In Gnostic doctrines, writes Prof. Hans Jonas,

the way of salvation leads through "generations" which life must endure before its lost memory is regained. To the unredeemed soul, this time perspective is a source of anguish. The terror of the vastness of cosmic spaces is matched by the terror of the times that have to be endured.[15]

Many western thinkers, from Joachim of Flore to Marx and Fr. Teilhard de Chardin, have tried to circumvent the linear concept by dividing history into phases, usually three. Each phase represents a new beginning, although they move in one direction and under one, all-embracing historical or evolutionary law. However, all such thinkers reveal their utopian bent when they assume that the last phase will be the truly decisive one and that it will mean,

[15] Jonas, *op. cit.*, p. 53.

in one way or another, a final purification of the human community and the end of history. The main characteristic of the final period is assumed to be immobility—that is, the rule of unchanging, absolute and absolutely good law. Karl Popper writes of this historical assumption that "it really looks as if historicists were trying to compensate themselves for the loss of an unchanging world by clinging to the belief that change can be foreseen because it is ruled by an unchanging law."[16]

So it is that the historicist—the utopian—manages to revive the pre-Christian ideal of an unchanging, a-historical, basically unfree world. He holds that after the rule of chance in which mankind ran wild, so to speak, and jeopardized its own existence, we have returned to the threshold of a new paradise, once more granting us freedom *from* choice. Thus, through tortuous ways, but never losing sight of the objective, the utopian succeeds in restoring, even if in modified form, the cyclical concept of history.

Unspoiled Beginning

The concept of the "unspoiled beginning" is not exhausted by insistence on the cyclical theory of time; it posits also an imaginary first ideal state of affairs, following which things degenerated; it is this original state which is to serve as a model for the inevitable restoration at the end of the cycle. The ancients, of course, as witness Ovid's *Metamorphoses*, believed that a Golden Age preceded the Silver Age, and that they themselves lived in an Iron Age. Virgil wrote in *Georgikon*: "Before Jupiter, no peasant farmed the land; it was a sacrilege to mark off the fields or divide them up; people shared everything." The Indians, the Aryan races and the Greeks, notably Hesiod, believed in a Golden Age and even tried to situate it in space. This theme became immensely popular

[16] Karl R. Popper, *The Poverty of Historicism*, Beacon Press, Boston, 1957, p. 161.

during the Middle Ages which introduced Christian elements into it. Jean de Meung, the thirteenth-century French poet, followed the ancients in telling of an egalitarian beginning. He wrote that "in the days of our first fathers and mothers, people loved one another with a delicate and honest love, and not out of covetousness and lust for gain; kindness reigned in the world." Even before Jean de Meung, Cosmas of Prague had portrayed the first settlers of Bohemia as living in an unspoiled, Communistic state. Norman Cohn tells of Cosmas' vision:

> Like the radiance of the sun or the wetness of the water, so the ploughed fields and the pastures, yea even the very marriages, were all in common. For, after the fashion of animals, they entered on matings for a single night. . . . There were no bolts to their shacks . . . because there existed neither thief nor robber nor poor man.[17]

Later, according to Cosmas, private property spoiled those idyllic farms; greed, avarice and jealousy became universal. Jean Jacques Rousseau also believed that men were born free, but that some men began to enclose the land and to proclaim the right to private property. This corruption of an unspoiled mankind had not been easy, however, and Rousseau's contemporary, the German Grimm, wrote (*Correspondance Littéraire*, Vol. V) that it took centuries to subdue the human race to the tyrannical yoke of the priests.

The "age of discoveries" suddenly gave concrete basis to the belief in the unspoiled beginning. The new lands and peoples in America and Oceania confirmed the belief that Utopia can, after all, be located, whether actually by Magellan or in fiction by Pantagruel who, in his travels, was also looking for the happy islands. Eighteenth- and nineteenth-century studies in ethnology,

[17] Cohn, *op. cit.*, p. 227.

archeology and ancient law and folklore did nothing to discourage the utopian belief in an original state of nature that was without laws, fraternal and spontaneous. The anarchist-revolutionary Peter Kropotkin held that the law is of comparatively young formation. Mankind lived for ages without any written law, and human relations were regulated by habits, by customs and usages which everyone learned from his childhood in the same way as he learned hunting, cattle-raising or agriculture.

All these writers have one common contention: because the beginnings of mankind were spotless, the present, all-important second beginning (of the second and final cycle) must also be spotless. Again the Christian element is unmistakable, although erroneously interpreted. Although modern man cannot believe in endlessly repeated cycles, he does feel authorized by Judaic and Christian doctrine to believe in two cycles: one before and one after the appearance of the Messiah. Christians believe that, given the Crucifixion (the fulfillment of the Old Testament), they now live in the second cycle (in which the New Testament will be fulfilled). Since they hold also that good and evil live side by side until Judgment Day will separate them, Christians cannot believe that they will live in an ideal and unchangeable earthly community before Judgment Day. And even Judgment Day, the end of history, will be relevant only for the individual soul—his salvation or damnation. Because the community has no such thing as a "collective soul," it cannot, as such, enter into either heaven or hell.[18]

18 Reviewing Bishop John Robinson's *Honest to God* in *Blackfriars* (July–August, 1963), Herbert McCabe, O.P., explains this point as follows: "Undoubtedly, the consequence of the incarnation is the abolition of a real distinction between sacred and secular; the religion which was central to the old law was fulfilled and transcended in Christ, but the absolute identification of the common world with the sacred must await the consummation of the kingdom to which we still look forward. The withering away of the Church which we await so impatiently is a feature of the parousia where there will be no temple in the city, 'for the Lord God Almighty and the Lamb are its temple.' For traditional thought, we are in an intermediate era in which,

It is different for the Jewish and other non-Christian utopians. Since the Jews live in the first cycle, they pin their definite hopes on the great entry into the second cycle, and this will happen when the Messiah arrives and opens the gates of the New Jerusalem, an earthly, yet spiritual community.[19] For other utopians, two roads are open, depending on whether they have religious beliefs or not. Where religious beliefs are held, the utopian expects the big leap to take place within his religion, and he expects, too, that the regeneration will strip from religion those accretions of time, tradition, and institutional forms which he considers the handiwork of men. Where religion is repudiated, the utopian will describe the big leap in the terminology of the social revolutionary (Marxist) or the scientific revolutionary. In subsequent chapters, varieties of contemporary utopianism will be examined, but, for the moment, it can be said that the big leap is represented by the proletarian revolution and, in scientific literature, by the invention of the nuclear bomb. These two events are shaping contemporary chiliastic thought.

The Utopian as Heretic

Not surprisingly, utopian literature is couched in either Christian theological language or a caricature of it, because fifteen hundred years of Christian thinking could not help but have some influence on the style and mode of expression for speculation about ultimate

---

while the new world is founded in Christ's risen body, we are not yet visibly and gloriously members of that world. The last things are not wholly to come as they were in the Old Testament, nor yet wholly realized as at the last day: hope is still an essential aspect of our divine life."

[19] It is well known that creation of the State of Israel has divided opinion on this matter. Many Jews hold that this is what was meant by the "rebuilding of Jerusalem," while others maintain that this purely secular event has nothing to do with the expected coming of the Messiah. The latter group, if they happen to be Israeli residents, even regard the new country as a kind of sacrilegious creation and refuse to obey the laws.

things.[20] More importantly, all utopian thinkers attempt, in one way or another, to modify Christian thought itself so as to justify their enterprise of psychological, social and political reconstruction. In pursuit of this, they go to the very roots of Christian doctrine and interpret this doctrine in their own way. Writes J. L. Talmon:

> The Messianic trends [of the nineteenth century] considered Christianity as arch-enemy. . . . Their own message of salvation was utterly incompatible with the true Christian doctrine, that of original sin, with its vision of history as the story of the fall, and its denial of man's power to attain salvation by his own exertions. The dichotomies of soul and body, etc. . . . stood condemned before the majesty of the oneness of life and oneness of history, and the vision of a just and harmonious society at the end of the days.[21]

Accordingly, the important utopian writers are heretics from the point of view of Christian doctrine; they want to restore man's original innocence—his knowledge and power—and, to achieve this objective, they want to abolish original sin and start with unspoiled beginnings.

Although of many varieties, heretics have all displayed characteristics which may be found among utopians as well. The

---

[20] For, roughly, the first five hundred years of Christianity, philosophical terminology was that of Greek philosophy.

[21] *Political Messianism*, Frederick A. Praeger, Publishers, New York, 1960, pp. 25–26. Dutch theologian, A. Hulsbosch, attempts to elaborate a new concept of original sin so that it may be compatible with the theory of evolution. Evolution, he holds (following the line of thought of French Jesuit Teilhard de Chardin), means that God has not yet fulfilled his own objective in creation; a new race of man ("as superior to us as we are to animals") will overcome original sin, that is, the refusal of the earlier-created man to conform to God's design. Hulsbosch, like Teilhard, detects in the present political, social and economic unification(?) of mankind a sign of moral advance, a new, perhaps last phase of evolution. Thus original sin 1) will be overcome here on earth; and 2) it will be overcome through collective, phyletic effort of all mankind.

principal common characteristic is to become like God in the knowledge of good and evil (Genesis 3:5). Thomas Aquinas (*Summa Theologica,* II-II, 163, 2) elaborates on this: "The first man sinned principally by seeking similarity with God concerning the knowledge of good and evil . . . in the sense that, by virtue of his own nature he should be able to determine for himself what is good and what is evil" and "in order that, like God who, by the light of his nature, governs over all things, man too, by the light of his nature, without the aid of external light, should be able to govern himself" (Commentaries on *Sententias,* II, XXII, 1, 2, ad. 2).

We may speak of heresy in its strict sense only in the case of utopians who admit to religious beliefs; but, in reality, all utopians follow the same pattern: the liberation of man from *heteronomy,* from the guidance and providence of a personal God, in the name of *autonomy,* of moral self-government. But since this would lead immediately to anarchy, the emancipated individual is necessarily plunged by the utopian into the collectivity which will assume his guidance and provide for him. To realize the main objective of establishing an ideal community, the collectivity attempts to usurp the prerogatives and attributes proper to God. Such a collective divinity—an idol in the scriptural sense—will then lay claim to unchangeability, to what Raymond Ruyer refers as the maniacal will to continue the system[22] guided and peopled by saints. The atheistic utopian does not mention God and heaven, except of course, as superstitious beliefs; he merely secularizes religious terminology, formulates a doctrine, devises ceremonies and recommends internal self-improvement and external conformity.

Having built his heaven (or at least the road at the end of which he promises heaven), the utopian sees no further justification for institutions, law, and the like, other than what flow from the communistic structure of the new society. Economic needs will be

[22] Ruyer, *op. cit.,* p. 276.

satisfied, and all vices arising from riches and poverty, inequality and exploitation will vanish. There will be dynamic and unquestioning obedience to the central authority which organizes not only production, distribution and consumption, but also leisure, culture and family life. However, utopian writers never speak of this central authority as a political institution, a term reserved for public bodies in unregenerated societies. In Utopia there will be no vices and no crimes—therefore, no laws. The socialist State of the Communists is not a political body, since only ruling classes need the State as a repressive arm; the State is, rather, an administrative extension of the classless society. And, of course, even that administration will wither away once the socialist *State* yields to Communist *Society*.

The religious utopian adopts the same attitude *vis-à-vis* the institutional aspects of his religion. He eliminates the Church as an intermediary between God and man, and, by the same token, most sacraments as well. What the atheistic utopian calls economically satisfied and, therefore, orderly people, the religious utopian conceives as saints. There is no need of institutions because inner virtue, directly illumined by God or liberated by the disappearance of crimes, suffices as a guarantee for an orderly, happy and saintly community. "Worldly governments," writes Msgr. Knox of the enthusiast's view, "being of purely human institution, have no real mandate to exercise authority. . . . Always the enthusiast hankers after a theocracy, in which the anomalies of the present situation will be done away, and the righteous bear rule openly."[23]

The desire for absolute purity is perhaps the utopian's main motivation. The history of heresies is really a long list of demands for purity—in body, soul, social life, political and Church organization—but it is such a purity as would so de-nature man that it would have to be enforced. The enforcement of purity would lead, in turn, both to loss of freedom for the members of the com-

23 Knox, *op. cit.*, p. 3.

munity and unlimited power and pride for the rulers—the Elect. In fact, the demand for purity often leads to abominable vices. In many medieval heresies, the "pure" felt authorized to behave immorally since their status as the Elect decontaminated them in advance of all stains which similar promiscuity would leave in the "unregenerated." The impossible demands made on ordinary people caused them to adopt hypocritical ways, obliged them to prove their virtue relentlessly and to spy on and denounce their neighbors. Utopian insistence on "purity" puts the majority of people in the category of scoundrels and finally corrupts them completely.

Millennium: Emergence of the New Man

The utopian mentality is marked, therefore, by the belief that mankind has not yet had the chance to make its own decisions and to live according to true standards of behavior. The utopian assumption is that man, potentially and ideally autonomous, has always been thwarted in the expansion of his "real" nature by a conspiracy of priests, by superstitious beliefs or by a political class. To these obstacles the religious utopian adds man's sinfulness which will be removed, however, by a dramatic new incarnation[24] or by biological-moral evolution such as Fr. Teilhard de Chardin teaches. This belief is called *millenarism*, and it usually finds expression in the fashionable terminology of the age. Millenarism manifests itself both in medieval chiliastic movements and in contemporary totalitarianism. As Norman Cohn writes, comparing medieval and modern chiliastic beliefs, "the old symbols and old slogans have disappeared, to be replaced by new ones; but the

---

[24] Cf. Cohn, *op. cit.*, p. 182. Ruusbroec makes his heretical opponent voice the highest possible claims: "It is the same with me as with Christ in every possible way. . . . All that God has given him he has given me, too, and to the same extent. . . . Christ was sent into the active life to serve me . . . whereas I am sent into the contemplative life which is far higher . . ."

structure of the basic phantasies seems to have changed scarcely at all."[25]

On St. Augustine's authority, the Council of Ephesus (431) condemned belief in millenarism as a superstitious aberration. Millenarism, whether religious or secular, invokes the necessity of a new Coming, a new World Drama, a new Passion at every turn of history much like the annual springtime purifying ceremonies in pagan religions. Instead of encouraging people to work out their salvation by resisting evil and doing good, as well as in gradually reforming the external conditions of their lives, enthusiastic millenarists look for short cuts and are ready to jump out of their natural condition at any slightest occurrence that seems unusual. The predisposition of the millenaristic mind is what Msgr. Knox called "ultra supernaturalism"—"the attempt to root up nature and plant the seed of grace in fallow soil." The ultra-supernaturalist believes, continues Msgr. Knox, that "to be born again makes you a new creature; that the seed of grace, ransomed from a drowning world, must not be confused with the unregenerate; they are a different kind of animal."[26]

To verify Norman Cohn's contention that in successive ages only the symbols and slogans change, but not the basic phantasies, the concept of millennium has been replaced by that of "revolution," whether socio-political or scientific. Although the term has changed, what has not changed is the assumption that all that has preceded the "revolution" was in some way not genuine; that mankind has been misled, that sin—exploitation, inequality and oppression—was universal, that the "revolution" will not only redress all ills, but will also create a situation from which sin will be definitively excluded. In holding that the French Revolution was the first modern event of chiliastic magnitude, the young Renan noted in his *L'Avenir de la science* that the French Revolution was

25 Cohn, *op. cit.*, p. xiv.
26 Knox, *op. cit.*, p. 584.

mankind's first attempt to take his destiny into its own hands and to govern itself, and that all that had preceded the French Revolution was the irrational period of human existence. One day, said Renan, this period in mankind's history would be considered as a baffling preface.

Marxism has, of course, been the most prodigious utopian doctrine of our times. Although it is the most thorough and systematic, its claim to be "scientific" reposes on very flimsy grounds. We shall deal with Marxism separately and shall show that its structure and tenets are no different from those of other utopian movements.

Although our contemporaries like to believe that modern man has "come of age," has "matured" for having assimilated the lessons of the past and has looked into such hitherto unimagined abysses as concentration camps, atomic destruction and global wars, we shall prove the chiliastic character of this conviction and that our age is no different from any other age either in the normal course of the events which fill it or in the declarations that it is peculiarly a "revolutionary" period. To former generations the events that would change everything were earthquakes or other natural disasters, ominous signs, like the appearance of a comet, the Second Coming of Christ, the French Revolution. In our times the portentous event is the atomic bomb which creates general insecurity and is credited with effecting a total change in mankind's destiny since it can no longer be called a "single event" but a permanent state with which we shall have to live from now on. Accordingly, voices are already heard that, living as we do "in the shadow of the bomb," our traditional moral assumptions will have to be reconsidered. Religious leaders declare that the existence of "the bomb" has so activated our awareness of science that, as Paul Tillich says, "we must forget everything traditional we have learned about God, perhaps even that word itself." Political leaders, fearful of the final cataclysm of nuclear annihilation, say that men must huddle together under a world government in the same way primitive hunting tribes gathered under the huge, jutting rocks which sheltered them from the fury of storms.

These comparisons will likely be held invalid by contemporary utopians who hold that previous dangers were only imaginary and, therefore, that earlier chiliastic moods and expectations had no foundation. To read the literature of medieval chiliastic movements, however, is to be convinced that they viewed their threats every bit as realistically as we view ours. Although their fears and hopes were permeated by religious experience, whereas ours are permeated by socio-political and scientific experience, the utopian character in both is identical.

- PART ONE -

1 - LIBERATION
FROM SIN

HE WHO MAY enter Utopia must be fundamentally different from pre-Utopian man. The latter is a being essentially dependent upon external compulsion, traditional inhibitions, circumstances of class, caste, background, education and occupation. On the other hand, the candidate for Utopia is self-determined in that he fulfills his essence by developing the potentialities which make him a human being. Since he has come into his own and coincides with himself, the candidate is not alienated; he is redeemed.

The concept of alienation is as old as Greek philosophy. It is contained in Plato's teaching of the *Idea* (Form), the copies of which are more and more imperfect in proportion to their distance from the original. Accordingly, *man* is alienated hopelessly from the *idea of man* since, in the course of subsequent changes, his degree of relative perfection decreases. When Greek philosophy in the Plotinian period became the articulator of other Mediterranean speculations—Jewish, Christian, Persian, Oriental—the Platonist *Idea* became assimilated with the Judaeo-Christian concept of God. Adherents of Plato, in consequence, became preoccupied with the degree of God's creativity and the autonomy of creatures in order to come to terms with such theological notions as creation, almightiness, the fall of the soul from grace and imperfection in the world.

Creation Is Evil

The basic problem for Plotinus and his disciples was the question raised in philosophical speculation since the time of Parmenides and so inadequately solved by Plato: How can the *One* create—that is, how can Being, which is itself immobile and indivisible, bring about movement and multiplicity without itself undergoing change? Plotinus solved this difficulty, but in a rather clumsy way: From the perfect nature of the One there flows a tendency to propagate and create; the result is a series of successive hypostases, each receiving its existence from the previous one, and each less perfect in proportion to its distance from the original starting point. The first of those hypostases is Intelligence (*Nous*), a kind of Creator in its own right since it possesses the entire creative potential of the One and originates the world below it.

If the *Nous* is an auxiliary god who does the unclean work for its master, then the One remains a non-being, in obvious contradiction to the Bible in which God says, "I am who I am," asserting thereby full existence.[1] The Judaeo-Christian concept of creation and of a creating God collided with Greek and Gnostic speculation and tried to overcome their objections and distortions. This was not easy because the various proliferating Gnostic systems went much farther than Plotinus. They taught that God was not responsible for creation, indeed that creation was a loss of the divine substance and, as such, evil. Responsible for creation was

[1] Early Christian thought was also affected by Plotinus. The consubstantiality of Father and Son received definitive formulation only at Nicæa in 325.

the Demiurgos (*artificer*), and he must be opposed and fought by men, his prisoners.[1a]

In order to free themselves, men—possessors of the divine light (*pneuma*)—must reintegrate themselves into the totality of Being by breaking out from under the despotic rule of the Demiurgos and his archons. In creation, men are alien, and even God's messenger is alien when he attempts to liberate them. Liberation is an extremely difficult enterprise, and only a few can achieve it (the pneumatics) by detaching themselves from all aspects of the created world. In the *Poimandres* of Hermes Trismegistus "the ascent is described as a series of progressive subtractions which leaves the naked true self, an instance of Primal Man as he was before his cosmic fall, free to enter the divine realm and to become one again with God."[2]

The Christian concept prevailed after heroic battles against the Gnostic doctrines, post-Hellenistic systems and heresies. But the problem of reconciling God's aloofness and providence, the contemplative and the active attitudes, the goodness of creation and the scandal of evil in creation was not solved to the entire satisfaction of Western man. True, the dichotomy between action and contemplation was abolished by Christianity which taught that man transforms the world for the glory of God and for his own contentment. *Ora et labora* was the Benedictine synthesis. Writes E. Underhill:

> Surely the real difference which marks Christianity from all other religions lies just here: in this robust acceptance of humanity in its wholeness, and of life in its completeness, as something which is susceptible of the Divine. It demands, and deals with, the whole man, his Titanic energies and warring

[1a] The title of Plotinus' treatise is *Against the Gnostics, or against those who say that the Creator of the World is evil and that the world is bad.*

[2] Hans Jonas, *The Gnostic Religion* (second edition), Beacon Press, Boston, Massachusetts, 1963, p. 166.

instincts; not, as did the antique mysteries, separating and cultivating some supposed transcendental principle in him, to the exclusion of all else.[3]

In fact, observes H. Gouhier, this characteristic feature is not proper only to Christianity, but to Christian mysticism as well, and it was this bent for action that made Bergson prefer it to Greek and Oriental mysticism wherein he saw action discredited. The primacy of contemplation in Plotinus' philosophy, says Gouhier, and the escape from life in Hindu asceticism repelled the philosopher of *élan vital*, particularly after he had met the great Christian mystics in whom action abounded.

Sin, the Work of an Evil Demiurgos

Yet, in the Middle Ages, the problem of alienation assumed a new form. Living in the climate of Christianity, medieval man was not concerned with the contradictions of action and contemplation. In his eyes the great scandal in the world was the existence of sin: the breaking of God's commandment, a deviation from the nature of man and alienation from the spiritual order for which man had to strive. The alienated man was now the sinner. The indignation over sin was, of course, exacerbated by the abuse of churchmen whose mode of living in a society permeated by religion became the more irritating as the gap between word and deed grew wider. Usury and lechery, violence and pride were monstrous scandals when committed by monks, clerics and ecclesiastical lords. Medieval utopian exhortations, therefore, have substance when they point to the absolute moral purity of the Perfect Society and to the necessary purification of its future dwellers.

Indeed, the Perfect Society was conceived not so much as

[3] E. Underhill, *The Essentials of Mysticism*, E. P. Dutton & Company, New York, 1960, p. 101. As far as both Platonists and Jews were concerned, God was hidden. To Platonists, God is an abstraction; to Jews, His very name may not be pronounced. Only for Christians is God revealed through Christ who assumed the human condition.

the antithesis of an imperfect civil society as of the Church. Just as radical critics of the Church, long before Luther, referred to Rome as "Babylon" and to the pope as "Antichrist," so the Perfect Society was defined as the true Church, with sinlessness as the condition of membership. To bring about adherence to their understanding of sinlessness, critics had to explain why the Church was far from a state of perfection and they had to devise new means for liberating man from the shackles of sin. For all intents and purposes, a new Church was the real objective of the critics since the existing Church was found wanting on so many counts.

At this point we are not yet interested in the utopian-heretical attacks against the Church as an institution, attacks which prefigure those against secular institutions. We are interested rather in the roots of man's sinning nature as viewed by the medieval heretics, although here we can but summarize their most important tenets.

Most of these movements, influenced by some revived version of neo-Platonism and Gnosticism, held that the world was created by a fallen demon and that, consequently, matter was evil. It was necessary, then, to disengage Christ and the soul from the material prison of the body.[4] Because Christ was not supposed to have had a body—which means that the Incarnation itself was denied—the soul's aspiration should be a gradual liberation from its physical bondage. The influence of Gnosticism was evident in the complete separation of the spiritual from the material realm: the Demiurgos became, in the heretical Christian imagination, the fallen angel, leaving to God the creation of the invisible world.

The Church of the Pure: Invisible and Spiritual

Accordingly, heretical movements strove to establish the "invisible Church" directly under God who rules over the society of

---

[4] According to Gnostic systems, the soul descends into the material world, then returns to the totality of the spirit.

the elect. As a community, the elect symbolically represented the soul, whereas sinners remained attached to the body, that is, to matter. In this light, it is understandable why the elect were so adamant against the baptism of children: only the elect, they felt, had given proof of purity and were alone worthy of admission among true Christians. Similarly, they denied to sinning priests the right to absolve or to bless because, if the world is again divided between the elect and the sinners, contact with the sinners would contaminate the elect.

The conflict between contemplation and action reappeared in all its acuity when, under the impact of modern atheism, attention was shifted from theological inquiry about God to anthropological inquiry about man. From Machiavelli to Feuerbach the assumption was increasingly articulated that God was merely a projection of man's aspirations—more precisely, that man was his own God. The question then became: If man is to come into his own and assume the characteristics of a creator, will he still remain a contemplative (religious) being, or will contemplation (religion) be absorbed in action? In other words, is the autonomous man *all* action or *all* contemplation? Is man to remain a philosopher who speculates about the world or a pure agent who transforms the world?

Hegelian Man Alienated by Nature

Utopian thinkers, on emerging from the philosophical turmoil of the French Revolution, formulated the concept of alienation in still another fashion: to them the pure, the elect, were those who had overcome alienation and had solved the contradiction and the scandal of the human situation. Hegel's system regards man as condemned to externalize himself, to cease being pure consciousness. Every interpersonal relationship, every relationship with the State, every economic relationship and every relationship with God and religion is a *reification* (objectivization) of man's subjective essence. Hegel must teach this since he made freedom something completely unattainable. In his *Logic*, Hegel writes that, to be free, one must be aware of no being other than himself. Since, postulates Hegel, finitude is bondage, the consciousness of something other than self argues to limitation, therefore to bondage. Freedom is that voyage into the open where nothing is below us or above us, and we stand in solitude with ourselves alone. Therefore, the entire Hegelian philosophy is an effort to overcome the alienation of consciousness; Hegel wanted to show that man *qua* consciousness alienates his self in the object-world, in the God of religion and in the State as an embodiment of objective will.[5] The German philosopher concluded that alienation could be vanquished only by what he considered to be "world-historical heroes." The Spirit (*Geist*), said Hegel, creates the conditions of alienation when it objectifies its relationships and reinforces its own antithesis, nature. On this point Marx refuted Hegel by claiming to have reconciled man and nature, the subjective and the objective principle, in one definitive, historical synthesis. It was the triumphal boast of Marx that communism had resolved the mystery of history.

Several critics of Marx have held that only the young Marx was concerned about the whole notion of alienation, and that was during the time when he was seeking to come to terms with Hegelian philosophy. Sidney Hook writes that, by the time Marx authored the *Communist Manifesto,* he had abandoned the concept of alienation. In fact, Marx later took the position in *Das Kapital* that "self-alienation" was the consequence of "the fetishism of commodities" and of "forces generated in a commodity-producing society."[6] Kostas Papaioannou reinforces Hook's estimate when he states that the "nihilistic implications" of young Marx's specula-

[5] Cf. Jean Hyppolite, *Etudes sur Marx et Hegel,* Librairie Marcel Rivière, Paris, 1955, p. 114.

[6] Cf. Introduction to the second edition of Sidney Hook, *From Hegel to Marx,* Humanities Press Inc., New York, 1950.

tions disappeared about 1847 and that he later defined "alienation" prosaically in *Das Kapital* as the gradimeter of the workers'
progress.[7]

Marxian Man Alienated from Nature

These are factual statements about certain modifications of
Marx's thought. But Sidney Hook further argues that the very
concept of alienation is incompatible with Marx's thought since the
latter did not believe in an unchangeable human nature from which
a man could be alienated. Regardless, it must still be held that the
entire thrust of the Marxian system is in the direction of utopia,
its pre-conditions and the delightful state afterwards. True, Marx
did not believe that there was a human nature *prior to* the establishment of a Communist society, but he most certainly did hold that,
after all the obstacles have been overcome, man will live in harmony
with nature—which nature is, in reality, his own nature. True, too,
Marx (*Misère de la philosophie*) held the entirety of history to be
the continuous transformation of human nature, and that human
nature, in turn, is the totality of transitory, ever-changing social
rapports. Still, Marx did envision at the end of the Communist
movement the classless society whose permanent social relationships would permit the restoration of original goodness and equality. Marx, therefore, did regard alienation as alienation from nature
with which we ought to be one, just as he held that the sum total
and essence of our knowledge was to be a kind of general anthropology, not an isolated subject with its own set of propositions,
but known by the mere fact that nature, transformed by man and
for his purposes, will not lie to him.

The utopian mind does not have to postulate human nature in
order to state the fact of alienation. Various evolutionists maintain,

[7] Cf. "La Fondation du Marxisme" in *Le Contrat Social,* January–February, 1962, p. 52.

for example, that God or mankind in their fullness do not exist yet, but that they will emerge at the end of a biological and/or historical process. Present forms, in this understanding, are imperfect in relation to the anticipated perfect type; they are incomplete or alienated in relation to the desirable. Furthermore, the notion of alienation does not always imply a past or an existing essence in relation to which a given form is considered alienated; the idea of alienation may imply merely the potential or future existence of a desirable essence.

Even though Marx, in his later years, heaped scorn and ridicule on the French socialists, Feuerbach, Moses Hess and on Hegel himself—that is, on those whom he then considered utopians and spiritualists—the system which bears his name simply cannot be described as an exclusively socio-economic analysis. For one thing, there is one continuous historical line which stretches from the early Marx of the 1844 manuscripts through Lenin, Trotsky and Bukharin right up to the current so-called Revisionists. For another thing, if Marxism had been nothing but an economic doctrine with a built-in sociological analysis, events of the past two or three generations would have made us forget the entire construction. That Marxism is far more than a socio-economic system is shown by its extraordinary spread to all continents and by the great variety of people, educated and uneducated, who have gathered under its banner. Most of the educated faithful have not been economists but philosophers, historians, social prophets and practical politicians.

When George Lukacs and others discovered the Marxian texts of 1844, a new impetus was given to Hegelian studies as well as a new, though more enigmatic, stature to Marx. In Hegel's view, reification was the tragedy of consciousness. The young Marx disagreed violently with this view and asserted that work—in the Heglian system a self-alienating activity!—was not an activity of man as a subject, but an action of nature manifesting itself through man. In fact, Marxist man is not a subject at all, but the *locus* of objective natural forces. In his *Nationalökonomie und Philosophie,* Marx contended that man creates objects because the objects create him, because, according to his origin, he himself is nature. In another connection, Marx noted that if industry is understood as the esoteric revelation of man's essential forces, then one must also understand man's natural essence and the human essence of nature.

Marx Reconciles Man and Nature

The young Marx, therefore, regarded man and nature as consubstantial. K. Papaioannou makes the point that, in the Marxian view, the natural object-world which industry creates is no longer a hostile and strange world; he goes on to say that nature created by industry is an anthropological (we would say "humanized") nature. Writing in the French magazine *Le Contrat Social* (November–December, 1961), Papaioannou contends that for Marx it is in this artificial world of raw materials and machines that we must recognize the most intimate nature of our being, for the technical reconstruction of the world assumes, with Marx, the meaning of a new creation where natural determinism and human finalities merge in a new unity. If nature is the object and man the subject, then the world of history created by industry—and by industry alone—is a subject-object, that is, reconciliation.

Now it is evident that work and the object-world it creates—"the technical reconstruction of the world by industry"—express man's essence and oneness with nature only if the worker labors for his own betterment. If the opposite is the case, says Marx, then the more the worker exerts himself, the more powerful becomes the alien objective world to whose creation he contributes; the poorer he and his inner world, the less he belongs to himself. In view of man's essential unity with nature, in the present capitalistic system labor and its product are alien to the worker; he himself is alienated. Therefore, work which normally should be man's function *par ex-*

cellence, replacing what the philosophers of the past meant by man's "substance" or "essence," has been traditionally considered as merely a useful activity external to man. And this was so because the philosophers were moving inside an alienated system, a perverted and absurd world where man exists in absolute opposition to his essence. Capitalist alienation has condemned man to an existence contrary to his essence and has obliged him to make of his essence (work) a means to secure his existence.[8] The result is absurd and humiliating: productive work which ought to be its own *raison d'être* has become a means of survival; and man finds himself in the paradoxical situation of feeling at home outside his work and feeling a stranger while working.

The Worker as the Natural Man

We begin now to grasp Marx's fundamental idea that man is alienated because the world is upside down. Speaking on the general subject of religion, Marx held that if man draws all knowledge and all sensation from the world of the senses and the experiences it provides, then what is really important is to organize the empirical world in such a way that man must acquire the habit of what is truly human. If man, he said, is shaped by circumstances, then circumstances must be created which are in harmony with his humanity. Accordingly, Marx attacked religion as the characteristic symptom of the upside-down world. The basis of anti-religious criticism, Marx felt, is the fact that man invents religion. The State and society create religion—that is, an inverted consciousness of the world—because the State and society themselves constitute an inverted world. Religion, then, is the phantasmagoric creation of the human being who does not possess the true reality. To combat religion, said Marx, is to combat indirectly the world

[8] Cf. *Nationalökonomie und Philosophie,* Kiepenheuer, Cologne, 1950, p. 146.

for which religion is a spiritual aroma. To demand that people give up their illusions about their situation is to demand of them that they turn their backs on a situation which needs illusions to make it bearable.

To put mankind back on its own feet would require that man become aware of being his own creator through work. He must first put an end to economic alienation, and this will lead to his liberation from religious alienation. Alienation, according to the French Marxist Henri Lefèbvre, has come about because, through a historically unavoidable perversion, the world is appropriated as ownership.[9] When society, observes Engels in *Anti-Dühring,* will take possession of and plan the totality of the means of production, thus delivering itself from servitude, then the last external power that religion reflects will have disappeared. Religion itself will then disappear because there will be nothing more for it to reflect.

Through the Revolution, as through one great thrust, the alienated man—the worker—will reappropriate the whole alienated world of private property. With that supreme act, not only the State, history and philosophy, but even evil itself will be abolished— evil which, according to Engels, is the form under which the motor force of history manifests itself. The new socialist man will be pure and will possess all virtue. In describing the post-revolutionary world, Marxist authors employ practically the same expressions which previous utopian writers used to picture the Perfect Society whence will vanish all collective ills, and where the individual will be joyous, healthy, honest and serene. Raymond Ruyer notes that in utopia the ideal man's domination over nature will be so complete that even weeds, harmful insects and poisonous plants will be things of the past. The perfection of the material world is not enough for Marx who sees the new man's relationship to nature as that of an artist to his material. As Prof. Tucker writes:

[9] Cf. *La Somme et le reste,* La Nef de Paris, Paris, France, 1959, p. 524.

Man will realize his natural tendency to arrange things "according to the laws of society." Economic activity will turn into artistic activity, with industry as the supreme avenue of creation, and the planet itself will become the new man's work of art. The alienated world will give way to the aesthetic world."[10]

Socialist Man Is Sinless

Going even further, Marx (in an early text quoted by K. Papaioannou) exclaims with Prometheus, "I have nothing but hatred for all the gods." Marx continues his defiance in proclaiming that he will confront all the gods of heaven and earth who do not recognize human consciousness as the supreme divinity.[11] This is not simply the cry of an immature enthusiast. Strictly speaking, "alienation" may be a meaningless term, as Sidney Hook says, when no essence is postulated as a standard from which man can alienate himself; but such a standard nevertheless exists. For the religious utopian it is the true believer and sinless creature; for the atheistic utopian—obsessed, in one way or other, by a divine being—it is God himself in whom he sees the norm of perfection. And though he does not believe in the actuality of such a norm, he does believe that somehow it exists, at least potentially, and that it can concretize itself in human beings. Thus we are confronted with this strange paradox: the Marxist utopian denies the existence of God, but he holds that man may become divine or may develop a combination of purity and power that will transcend any human form and accomplishment ever witnessed in the past. We are entitled to say, then, that the Marxist utopia, or Communist society, is supposed to be peopled by quasi-divine beings, which is the sup-

[10] Robert Tucker, *Philosophy and Myth in Karl Marx,* Cambridge University Press, 1961, p. 158.
[11] Cf. "L'Idéologie froide" in *Le Contrat Social,* July–August, 1961, p. 199.

position of all utopian systems. Nor is Marx particularly original in contending that this quasi-heavenly existence is constructed over firm material foundations. If this is what provides scientific mooring to the Marxist conception of Communist society, then it is not alone among utopian systems in possessing such qualifications. Almost all utopias consider excessive physical work as a sign of man's lack of power and, therefore, a defect of technical ability rather than a divine curse. Most utopian systems introduce science as a remedy for the ills of society, automatize most functions and turn society into a technological paradise as egalitarian as that of Marx.

True, Marx considered his socialism to be scientific because it revealed the mechanism of class struggle and the relationship between systems of production and economic crises. So completely, however, did Marx believe that he had solved the "riddle of history" that his claim to scientific analysis vanishes by the supreme claim that science renders superfluous everything else—religion, law and State—and that it brings man's untarnished happiness on the scene. In fact, Marx uses the concept of science in the same way as earlier utopians used the concept of purity and sinlessness; he and Engels are unable to repress their enthusiasm when speaking of the unlimited perspectives which science opens up, whether in the domain of pure research (for example, chemistry will find the formula of life) or of technology. The utopian element in these predictions is not so much the anticipated accomplishments of science as the unconditional belief that the human situation will become "scientific" and, therefore, one without problems. In the language of Marxism, "science" means not only the activity produced in laboratories; science is also man's reconquest of his essential unity with nature. When man conquers nature, he acquires the decisive victory over himself; he possesses himself. And through industry this possession is an active one, so that the new divinity never ceases to create.

2 - SECULARIZED RELIGION: PANTHEISM

NO MATTER HOW the utopian defines sin and sinlessness or alienation and integration, the essential element in his definition is the
definitive and collective evolving from the first to the second. In
urging the distinction between perfection so achieved and everyday
efforts to pursue values and virtues, Aurel Kolnai (in *La Table
Ronde*) rightly perceives that an exaggerated thirst for values and
a similarly exaggerated contempt for reality do not characterize
the utopian. Rather, the utopian mentality is fascinated by that
reality which consists of values, including the value of their complete realization. In other words, the utopian is convinced that,
once we acknowledge the desirability of an ideal state of affairs,
we must immediately proceed to bring it about; any hesitation or
reckoning with obstacles is an unforgivable scandal in his eyes.
Once opportunity for perfection is given, it must be seized immediately and resolutely; therefore, the non-perfect deserve the most
severe punishment and must be pointedly set aside from the elect.

43

That anonymous medieval religious agitator, the "Revolutionary," once declared that the Emperor will issue an annual decree for the purpose of unmasking sin. Unquestionably, one aspect of medieval "perfectionism" did develop as a repudiation of the alleged loose living of clergy and hierarchy. Emperors and kings had indiscriminately placed their favorites in bishoprics and other ecclesiastical posts, with the result that feudal-age *mores* penetrated the higher ecclesiastical ranks. From the time of the foundation of Cluny, however, and especially after the reforms of Gregory VII, there had been a vigorous movement toward renovation within the Church—a fact which the leaders of heretical sects consistently failed to appreciate. A second fact that must not escape notice is that sectarian fanatics had gone beyond simple advocacy of reforms and had attacked both institutions and the social framework, as such, on the grounds that they originated in the material and corrupt side of creation. In consequence, they sought to oppose to them pure morality and pure spirit which sustain themselves by their mere spiritual superiority.

Separation of Sinners and Sinless

It was natural for religious fanatics to turn to the laity and to set their "purity" in opposition to the depravity of churchmen. The propaganda of these sects consisted, as Georges de Lagarde notes, in a spectacular display of the ascetical lives of their leaders, the so-called perfect ones who believed that they had been called to fulfill the moral law before the eyes of the faithful.[1] Invariably, these sects drew inspiration and belief from some form of Manicheism and had already determined who were evil and who were good. Such a determination meant, in turn, that these sects must set about to abolish institutions, particularly all religious institutions. The so-called Lombard sects, with which the Waldensians

---

[1] *La Naissance de l'esprit laique*, Ed. Nauwelaerts, Louvain, 1956, I, p. 85.

merged at the beginning of the thirteenth century, rejected not only the Catholic hierarchy, but all forms of the priesthood as well. They elevated those laymen whose mode of life was judged dignified and entrusted them with the sacraments. The real priest, they declared, is the morally perfect man.

Msgr. Knox remarks of the Puritans—whether those in Geneva, Edinburgh, or America—that they meted out punishment to sinners on the understanding that these enemies of God, "being unsaved, had lost the common rights of humanity."[2]

This absolute separation of the sinner from the sinless, together with the urgency attached to the process, is to be expected from the utopian. "If only everybody would bear witness," wrote Tolstoy,[3] "to the truth that he knows, or at least not defend as truth the untruth in which he lives, then in this very year [1893] there would take place changes toward the setting up of truth on earth." Urgency is now coupled with exclusivity: perfection, toward which all human efforts are directed, is man's only worthy objective. The great, true goal of history, as Michael Bakunin sees it, the only justifiable goal is our humanization and deliverance—the genuine liberty and prosperity of all men in society.[4]

Self-divinization of the Pure

It would be a mistake to imagine that perfection, or sinlessness, thus conceived is a slow and painful rise in the direction of such a norm as that expressed by Christ—"Be ye perfect as your heavenly Father is perfect"—a noble aspiration and recognized as impossible of earthly accomplishment. On the other hand, utopian perfectionism believes in what is actually a conscious and concentrated form of *self-divinization*.

Louis Salleron has pointed out that, while one term in the

[2] *Enthusiasm*, Clarendon Press, Oxford, 1950, p. 133.
[3] As quoted by Paul Elzbacher in *Anarchism*, Libertarian Book Club, New York, 1960.
[4] *Dieu et l'Etat*, Geneva, 1882, p. 65.

utopian's religious imagination remains fixed—God—the process of becoming perfect consists of continuing progress by man toward the same level.[5] In fact, mankind and nature ascend the path of progress together until the cosmos will be indistinguishable from God.

As noted in the Introduction, Fr. Herbert McCabe, O.P., has pointed out correctly that, even for the Christian, our common world is not yet identifiable with the coming sacred world. Virtue still requires effort because it is not yet man's ordinary condition. Yet, the utopian believes that it is enough simply to demand that the world become virtuous, since our original moral purity has never really been sullied (as the doctrine of original sin teaches) so much as only obscured and rendered more difficult by unfavorable circumstances. For the utopian, then, it is intolerable that moral perfection, which lies just beneath the surface, so to speak, has not yet been uncovered and allowed to shine as an ineffably splendid piece of gold retrieved from the mud.

Since the utopian has no reason to believe that it is man's own fallen nature which is the real obstacle to human goodness and perfection, he assumes that perfection is easy. Nor is it surprising that he attaches his hopes for mankind's regeneration to sufficiently impressive and spectacular events or to techniques which strike the imagination and affect the external aspects of our existence.

The impact of modern science, for example, leads the utopian to believe that the path to perfection has become considerably shorter and the objective more clearly visible. With an almost disarmingly naïve faith, he assumes that communications techniques and ease in travel forge a new mankind, a global melting pot to which each man brings his own unique contribution and receives the imprint of the communal consciousness. More than a hundred years ago, the early stirrings of democratic liberalism prompted the same illusion: on the threshold of the 1848 revolution, Georges

[5] *Les Catholiques et le capitalisme,* La Palatine, Paris, 1959, p. 15.

Sand, friend and patroness of the French utopian socialists, greeted the dawn of a "unanimous mankind" whose artisans and members would be "nobler than the sages of Greece." Today, science and technology have taken the place of ideologies, and the new enthusiasts greet an age when cooperation will be prompted by a mixture of good will and material necessity. The Jesuit priest Teilhard de Chardin imagined that, following the model of cooperating teams of scientists, all men would gradually become one in aspiration and method and rise together toward the last phase, the emerging "super-mankind." Such prominent Protestant theologians as Dietrich Bonhoeffer, Paul Tillich and Bishop John Robinson, similarly impressed with the stupendous achievements of modern technology, conclude that mankind has come of age and must now shed its "traditional religiosity," perhaps even the very term, *God.* These theologians hold that adult man has no need of what biologist Julian Huxley has called "the umbrella of faith" under which God, like a *paterfamilias,* assumed ultimate responsibility; rather, adult man nears perfection precisely by loosening his ties with the concepts and images of traditional belief and by developing an autonomous "morality of love" conceived as the "ground of his being."

Perfection through Science

Throughout the pages of Bishop Robinson's little best-seller, *Honest to God,* is his unconcealed admiration for modern science, not, however, as a cure-all, as it was regarded in the eighteenth and nineteenth centuries, but as an aid to purify us of our moral imperfections and to force us to face the impossibility of a "God above and/or outside." In light of the technological revolution in general, Bishop Robinson seems better able to suggest that we re-examine all our previous judgments and attitudes about good and evil and that we pronounce no final judgment until we have measured our acts against the only valid standard: the amount of love in our action. However, the good bishop fails to explain how this amount is to be measured. And why should he? Presumably we are all "adult men," able to judge our own actions according to our own lights. If he continues to mention "love" as a standard of religiosity, it is probably because this term, taken out of its theological wrappings, can be easily secularized, that is, identified with social actions on which all may agree, regardless of religious or irreligious commitments.

Perfectionism in our time is not essentially different from that of other ages. Invariably, some new invention, discovery or event— the expectation of the millennium, socio-political revolution, or new technological advances—offers the utopian his pretext for announcing the need of a new and final set of moral values worthier of a purified, sinless, mature, autonomous, perfected mankind than any previous set of moral imperatives. As Pope Pius XII viewed it, modern technology seems to communicate to man, kneeling at its altar, a feeling of self-sufficiency and satisfaction in his insatiable desire for knowledge and power. Through its many uses, the absolute trust it prompts and the possibilities it promises, modern technology spreads before contemporary man such a vast vision that its beholders may easily confuse technology with the infinite.

The real issue, then, is not one of opposition between exaltation of and contempt for technology. The issue is whether the laws of morality are likely to undergo and, in fact, ought to undergo fundamental changes because of technological progress or some startling development. For example, why should a strikingly new means of communication require us to adopt a different attitude toward our fellow human beings? The currently standard answer to this question is that a more perfect system of communications leads to a multiplicity of contacts; these contacts lead, in turn, to a better knowledge of others; this better knowledge, in turn, leads to mutually friendlier attitudes. With the same likelihood it could be argued that a mere quantitative increase of contacts yields opportunities for antipathy as well as for sympathy, for injury as well as for charity; in other words, the perfecting of communications media may have merely intensified feelings for better as well as for worse, without even considering the question of qualitative improvement.

Another argument advanced is that technological advances in communications assures more knowledge and better information. Again, however, knowledge and information do not necessarily prompt good action: while it is true, for example, that the modern stock market developed because information was more quickly received about the conditions in distant points of the globe, this meant only that speculators could sometimes take advantage of even a few minutes' advance information. In the same way, the Rothschilds of London increased their fortune and prestige because news of Wellington's victory at Waterloo had reached them before it reached their competitors. It is also undeniable that the very rapidity of today's communication leads to misunderstanding and confusion, since those in charge of the communication centers of operation (news agencies, journalists, government spokesmen) often launch false information or are tempted to exploit their position at the sources of information.

Instant Utopia

If the utopian seizes upon fashionable ideologies, scientific inventions and technical improvements to shorten the way toward the desired perfect state, it is because he holds all intermediary situations in contempt. He does not proceed, like the usual reformer, in piecemeal fashion because he lacks the patience to adjust concrete realities to new requirements. He is intent on abolishing every part of an existing situation because only in this way can he prevent the radically new from being contaminated by the necessarily old. The utopian is, therefore, the great demolisher of institutions in which he sees congealed forms of vested and pernicious interests which stifle the fresh sources of spontaneity. He particularly attacks those institutions which seem to block man's higher aspirations, because he believes that the dynamism of these aspirations suffices to create the atmosphere in which morality and goodness may become as natural as breathing.

Charles Maurras warned against the folly of those purely moral philosophies which try to bypass institutional mediation and to bring about at once the desired result of ethically perfect creatures.[6] The objective of purely moral philosophies is, he warned, to eliminate the web of relationships by which the individual is aided in his understanding of and positive attitude toward the fundamental problems of his being. Granted, he continued, these philosophies may correctly assume that the foundations of the moral problem are rooted in the individual conscience; granted, too, that they strive, in consequence, to secure a more intimate tie with the source of our being, unassailable by the hazards and vicissitudes of ordinary existence; at the same time, these purely moral philosophies so strongly insist on the sufficiency and exclusiveness of the individual's relationship to God that they put an unbearable strain on it.

God Exalted and Dismissed

In his attempt to eliminate everything "artificial" and to remain honest to the point of moral nakedness, the religious utopian relies entirely on God. This is, of course, an adequate support. In our human weakness, however, we need around us the example and inspiration of our fellow men on every human level. Not so the religious utopian: "the enthusiast . . . expects more evident results from the grace of God than we others. . . . He has before his eyes

[6] Cf. Henri Massis, *De l'Homme à Dieu*, Nouvelles Editions Latines, Paris, 1959, p. 101.

a picture of the early Church, visibly penetrated with supernatural influences; and nothing less will serve him for a model."[7]

In our own time, too, the religious utopian desires to strip the relationship between God and man of its religious dimension. Today, like in times past, he stresses faith at the expense of reason and opposes austerity to the aesthetic dimension. The pretext today is that modern man "has come of age": technological inventions are modifying the structure of his thinking and behavior; science answers most of his questions which were hitherto shrouded in a God-protected mystery. To save both God and the believer from future embarrassment, the religious utopian would like to limit their relationship to a purely moral one because—who knows?—science may tomorrow be able to answer *all* our questions, thus further restricting God's "religious" domain. It may be a significant coincidence, for example, that the Soviet astronaut Titov declared he had found no God in space at about the same time as Bishop Robinson published the view that modern man dismissed the concept of "God above" as childish. Several critics of Robinson pointed out that most people—and certainly theologians, churchmen, and the intelligent laity—never had thought that "God is above" in a spatial sense. But that, of course, is not the issue. Robinson and his fellow theologians have posited such an ineffable, irrational, and abstract concept of God that the religious believer, if he wants to follow them, must feel compelled to give up religion altogether and suffer even his belief in God to be shaken considerably.

German theologian Dietrich Bonhoeffer put the thesis in its boldest form. Modern man, he argues, has been increasingly capable of solving all those problems (technical, political, economic, and the like) in which he once asked God's help. Accordingly, God "is being more and more edged out of life, losing more and more

[7] Knox, *op. cit.*, p. 2.

ground."[8] What will happen, asks Bonhoeffer, when even the so-called ultimate questions—death, guilt—will have been answered without recourse to divine explanation? We must prepare for that day, Bonhoeffer urges, by recasting God in his new role and, indeed, with his authorization, for in this twentieth century God is decidedly calling us to a form of Christianity which is independent of religion's premises. As Bultmann would have it, Christianity must be de-mythologized and the entire conception of a supernatural order which invades and permeates this order must be abandoned.

Dissolution of Christianity

What role, then, will remain for God and the entire Christian religion? The question implies that religion does not constitute a total and permanently valid approach to man's problems and is only partially and conditionally relevant to human existence. It implies also that this relevance is shrinking. "To be a Christian," Bonhoeffer continues, "does not mean to be religious in a particular way, to cultivate some particular form of asceticism, but to be a man. It is not some religious act which makes a Christian what he is, but participation in the suffering of God, in the life of the world."[9]

If we now add to Bonhoeffer's statement one by Paul Tillich, we may conclude that the doctrine of this new school is apt to create the greatest confusion. "There is no religion," writes Tillich, "as a special spiritual sphere. Everything is secular and every secular thing is potentially religious. The relation to the unconditional permeates every moment of the daily life and makes it holy. The

---

[8] As quoted by Bishop John Robinson in his *Honest to God*, SCM Press, London, 1963, p. 24.

[9] *Ibid.*, p. 83. And, in this connection, Teilhard de Chardin remarked that if he lost faith, successively, in Christ, in a personal God and in the Spirit, he could still continue to believe in the world.

'holy' is not one value beside others [but it appears] in all values [and] being."[10]

It is no wonder that the average Christian loses his bearing when he is told by Bonhoeffer and Tillich that Christianity is both everything and nothing, that it is not religion, but life—everyday life; yet it is participation in the suffering of God. The very people who most profess to be worried about the de-christianization of modern man are those who push him farther away from religion. And there is no little irony in Bishop Robinson's warning that "If Christianity is to survive, let alone to recapture secular man, there is no time to lose in detaching it from [its traditional] scheme of thought, from this particular theology or *logos* about *theos*, and thinking hard about what we should put in its place."[11]

In 1960, prior to Bishop Robinson's *Honest to God*, another Protestant theologian Prof. Hans Hoekendijk said in a speech at Strasbourg:

> We will not be able really to get alongside man in our modern world unless we begin to "dereligionize" Christianity. Christianity is a secular movement, and this is basic for an understanding of it. We have no business to make it a religion again. That would mean a correction of what Christ has done. And we have no business to make a Christian into a *homo religiosus* again, a religious man, a normal human being plus something. The Christian is simply a man who is in the process of being restored to normal manhood.[12]

These theologians are convinced that the most urgent task is to abolish religion or, rather, to dissolve it in "everyday life." If we re-read the above statements by Robinson, Tillich, Bonhoeffer and

---

[10] *The Protestant Era*, University of Chicago Press, 1948, p. 175.
[11] Robinson, *op. cit.*, p. 43.
[12] Quoted in Edwards-Robinson, *The "Honest to God" Debate*, SCM Press, London, 1963, pp. 272 ff.

Bultmann, we must conclude that the following are synonymous with religion: childish concept of God; non-scientific answers and solutions; mythology; the supernatural order; traditional theology; an abnormal concept of man. Such ideas should be removed from religion as religion is conceived by such as Robinson, Bonhoeffer, Tillich and Bultmann because these ideas represent that "plus" which, in Prof. Hoekendijk's derisive remark, is unnecessarily added to the definition of the religious man and of the Christian. By similar logic one might say that a healthy individual is one who lacks arms and legs, or that a thinking man is one without a brain. Notes omitted from the definition of the normal human being are not a plus"; they are inseparable from man's essence and, conversely, man is incomplete—that is, no-man—without them. Prof. Hoekendijk's statement would have been acceptable perhaps by the ultra-materialists of the eighteenth and nineteenth centuries— and certainly by the Marxists—but man's religious dimension has been confirmed by ethnology, depth-psychology, art, and any number of other disciplines, each in its own way.

When such theologians as Bonhoeffer and Tillich eliminate the traditional and traditionally rich concept of religion, it is done, they say or imply, for the greater glory of God. Not only man, but also God must be purified to satisfy the utopian. They regard religion as a complexus of ceremonies, precepts for singular living, sacraments and institutions which sully man and God alike: religion detracts from man's purity of intentions and renders God more remote by emphasizing attention to intervening distractions. However, utopian efforts to simplify matters succeed not in bringing God and man closer together so much as in alienating man from God. In his weakness, man needs crutches—crutches by which he walks toward his God. Thus we pay the heavy price of sacrificing religion in order to obtain a supposedly clearer view of God and a more solid, reliable link to him. Yet the God who emerges from these efforts—or, rather, what remains of God after religion has been swept away as an embarrassing remnant of a primitive age —is a strangely impoverished one. When Luther struck out at saints, sacraments, Church and clergy, there remained in his beliefs an unforgiving God, frightening in his might and inexorable to the sinner. When Paul Tillich writes of theology, one wonders why he needs three bulky volumes (*Systematic Theology*, 1953) to deal with the extremely rare instances of man's encounter with God. Tillich's "God above the god of theism" is a remote and abstract figure which frustrates our religious imagination and disappears when, in this puppet show, the theologian draws back the string at the end of which his God was dangling. We should be aware, Tillich writes, "of the paradoxical nature of every prayer, of speaking to somebody to whom you cannot speak because he is not 'somebody,' of asking somebody of whom you cannot ask anything because he gives or gives not before you ask, of saying 'thou' to someone who is nearer to the I than the I is to itself." And he concludes: "Each of these paradoxes drives the religious consciousness towards a God above the god of theism."[13] One might add that there seems to be no reason to stop here: as with the bottle's label on which the bottle label is reproduced, and so *ad infinitum,* so we might look for another God above the one who is himself above the god of theism, and so on.

Return to Gnosticism

Tillich's position is not original; it is a modern formulation of the Gnostic idea of the *deus absconditus,* the transcendent God hidden from all creatures, knowable only by a few elect through supernatural revelation. The Gnostics taught that the created world is imperfect and evil; God, consequently, cannot be held responsible for it; he cannot have created it. The "real" God is

[13] *The Courage to Be,* Yale University Press (paperback), New Haven, Conn., 1959, pp. 180–181.

one above creation, ineffable, and accessible to the specially illumined possessors of knowledge. Cerinthus, the Christian Gnostic,
taught that "the world was made, not by the first god, but by a
power which was far removed and separated from the source of
being and did not even know of the God who is exalted above
all things."[14]

The position of Tillich and those of similar leanings resembles
that of the heretic Marcion of Sinope who taught the opposition of
the idea of the unknown god to that of the cosmos. Man's salvation, Marcion held, consists in his liberation by the superior god
from the power of an inferior and oppressive creator.

Clearly, God is not hurt by this proposed isolation, but its effects
on man are devastating. For all practical purposes, a God man
cannot reach is a God who does not exist, and the practical result
is agnosticism or atheism.

> For Tillich, belief in God has been evacuated of all its
> traditional content. It consists now in moral seriousness and
> nothing more. Even if we were to concede Tillich a verbal
> triumph over the atheist, the substance of atheism has been
> conceded. Just as Bultmann's view of the New Testament
> points towards scepticism, so does Tillich's analysis of the
> doctrine of God. It seems that Dr. Robinson is not alone as
> a theological atheist. . . . We should expect to find continual
> attempts to use religious language to make an atheistic vac-
> uum, and sooner or later someone was bound to try to pre-
> serve the religious language and the atheistic content together
> by suggesting, although not of course explicitly, that the latter
> simply *is* the meaning of the former.[15]

[14] Quoted by Hans Jonas, *The Gnostic Religion* (second edition), Beacon
Press, Boston, 1963, p. 136.
[15] Alasdair MacIntyre, "God and the Theologians," *Encounter*, Sept.,
1963.

The "God is dead" theology claims to salvage whatever remains of God in this secularized, scientific and anxiety-filled age. This trend is especially popular in the United States[16] since it consists of a series of attempts by individual theologians to adjust the remnants of God-belief to modern industrial society. But there is very little that is original in these well advertised attempts; American theologians follow either Tillich or some scientific, evolutionary theorist like William James or Alfred North Whitehead, and they find God in the "ultimate concern" (that is, in subjective sentiment and enthusiasm) or in the ever-more-perfect domination of man over nature (that is, in science and technology). At the end of both approaches there is the replacement of God by man, the latter's self-divinization.

All this is as old as the Garden of Eden and the Tower of Babel, and it does not mean that "God is dead"; it means only that age-old temptations are presented in modern terminology. The "God-is-dead" theologians are not theologians, but the last and desperate disciples of earlier humanists. Having lost faith in God, they have succumbed to the dreadful alternative of deifying man. Their "concern" for the modern world is not so much based on charity as on their own *libido dominandi*.

Replacement of God with Personal Enthusiasm

The pseudo-exaltation of God stripped of religion is an enterprise launched not merely to "de-mythologize" religion and to "de-religionize" Christianity, but to *dissolve the concept of God*. The entrepreneurs of this dissolution, as MacIntyre warns, are anxious to remain religiously respectable: their proclaimed motive is so to re-define the concept of God that it is unassailable. Nor will the immediately resulting bewilderment, despair, and scandal deter them in their objective to establish an invisible church whose

16 *Time* magazine devoted its cover story to this subject, April 8, 1966.

faithful are tranquil before the vague and illusive God known only to the heart. But this is not God; this is nothing but an outgrowth of personal enthusiasm, and his existence has endurance commensurate only with the endurance of whipped-up enthusiasm.

The very term, "God," Tillich advises, is sullied by anthropomorphic associations,[17] and it should be abandoned in favor of "ground of our being." The faithful are given precious little help in being told that the "ground of being" is love, since love has always been fundamental and central Christian teaching. But matters become still more difficult when love is identified with God, because then a basic shift in doctrine has taken place. The teaching is no longer that "God is love," wherein God has many other attributes besides love; rather, the current teaching is that "love is God," and this is the exaltation to divine status of a personal feeling which is subject to change and whim, which may expand or shrink, which may even turn into hatred. This "love" may mean one thing to one person and something else to another, as witness the comment by an agnostic English Free Church minister on Bishop Robinson's *Honest to God*:

> This is one of the most happy things—a sense of identification with absolutely everybody. I can understand the "trad" [*sic*] Christians because I was one, the gnostics and atheists because in a real sense I am one, and the perfervid evangelical because I have in common with him a quite unavoidable sense of being "in God," "in Christ," or however you choose to describe it.[18]

[17] In the July 3, 1964 issue of *Commonweal*, I pointed out what I regarded as a surprising eagerness on the part of these theologians to drop the name of God. Michael Novak, a Catholic writer of the "new wave" in matters religious, answered my letter to the editor: "It does not surprise me that some theologians blush when they say 'God,' in view of the uses to which that Holy Name is put by demagogues and cynics." But shall we also abandon *virtue* or *honesty* because these words too have been put to immoral or cynical uses?

[18] Quoted in Edwards-Robinson, *op. cit.*, p. 79.

This quotation illustrates the typical utopian contempt for language and rationality. The greatest thrill may be obtained by "identification with absolutely everybody"; instead of precise knowledge, it is enough to have a "sense" of this or that, "however one chooses to describe it." The inevitable satisfaction displayed by utopians in the use of fuzzy language, blurred notions, irrationality and inordinate stress on sentiments is characteristically present in the above quotation, along with the predictable impulse to identify oneself with a nebulous substance. To paraphrase Msgr. Knox, once the interlocking relationship of reason and revelation is loosened, so that one no longer controls the other, anything is possible in the domain of theology and its adjuncts; in the case of the enthusiast, the speculative intellect is dethroned and only those impressions are valid which are authorized by the individual's "light."

The upshot of all this is usually pantheism, for pantheism authorizes the individual to identify himself with everybody and everything elevated to the status of the highest existence. Despite the impression conveyed by Bishop Robinson's language, this form of reasoning may be detected: when Robinson writes that "assertions about God are, in the last analysis, assertions about love—about the ultimate ground and meaning of personal relationships," he means to say that "all personal relationships are expressions of love," that "love is God," and, therefore, "personal relationships express God."

Pantheism

God's dissolution in pantheism is a most fascinating mental exercise, although, as C.S. Lewis remarks, "so far from being the final religious refinement, pantheism is, in fact, the permanent natural bent of the human mind."[19] The reason is obvious: once

[19] *Miracles,* The Macmillan Publishing Company, New York, 1947, p. 85. This is illustrated by Cicero's statement (in *De Natura Deorum*) that the

the equilibrium of reason and faith is upset, man loses his gravitational center, so to speak, and believes that everything is part of a self-contained and self-sufficient universe. Whatever exists, he says, is part of the universe; therefore, God, too, is a part. It is a contradiction, continues Lewis, to say that something exists which, not a part of the totality, has created it and now moves it from an impossible "outside." The pantheist, therefore, is led to state either that everything is God or that nothing is God, but in neither case is he able to give any precise meaning to his concept. For, if it is maintained that "every object in this room is a table," then there is no longer a distinction between an actual table and a chair, a bed, or a desk lamp; everything in the room must be a "table" because it was arbitrarily so decided; yet nothing would be a table and nothing could be used as one by the rules implicit in the statement. Similarly, if everything is God, then everything exists in its own right; there can be no subordination, no political community; if, on the contrary, nothing is divine, then the universe is a chance encounter of atoms, an ephemeral phenomenon, and all man-made structures are artificial, illusory and without justification.

In consequence, the pantheist is apt to think of the world as being better or as being worse than it actually is; it is either a world of saints and of perfection or it is merely illusion and vanity from which one should try to escape.

The first type of belief was exemplified by many medieval heresies. One example is the thirteenth-century Amaurians who professed that all things are One because whatever is, is God.[20] Drawing a legitimate conclusion from this pantheistic belief, one

---

cosmos is all there is, there is nothing beside it, and nothing which is not part of it. This all-embracing whole is God.

[20] Norman Cohn, *The Pursuit of the Millennium,* Harper & Bros., New York, 1961, p. 159. "All that is known for certain of Amaury's doctrine is that it was a mythical pantheism which owed much to Neo-Platonic tradition" (*ibid.,* p. 157).

leading Amaurian held that "he could neither be consumed by fire nor tormented by torture, for insofar as he was, he was God." In this he echoed the first heretic Simon Magus, a contemporary of the Apostles, who said of himself that he was "the Power of God that is called the great." The Amaurians held also that Christ's Incarnation had been superseded because it was now being repeated in each one of them. And similar expressions are basic to the creed of the Brethren of the Free Spirit who believed that "God is all that is," that "every created thing is divine," and that from all eternity man was "God in God." Accordingly, these Brethren taught that man was not begotten and that "he is wholly immortal."

In the practical order, these two visions—the optimistic and the pessimistic—show identical contempt for reality. While it is not practical in everyday living to deny the existence of the object-world, it is quite tempting to deny legitimacy to human accomplishments, to civilization. Pantheists regard civilization as an arbitrary construct, arbitrary because men choose the values by which they live. "Why these values rather than those?" asks the pantheist, and he concludes that values are mere illusions: either values do not exist or else any autonomous act, as the existentialists say, is a value. This creates, of course, a confusion between good or evil when, as in Sartre's system, a criminal and a pervert, a Hitler and a Stalin are placed on the same ethical level as ordinary good people or even saints.

Buddhism

The pantheistic doctrine *par excellence* is Buddhism, the perfect illustration of the belief that the world is illusion. It should be observed that, in times of crisis, Buddhism and its variants at once begin to exert their attraction in western Christian thought and outlook. Germs of a destructive vision find it easier to penetrate a body of thought when it is in a weakened condition. The fundamental belief of Buddhism is that all is matter, including the individual. The Venerable Nyanatiloka Mahathera (*Présence de Bouddhisme*, 1959) wrote that there are no individuals, only perpetually changing combinations of bodily conditions, sensations and states of consciousness. To speak of "I" or "self" is merely a conventional way of referring to a changing assemblage of sensations. The self, or ego, is an illusion, and contemporary Buddhists consider the non-substantiality of the ego as the tenet which contains the essence of the entire doctrine.

If the "self" is nothing but illusion, a segment of the permanent flux of atoms which gains consciousness of itself only by suffering (it suffers because it knows it is pure illusion), then it is advisable to terminate this flux and its exasperating repetition. Individuals must annihilate in themselves the *kamma,* the vitalizing *élan,* the ardor which drives life on and on. The sages have completed this annihilation and their continuing activity is meant only to enable others to choose the same Noble Path. Ignorance of the Noble Path is at the source of desire, and desire makes us live—in fact, desire makes us live even several existences in the hope of finally possessing wealth, beauty and all by which the world tempts us. Yet, how can the self possess anything whatsoever when the self does not even exist? All possessions, therefore, are illusory, and the endless string of desires is, in reality, an endless pain, the very sickness of existence.

The devastatingly negative character of such belief is obvious: it allows for no God, not even for meaningful human life, and it rejects action at its very source for the reason that action would lead to an illusory possession, to unnecessary extension of an equally illusory self. Needless to say, Buddhism refuses to consider such a self as a social being, since all that the self can reasonably do is to enter more and more into itself and learn the techniques of asceticism by which it may decrease its suffering in the next incarnation. The ultimate hope of the self is to extinguish in itself all desire and put an end to the inexorable series of consecutive existences.

Dissolution of the Self

In the Buddhistic brand of pantheism, the dissolution of God leads directly to the dissolution of the self and all the attributes which make the individual a multi-faceted human being; it leads to a thorough nihilism. Msgr. Knox remarks that the "oriental anti-thesis between spirit as entirely good and matter as entirely evil . . . brings with it grave dangers, speculative and moral, leading away from Christianity to pantheism."[21] But in Buddhism there is not even room for this antithesis: one of the terms, spirit, is missing. Manicheism recognizes the reality of good and evil and recommends escape from one and adherence to the other. Even Brahmanism acknowledges that the self seeks union with Totality; in other words, it recognizes movement and, therefore, action. Only Buddhism denies the self and urges the annihilation by which it can be dissolved in the "nibbana" (nirvana). After decisive encounters with this world's suffering, Gautama, founder of Buddhism, felt an incurable repugance for suffering. His very first discourse, at Varanasi, dealt with pain, the result of successive rebirths, and how to escape it.

The root of suffering, according to Buddhism, is the impossibility of possession by a phantomatic self. However, as thoroughgoing materialism, Buddhism does not deny the here-and-now existence of such and such an object. The object is illusory in this sense, that, granted its existence today, it will not exist thousands of years hence. The same may be said about societies, movements and empires. Mircea Eliade makes this clear when he writes[22] that,

[21] *Op. cit.,* p. 93.
[22] *Images and Symbols,* Sheed and Ward, New York, 1961, p. 68.

in Indian idealism and the Vedanta, the historic world, its societies and civilizations, so painfully reared by the efforts of countless generations, are all unreal because they last but for an instant in comparison with the cosmic rhythms. The Vedantic, the Buddhist, the riski, the yogi and the sadhu conclude from the lessons of infinite time and from the Eternal Return that they must renounce the world and seek the Absolute Reality, for only knowledge of the Absolute can help free them from illusion to pierce the veil of Maya.

Atheistic Existentialism

Parenthetically it may be noted here that the contemporary expression of Buddhist teaching in the western world is atheistic existentialism. Despite its somewhat different language, atheistic existentialism expresses the same basic convictions and preoccupations. The world is matter and psychic relationships; life is absurd; the self is morbidly engulfed in itself and, when it emerges, it is absorbed (Sartre) in the traps of illusion, in bad faith, or in impersonalness (Heidegger); selves are enemies of one another and are intent upon greedy conquest; whatever is created is built on the quicksand of time and renders human effort futile in retrospect (Camus). Further analogies—and, in fact, influences— can be found in Hegel, Schopenhauer and Fontane.

The teachings of these men, apart from frequent points of similarity, are commonly pessimistic. "Escapism" seems to be the current favorite word for pessimism. Regardless of the nomenclature, the fact remains that, as noted before, pantheism of the materialistic variety soon develops an incurable repugnance for suffering; now, since suffering is but another term for reality as it presents itself to us, repugnance is directed to reality itself.

Not every expression of pessimism need be as thorough as Buddhism. For example, pessimism of the Calvinistic variety teaches that man's rational lights were so completely obscured by original sin that, unable to comprehend divine justice, man can conceive only meanness, iniquity and corruption. From this premise of perversity, Calvin concluded that any society of men must be governed with mailed fists. Accordingly, he excoriated Luther for holding that no law would be needed in a society of true Christians.

The reason for devoting so much space in this chapter to Buddhism and other pessimistic doctrines is simply to cast greater light on pantheism, the dissolution of the concept of God. When religious utopians insist on clearing "religion" out of the way in order better to approach God, pantheism inevitably follows.

The next logical concern, the matter of the next chapter, is the elaboration of secular religion and man's self-divinization when God has been dissolved in pantheism and man alone is master of his destiny.

3 - MAN-GOD

IN MÉMOIRE SUR LA SCIENCE DE L'HOMME, Saint-Simon assumed that in every age a new set of beliefs gives mankind the strength to live, work and accept his society. Crisis inevitably precedes and attends the birth of these beliefs, so that with each crisis mankind becomes more perfected as its concept of religion becomes purer, more precise, more scientific. What men of his own time most needed, according to Saint-Simon, was a synthesis of all positive—that is, scientific—knowledge. Science, he held, is a collective enterprise, so that the religion of the future must, negatively stated, cease to be individual aspirations for eternal life without regard for the social framework and, positively stated, must become collective will to protect itself against external perils.[1] This implies religious unity, and when such a unity breaks down, as in the Roman Empire and in sixteenth-century Europe, a crisis in leadership occurs. When, as a result of new basic dogmas, religious unity is restored, a new sacerdotal caste assures "the monoploy of spirit-

[1] Ernest Renan maintains that the universal task of all living beings is to make God perfect, that is, to bring it about that the cycle of things will be closed and unity imposed. Reason is the agent to bring this about and, after reason has organized mankind, it will set about to organize God. Cf. *L'Avenir de la science*, Vol. III, Calmann-Lévy, Paris, 1890, p. 757.

ual activity." In Saint-Simon's view, then, the religious institution of a historical period is, at the same time, its principal political institution.

The New Religion: Faith in Mankind

In Saint-Simon's judgment, the future religion will be a mere auxiliary of the most important task: the industrialization of the West. Nor was Saint-Simon the first to propose that religion be removed from the sphere of the divine and integrated into a system of disciplines directed toward socio-political goals. His most illustrious predecessor in this line of thinking was Machiavelli who held that a religion is good only when it serves the State by encouraging civic virtues. The Roman religion, practiced at the height of Rome's greatness, was Machiavelli's model for every State to emulate.

For our present purposes, it is important to note that an inherent logic is at work in the development of the utopian idea, for, when God and religion are dissociated, two phenomena take place: the notion of God dissolves into pantheism; the concept of religion is secularized. We shall shortly see what fate is reserved for the notion of God. As far as secularized religion is concerned, both Saint-Simon and Machiavelli seem at least honest in their positions. Saint-Simon, Machiavelli and Renan express their faith in mankind exclusively; they are not really concerned with religion and are quick to introduce such substitute terms as science, industry, statecraft and social cohesion. Religion, in their terminology, is merely a phase in man's gradual understanding of himself and his environment, and this places them in basic agreement with Julian Huxley:

> The god hypothesis is no longer of any pragmatic value for the interpretation or comprehension of nature. . . . It will

soon be as impossible for an intelligent, educated man or woman to believe in a god as it is now to believe that the earth is flat. . . . Gods will doubtless survive, sometimes under the protection of vested interests, or in the shelter of lazy minds, or as puppets used by politicians, or as refuges for unhappy and ignorant souls.[2]

As Huxley views it, then, religiousness is to be equated with cynicism, stupidity, dishonesty and ignorance. The same Huxley, as quoted by Bishop John Robinson, wrote that "gods are peripheral phenomena produced by evolution," leaving us to conclude, therefore, that cynicism, stupidity, dishonesty and ignorance— all shelters for religious belief—are also only peripheral phenomena, manifestations of an inferior phase in evolution, all of which, except for a few fossilized specimens, will vanish when higher phases have evolved. In these higher phases, men and women will reject the "god hypothesis" because they will be "intelligent and educated."

The Last Phase: Socialization

This is, of course, an extraordinarily simplistic, unrealistic and crude picture to which the spiritual utopian cannot subscribe. Taking his own detours, however, the spiritual utopian must arrive at the same conclusion, that is, at a secularized religion. Now a secularized religion, as earlier indicated, undergoes crises and basic alterations in each great historical period. Accordingly, we may not speak of one secular religion, but of secular religions in an ever-ascending line. For each historical (bio-psychological, etc.) period is supposedly more perfect than the preceding one, and, therefore, each religion which is attached to a given historical period becomes also more perfect than the preceding religion.

[2] *Religion without Revelation,* Harper & Bros., New York, 1927, p. 62.

Perfection here means, as evolutionary pantheism teaches, "socialization" and "humanization": to the secular utopian, socialization is the cooperation of all men in all great common tasks along the lines laid down by science; to the spiritual utopian, socialization is that increase in moral substance among men which will enable them to be like brothers in a kind of "divine milieu." However, since there is no adequate image by which to visualize the coming fraternity in the "divine milieu," the spiritual utopian must concretize his image by urging social, economic and cultural achievements. Thus Teilhard de Chardin looked forward to the Geophysical Congress of 1955, at which scientists of all nations would convene and exchange ideas, to provide a model for his noosphere. Teams of scientists who, in Teilhard's own experience, united for common paleontological research provided a working model of the noosphere.

Such images and models, characterized by certain religious features, may be adopted by the secular utopian also, because they are so vague that practically any interpretation will be considered acceptable. Among the available interpretations, the socially more concrete secular model is likely to prevail. My own feeling is that so many atheists, gnostics, anarchists and secular utopians welcome the statements of Teilhard de Chardin because the evolutionary outcome he proposes (and couches in religious imagery) is a million years away. There is no danger that Teilhard's "Super-Christ" will emerge very soon; and, in the meantime, the secular utopian enthusiastically underwrites Teilhard's statement that the eventual establishment of the noosphere will signal the emergence of "super-mankind."

The spiritual utopian is singularly restricted in his proposals. If he wants to appear at least quasi-religious in his language, the best he can do is to add religious flavor to fashionable secular terminology. The Sabellian heretics in the fourth century explained God as an expanding monad. Marcellus, Bishop of Ancyra, spoke of the "dilation of the divine" and of the *logos* externalizing itself through an active energy, though always remaining God. The Arians believed that Jesus Christ and the Holy Ghost were subsequent emanations of God the Father, that Jesus Christ is a man whose soul is the *logos*, which meant that Christ was a perfect man in direct communion with God and that, as a unique man, Christ would facilitate our own communion. All of this was nothing more than post-Platonic philosophy lightly dipped in holy water.

The religious utopian today speaks the sentimental language of *socialization* and asserts his belief in the dawn of a new *scientific* era. He seeks the invalid baptism of evolutionism when, with Teilhard de Chardin, he speaks of the "ascension of the living" toward the "ultra-human" or of a "finally awakened human intelligence" at the "threshold of a greater consciousness." In all this, man, not God, is exalted; in currently fashionable philosophical vocabulary, man's ordinary qualities are blown up to cosmic proportions, and the swollen result is then called divine. This procedure is not haphazard: the notion of God must first be made sufficiently meaningless before man will undertake to put himself in God's place.

Teilhard de Chardin performed this work of secularization, of rendering the idea of God meaningless, by ingeniously combining contemporary admiration for science, socialism and irrationality with their respective vocabularies. The result, condemned by every line of the Old and New Testament, is the very content of the original sin. But this age believes in what the French existentialists call *dépassement*, that is, the necessity of leaving behind traditional forms. It is not difficult for the religious utopian to forget that he is, himself, a permanent type in the struggle of belief and disbelief. His public forgets even more easily that man cannot step out of the human condition and that no "universal mind" is now being manufactured simply because science has permitted the building of nuclear bombs, space ships and electronic computers.

*Teilhard's God: Spiritualization of Matter through
Evolution*

What Teilhard did was to identify God with the universe—
standard pantheistic procedure—not a static, but an expanding,
universe, not a space-and-time universe, but a mental-moral continuum of his own devising. As Bishop Marcellus tried to come to
terms with Plotinus, calling this supposed expansion "dilation," so
Teilhard sought to come to terms with Darwin and Marx, calling
this expansion "phyletic effort" and "totalization." Teilhard is
certainly explicit in teaching evolutionism or collectivism; in
addition, his forced and empty neologisms, his unwarranted comparisons and *non sequiturs*, all couched in that vague language so
beloved of all utopians, has appeal for the untutored, for those who
are so easily impressed by emotional appeal, allusions and poetic
style and who confuse these qualities with substantial speculation
and rational analysis.

The God of Teilhard's system is tied to the evolution of matter,
for God could not create life and, later, man unless the material
preconditions were ready. Similarly, in this view, God cannot save
mankind until its moral condition has reached the dizzying heights
of what Teilhard calls noosphere, that improved world of men,
morally and intellectually united, who await further "centration" in
Omega Point, the end of evolution when "superhumanity" meets
"Super-Christ." It is, then no exaggeration to say that, for Teilhard,
God *is not*; more accurately, God only *becomes*, he grows, so to
speak, along with his own creation; he is a non-rational God, partly
aloof from man's difficulties, partly powerless. Sooner or later the
heretic and enthusiast will identify this with a more understandable
term, such as nature, evolution or history. In the name of an
evolving God, or a *pan-Theos*, or a God which is the unfolding
of Absolute Spirit in history, every personal experience is exalted

as an increase in goodness and consciousness and every hallucination becomes interpretation of the divine will. Once the rational standard is eliminated, the idea of a personal God is discarded, too. Corresponding to the concept of God identified with nature, evolution or history is the concept of collective salvation or collective perdition.

Teilhard's thinking decidedly takes its direction from confidence in the collectivization of mankind. He speaks of "phyletic effort," of "totalization," and in *The Future of Man* (as seen by a paleontologist) he who is not yet completely socialized is regarded as a lower form of evolution. The fundamental choice, says Teilhard, belongs not to the individual, but to the "human mass." In the quasi-Marxian terminology of *The Divine Mileu*, man's alienation and frustration are cries that find no echo. The reader will easily note also the atheistic, existentialistic spirit of Sartre and Camus in such a description.

In numerous places throughout Teilhard's works,[2a] the Second Coming is predicated on the coalescence of individual men in one Whole, the coalescence of individual consciences in one "cosmic conscience." Thus we are caught up in a "super-evolution" tending toward a super-organism in which individual thought becomes unanimous thought at the phase of socialization. Only at this point in the evolution of a "super-humanity" may the "Super-Christ" finally emerge.

Teilhard de Chardin, the enthusiast, saw everywhere signs of incipient collectivization which made him confident of the future. He calculated that in a "few hundred thousand years" we shall have taken enormous steps toward an "enlarged consciousness," which he visualized as a kind of globally organized and permanent, scientific research project. Like every "enthusiastic" doctrine, whether it be the Albigensian heresy, Anabaptism or the modern variants, "Christified evolutionism" exalts the individual's "unique experiences" without benefit of rational norms.

[2a] In *Notes for Progress*, as an example.

The New God: Mankind

The contemporary variant of secular religion retains the name of God, but permits mankind, as a collectivity, to identify itself with God. Mankind, as such, seldom appears as an object of worship, however, at least in the crude form of such religion; worship is more often addressed to a society, a race, a nation, or to some hypothetical State to appear at evolution's end. The only difference among secular religions is the form of worship: a given nation, race or regime may demand, as shown in Nazism and Communism, an elaborate ritual, specific slogans and gestures; mankind as such, particularly an evolving mankind, offers no precise object that may be displayed for worship. Robespierre tried to organize elaborate ceremonies in honor of the Supreme Being, a kind of super-mankind, but the rituals collapsed into obscenity and ridicule. Thus, a vague reformist attitude dictates good deeds and respect for other people as precepts to be observed in secular religion.[3] Unwittingly, perhaps, John D. Godsey hit upon the only coherent attitude which the modern religious utopian may assume concerning Christian teachings: "The continuance of a religious interpretation of the Gospel in a non-religious world may be at once a misunderstanding of the Gospel itself and a default of the Church's responsibility *vis-à-vis* the world."[4]

If speaking of religion is admittedly out of place and an almost indecent and reprehensible enterprise, what is left? In the debate occasioned by Bishop Robinson's *Honest to God*, T. E. Utley answered this question:

[3] The Freemason's creed is perhaps the end of the line in religious feelings. As summed up by Serge Hutin in *Les Francs-Maçons* (Editions du Seuil, Paris, 1960, p. 180), this doctrine is an eclecticism at the mercy of all new ideologies; its practice accepts a soulless ritualism; its internal discipline consists of vague recommendations for improving oneself.

[4] *The Theology of Dietrich Bonhoeffer* as quoted by Robinson, *Honest to God*, SCM Press, London, 1963, p. 124.

Where, one must ask, will the ravages of liberal theology end? The Devil and Hell went long ago; the position of the Blessed Virgin has been seriously undermined; God, who until last week was invulnerable, is now distinctly on the defensive. What will ultimately be left except the belief in the need for bishops, if only to give evidence in trials about obscenity and to talk to pop singers on television?[5]

This may seem like caricature and cruel sarcasm; actually it expresses the only logical position open to the religious utopians. Nor are the latters' attacks against religion limited to Christianity: the Gnostics caricatured Judaism, for example, by converting the names denoting Jahweh into demonic entities and by reviling the Mosaic Law as a network of institutions and precepts intended to enslave men to the Demiurgos and other archons. On the one hand, the utopian objective is to show a frightening distance between God and man, bridgeable only by those few Elect who possess the divine knowledge; for ordinary people, God is no longer available because utopian designations have completely obscured any meaningful discourse about him. On the other hand, the individual and mankind are held to be increasingly exalted as they stand on the threshold of a brilliant cosmic career, developing new mental and moral faculties in the processes of mutation. Is it any wonder, then, that Bonhoeffer, as summed up by Robinson, should state: "The eternal Thou is met only *in, with and under* the finite thous, whether in the encounter with other persons or in the response to the natural order."[6] In other words, God, for man, is man himself, exactly as the atheist Feuerbach—Marx's mentor in this matter— had written.

Robinson, Tillich and their fellows protest against this interpretation as one belonging properly to naturalism. But what is

---

[5] *Sunday Telegraph*, London, March 24, 1963.
[6] *Op cit.* Italics by Robinson.

their own interpretation? They contend that one must go beyond the naturalist critique of supernaturalism, yet they welcome this naturalistic critique as valid. In Tillich's own words, "Our period has decided for a secular world . . . a great and much-needed decision [since] it gave consecration and holiness to our daily life and work."[7] The only reason they give for warning against naturalism is that there is some "necessity for the name 'God' " because "our being has depths which naturalism, whether evolutionary, mechanistic, dialectical or humanistic, cannot or will not recognize."[8] Paul Tillich enumerates these "depths": "the feeling for the inexhaustible mystery of life, the grip of an ultimate meaning of existence, and the invincible power of an unconditional devotion."[9]

The Social Gospel

These reasons are hardly sufficient for preserving the name "God," particularly since Tillich himself rejects this name and prefers—because he is fond of speaking of depth—"ground of our being." In reality, however, interpersonal relationships are substituted for relationship with God, because, one may assume, "love of God" has lost all meaning where God is emptied of all significance. One cannot love an abstraction, particularly when that abstraction is discoverable only at the peak of evolution. One can, however, love his fellow men, as witness Bishop Robinson's statement that "assertions about God are, in the last analysis, assertions about love—about the ultimate ground and meaning of personal relationships."[10] This is, of course, the purest pantheism because, as Herbert McCabe, O.P., explains in *Blackfriars* (July-August 1963), if all statements about God can be converted into

---

[7] *The Shaking of the Foundations*, Charles Scribner's Sons, 1948, p. 181.
[8] Robinson, *op. cit.*, p. 54.
[9] *The Shaking of the Foundations*; see note 7 *supra*.
[10] *Op. cit.*, p. 105.

statements about interpersonal relationships, then such relationships are God—or else the sentence is a tautology. And, indeed, Robinson himself confirms this analysis: whether one has known God, says Robinson, is tested by one question only: How deeply have you loved? He concludes: "encounter with the Son of Man is spelt out in terms of an entirely 'secular' concern for food, water supplies, housing, hospitals and prisons."[11] An astonishing anticlimax in view of the fact that we have been told that the name "God" still stands for a "feeling for the inexhaustible mystery of life." Robinson tries to save the situation by putting the word "secular" between quotation marks, indicating thereby, one assumes, that concern for food and the like is not a purely secular preoccupation; at the same time and insofar as these concerns are associated today with the activities of social workers and agencies of the welfare state, one would like to know what Bishop Robinson and his fellows regard as the difference between social work, governmental functions, and religious devotion. There is no difference, judging from the Bishop's statement. Is one to conclude that the relationship with the "finite thou"—social work—is the only meaningful way of encountering the "eternal Thou?"

That very conclusion seems inescapable in light of the purely social nature and moral relativism contained in the foregoing statements. The character of social work today does not posit the question of right and wrong; its sole concern is alleviation of what it regards as the ill effects of urban living, slum conditions, delinquency and similar social conditions. This thinking may be right as far as it goes, but it does appear to be neutral in the religious sense. In fact, Bishop Robinson goes no farther than the average social worker when he declares:

Nothing can of itself always be labelled as "wrong." One cannot, for instance, start from the position "sex relations

[11] *Ibid* p. 61.

before marriage" or "divorce" are wrong or sinful in themselves. They may be in ninety-nine cases or even a hundred
out of a hundred, but they are not intrinsically so, for the only
intrinsic evil is lack of love.[12]

How, indeed, could anything be "right" or "wrong" in the context
of evolutionary pantheism when these labels are supposed to cover
different items throughout the advance of moral, psychological and
social evolution? Perhaps their true nature—unless "true nature"
is inappropriately static in an evolutionary context—will be revealed at Teilhard de Chardin's Omega Point. For that matter,
perhaps even the elements of Tillich's "ultimate concern" will cease
to be ultimate as science (considered as broadly as the evolutionary
pantheists speak about it) provides answers for them. This, at least,
is the assumption to be noted in a text by Bonhoeffer:

> Our whole nineteen-hundred-year-old Christian preaching and
> theology rests upon the "religious premise" of man. . . . But if
> one day it becomes apparent that this *a priori* "premise" sim-
> ply does not exist, but was an historical and temporary form
> of self-expression, that is, if we reach a stage of being radi-
> cally without religion—and I think this is the case already,
> else how is it, for instance, that this war, unlike any of those
> before it, is not calling forth any "religious" reaction?—what
> does that mean for Christianity? It means that the whole
> linchpin is removed from the whole structure of our Chris-
> tianity to date.[13]

[12] *Op. cit.*, p. 118.
[13] *Ibid.*, p. 122. What Bonhoeffer regarded as the complete lack of religious reaction to the atrocities of World War II was sufficient reason for
him to judge the almost two thousand years of Christian teaching as wrong.
Bonhoeffer was executed in a Nazi prison in 1944 and, therefore, was in no
position to have witnessed the strong religious reactions. Too, why should a
failure of religious people to react, as Bonhoeffer felt they should, invalidate
the body of Christian truth? Finally, if Bonhoeffer felt that Christianity and

The logic of the evolutionary pantheist's attitude, as it appears from these analyses, leads to a secular religion, that is, to the worship of mankind. In their tremendous impatience with traditional religions (the worship of God) which do not deliver the expected goods—namely, the transformation of humanity into a community of saints—the evolutionary pantheists are ready to jettison the religious luggage and to look for something else, the only one alternative: a secular religion—the worship of man—in which the tensions and contradictions of the *homo religiosus* are, if not solved, at least ignored. And there is, of course, no way back from a secular religion because it has its own logic and its own program.

The religious man believes that freedom leaves us in a permanently precarious situation because of the everlasting tension between what he wants and what he can achieve. He trusts God in the same way as the child puts his trust in his parents, and not because he expects God to work a miraculous cure; he knows his parents' love for him, a love which will guide him through his difficulties.[14] But man also knows that his own wrong decisions may wreck the intentions of divine providence. The same holds for society and mankind as a whole: Dominican Father Calmel holds that the goal of civilization and religion is not to promote a brilliant and prestigious mankind which is free, from the present century onward,

---

other moral teachings had failed so miserably, why did he feel that man was "mature" and able to define his own religion?

[14] Claude Lévy-Strauss, a prominent French anthropologist, recently declared that there is no meaning in the world or in life, and that whatever meaning the individual assigns is meaningful only for him. The famous biologist, Jean Rostand, declared on the same occasion that our brain is perhaps a mad mechanism, making us mad, too, and rendering all science, philosophy and faith illusory. What remains, says Rostand, is only our anguish in the face of this meaninglessness, although we cannot even account for this anguish.

In the statements of both scientists, interviewed in *La France Catholique* Oct. 23, 1964, are to be found not only the roots and form of contemporary atheism, but also elements of Buddhist, Gnostic, etc., style characteristic of all atheistic thought.

of the miseries and defects inherited from Adam, but to allow a permanently imperfect humanity to remain faithful to God in the spiritual and temporal order.[15]

Secularized man, on the contrary, seems to have adopted religion in the hope that it will bring about mankind's autonomy. In the opinion of secularized man—Julian Huxley, Freud, Bonhoeffer—religion has been given its necessary and fair trial period (which corresponds to mankind's childhood) but now, as it also seemed in the fourth and thirteenth centuries, this trial period is over. Religion has ceased to pay dividends on man's investment, and, at any rate, he has come of age: science explains rationally what, in the past, were considered miracles and mysteries; psychology dispels the darkness which man once confused with the soul; technology benevolently compels man to create the universal society by making him recognize the needs of his fellow men. The things expected of religion have come to men without religion and the religious world view—in fact, in opposition to them. Hence, nothing may stand in the way of an emancipated humanity to reach the "ultra-human," to realize its limitless potentials, to become its own goal, to worship its own achievements, to worship itself.

The True Motive of Secularism: Disappointment with God

None of this is surprising to the secular utopian. He expected for a long time that the "revolution of science," the discoveries of psychology and the affluent society would bring about the emancipation of man from what Freud called "illusions" and from what Marx called the "opium of the people." Although the secular utopian regarded these developments with great satisfaction, and

[15] Cf. "Première approche du teilhardisme: la distinction des trois ordres," in *Itinéraires*, March, 1962, p. 162.

by no means with astonishment, they did come as a tremendous shock to the religious utopian who was hoping all along that God would somehow appear, take over personal leadership of the modern world and explain how, from all eternity, he devised the laws of science. But things simply did not happen as he had envisioned, and science seemed to do quite well without proclaiming its fealty to God. Shock followed shock, and God was not found in the depths of the psyche, in the altitudes of space travel or in the mechanism of the modern welfare State. Disappointed and scandalized at this point, the religious utopian is ready now to switch his allegiance to secularism. He now transfers to society and mankind the passion he once felt for God. Bishop Robinson speaks for them all when he declares in his own summary of the debate which developed around his *Honest to God*:

Accepting the fact that modern man has opted for a secular world, Bonhoeffer refuses to deplore this. On the contrary, he agrees that the period of religion is over. Man is growing up out of it: he is "coming of age." By that he does not mean that he is getting better, but that, for good or for ill, he is putting the "religious" world view behind him as childish and pre-scientific. Till now man has felt the need for a God, as a child feels the need for his father. He must be "there" to explain the universe, to protect him in his loneliness, to fill the gaps in his science, to provide the sanction for his morality.[16]

The God of Utopians: the Socially Integrated Man

The assumption that the period of religion is over appears, significantly and almost verbatim, in the writings of Friedrich

[16] Edwards-Robinson, *The "Honest to God" Debate*, SCM Press, London, 1963, pp. 270–271.

Engels. Marxism's founders were really convinced that Christianity was the most advanced accomplishment, the very synthesis of the religious spirit, and that no other religion could surpass it or take its place. After 1874, Engels expressed the opinion that the European working class was simply finished with God. This means to the Marxist that the idea of God in its entirety may now be translated into a secular language and projected into the world. In this sense, Christianity is the reverse side of the coin of what Marxists and secular utopians generally consider to be the *true* nature of man, the nature he would have had if religious belief had not usurped it and made it into a distorted reflection of reality. Marx himself thought that Christian theology contained valuable information about the men who conceived it: for example, the Holy Family is a model for the average Christian family, and religion is the consciousness of man who has not yet found himself.

Consequently, it must be re-emphasized that the God of secular utopians is man himself. Needless to say, there are deep reasons for this exaltation of man. In the religious conception, as earlier noted, there always remains a tension between what man desires and what he can achieve. This tension is, of course, heightened in the case of collective desires and achievements, for then the element of the unknown, inherent in the individual, is multiplied by the number of the participants. Basically, this is the price of freedom, itself the result of the distance separating man from God. In the concrete worldly contact, this freedom appears as chance, as an element of incalculability in human actions. This very incalculability, this margin of uncertainty which is inevitable in all human enterprises, is offensive to utopians in their planning of the perfect society. This margin is recognized as flowing directly from the distance between man and God expressed in the human conscience—a tabernacle of God and a private laboratory of invisible and inscrutable decisions. If this distance could be suppressed and God "brought down" from Heaven[17] and made to coincide with man, the rule of chance could be eliminated from human affairs.

Leo Strauss suggests, for example, that "Machiavelli's lowering of the standards is meant to lead to a higher probability of actualization of that scheme which is constructed in accordance with the lowered standards. Thus, the dependence on chance is reduced: chance will be conquered."[18] Saint-Simon foresaw the same development as the next and last phase in the history of religions: a socialized religion. Auguste Comte also grappled with the problem: if God exists, he thought, mankind cannot establish a fully rational and secular society, because the selfish concern for personal salvation and the absolute interest in a Divine Absolute demanding this interest prevent each from giving himself entirely to the common task.

Only a *man-god,* therefore, would be a guarantee that the common task could be carried out as conceived, since not only an extra amount of energy would be liberated by not being spent "outside" the human enterprise, but the loyalty of man would also be naturally channeled into the construction of a purely this-worldly society. The resulting network would be the highest achievement in the universe and credited to man as sole creator.

Leo Strauss mentions that Savonarola already denounced the "wise of the world" who opined that "speaking philosophically and disregarding the supernatural, the world is eternal, God is the final and not the efficient cause of this world, and there is only one soul in all men; they say that faith is nothing but opinion."[19] This rejected belief is an early affirmation, somewhat timidly expressed, of the doctrine of the collective soul and its divine character. The terms are still theological, but a few centuries later Hegel drew the

[17] In *Brothers Karamazov,* Dostoyevsky observes that socialism is the contemporary incarnation of atheism, that it is the rearing of the Tower of Babel not to reach Heaven from earth, but to lower Heaven to earth.

[18] *What Is Political Philosophy?* Free Press, Glencoe, Illinois, 1959, p. 41.

[19] *Thoughts on Machiavelli,* Free Press, Glencoe, Illinois, 1958, p. 175.

logical consequences: if mankind is on its way to becoming divine, then, first of all, the traditional dualism of God and man must be rejected; the second step is the description of mankind's self-elevation from finite to infinite life presented as world history. World history must then be conceived as God's progressive self-realization.

Feuerbach shifted the emphasis only slightly, yet it proved decisive. While Hegel still spoke of God as a world spirit which seeks plenitude in the material that mankind provides, Feuerbach looked at the problem from a strictly human point of view: God, he said, is the result of man's thought, its projection. But projection means alienation since the ideal thus projected makes man realize his own limitations. The task for Feuerbach, as it must be for the Marxists, was to re-absorb this ideal and to assure man that he possessed the projected qualities. "Religion is the disunity of man from himself; he sets God before him as the antithesis of himself. God is not what man is—man is not what God is. God is the infinite, man the finite being; God is perfect, man imperfect; God eternal, man temporal; God almighty, man weak; God holy, man sinful."[20] But if God were really so different from man, this perfection would not trouble the latter: "God is nothing other than the prototype and ideal of man: as God is, so man should be and desires to be, or at least hopes to become some time."[21] The turning point of history, says Feuerbach, will be the moment when man will realize that his only God is man himself, *Homo hominum Deus*.

Proudhon's convictions were substantially the same as Feuerbach's. He, too, regarded history as one prolonged error of imperfect societies which attributed to an imaginary being their own qualities and vices. But now, Proudhon continues in his *Correspondance* (V, 299), society is on the way to becoming perfect;

[20] *The Essence of Christianity*, K. Paul, Trench, Trübner & Co., London, 1893.

[21] Feuerbach as quoted by Robert Tucker, *Philosophy and Myth in Karl Marx*, Cambridge University Press, 1961, p. 89.

it is time to substitute mankind in flesh and blood, in thought and action, as an organism and a system for the supernatural Christ of the Gnostics and the God of Rousseau and Spinoza. The cult of the Supreme Being should now yield to the culture of mankind which Proudhon saw as the comprehension of the universe.

These conclusions seemed to be in the air. Saint-Simon, Auguste Comte and Proudhon in France advocated them, as did the Russian characters found in the novels of Turgenev and Dostoyevsky and English writers of the leanings of Godwin. Engels wrote in an early article: "Hitherto the question has always stood: What is God?— and German philosophy has resolved it as follows: God is man. . . . Man must now arrange the world in a truly human way, according to the demands of his nature."[22] Several decades later, in his introduction to *Literature and Revolution,* Trotsky echoed Engels when he held that the revolution must start from the central idea that collective man must become sole master and that the limits of human power are determined by man's knowledge of natural forces and by his capacity to use them.[23] Mankind is definitively enthroned in the place of God, and from this point on, as Marx said, all will depend on the development and organization of the productive forces. This represents the shift in governmental and social functions which Saint-Simon had predicted when he said that, because *government of people* is a thing of the past, the task of the new era is to organize the *administration of things.* The utopian element in this position, as Michel Collinet remarks, is the abandonment of the Aristotelian contention that man is a *political* animal in favor of the tenet that man is an organic animal.[24] Indeed, the utopian believes that organization is the last word in everything pertaining to man.

[22] As quoted by Tucker, *ibid.,* p. 73.
[23] Cf. the Introduction to Trotsky's *Literature and Revolution,* Russell and Russell, New York.
[24] "Saint-Simon et l'évolution historique," *Le Contrat Social,* Sept., 1960, p. 294.

4 - THE END OF
PHILOSOPHY

IN THE preceding chapter we saw that the apotheosis of mankind is
the natural objective of all utopian thought. Now some questions
arise, as they must not only with all religious systems, but also
with all fields of human knowledge: How may we obtain reliable
data concerning our subject, "man-god"? How may we organize our
knowledge of this subject? How shall we formulate the discipline
devoted to it? The discipline devoted to the study of the divine
attributes and manifestations is theology. Now, when man occupies
God's vacated throne, shall we call the new science "anthropology,"
as Marx seems to suggest, or shall we regard it as some form of
lay philosophy which would exclude speculation about the divine?

Theology and Philosophy Cannot Speak of Man-God

Obviously, the term "theology" would no longer make sense. In
the utopian perspective, everything about man and the universe is
discoverable, knowable, provided prejudices and superstitions—
and here religion leads all the rest—are discarded and the right

87

scientific instruments devised. In western religions, God always remained the *Deus absconditus* of the Bible; but man must stand in the full light of scientific investigation; nothing about him may be considered mysterious. In fact, only by exploring and exposing everything about him, and in the smallest of details, may mankind hope to become absolute master of its own destiny, for mastery means power, and power, so Bacon taught, reposes in knowledge.[1]

Would the discipline which organizes knowledge about the newly conceived mankind be properly called philosophy? Traditionally, philosophy has always approached the problem of man by setting him in perspective as a being in relation to realities and powers which transcend him. The philosopher has held, either as assumption or explicit teaching, that man is a created being—or, if not created, man at least *feels dependent*—partly mysterious in origin and constitution, but in a certain way free of his creator as well as of the elements which constitute him. We earlier noted the *distance* which separates man from God and which is responsible for the freedom that man enjoys and under which he suffers, an attribute which makes man ultimately immeasurable, unfathomable and incalculable even to himself.

A new philosophy, then, or even some new discipline is needed to discourse meaningfully about the new mankind. It must be a

---

[1] The entire notion of mastery of man over man is ambiguous. It not only means that we know everything about man, but also that, in the name of this knowledge, some men lord it over the rest whose knowledge is comparatively deficient or judged to be insufficient. This opens up the possibility of tyranny in the name of knowledge, of the right interpretation of what is "man." Theoretically, this danger could be averted if everybody knew everything about man, that is, if everybody were equally well educated and knowledgeable. Hence the utopian's commitment to education which he regards as his true religion. However, even if all men were equally all-knowing, there remains the factual element of the *appetite* for power to be found in some men, and this element is not something which education may extirpate; in fact, education may well whet this appetite. Given this appetite for power, its exercise determines whose knowledge is right knowledge, whose knowledge is harmful, so that the situation has come full circle. Power, the central issue of politics, is not solved by knowledge.

science organized according to an ever-increasing number of facts,
building its conclusions on previously established sets of verifiable
knowledge, incorporating what has been acquired, and progressing
toward a phase where this knowledge will be increasingly ap-
plicable, and in an increasingly precise way. Of course, philosophy
has never proceeded in this manner, because it is not one of the
natural sciences; it does seem significant that every philosopher,
sooner or later, writes a volume on the question "What is philosophy?" Each philosopher feels the need to redefine his discipline
not only because of his acquired competence, but in view, too, of
the wisdom and experience he has accumulated as a human being.
This does not mean that philosophy is a meaningful word only
when it is the expression of personal tastes and values; far from it,
because philosophers are able objectively to discuss their respective
systems and positions, to agree and disagree. In fact, philosophers
even write histories of philosophy, that is, they select from among
themselves those whose great contributions to the stream of
speculation are recognized. Yet, philosophy is always a personal
view of God, man and the universe, of knowledge and values; yet
mankind is sufficiently one in its mental structure and its aspirations to offer topics which all philosophers may recognize as
genuinely theirs.

Science as Total Knowledge

The ideal science for the new mankind, as the utopian conceives
it, must, on the contrary, be entirely *objective*. Objective, that is, in
the clearest sense of the word: directed at the object with neither
personal distortion, ulterior motives, nor the distance which seems
to be inevitable simply because the observer is detached from the
object he observes. Objective, too, in the sense that, in contrast to
the philosopher who often remains tainted by Platonism, the man
of science should not regard his object as the reflection of some

superior entity, as having a "meaning" beyond the observable and verifiable. In summary, the new science should be concerned with *facts*, physical or social, and should elaborate the laws which co-ordinate and organize all facts into one world-system, one all-embracing science. Preferably, there should also be only one law accounting for all phenomena, their movements and transformations.

Although science and philosophy can live in comfortable neighborly relations, the utopian must naturally reject philosophy and teach its absorption by the all-embracing science which we have tried to characterize. Religions consider God as all-knowing; man-god, the religious object of the utopian, must also be all-knowing, one who cannot settle for approximations or engage in uncertain meditation about himself and about nature whose master and re-creator he believes himself to be. Thus, philosophy becomes in the utopian's eyes the uncertain knowledge *par excellence*, unworthy because of its fragility to be called full knowledge. As Marx viewed it, philosophers had been, at best, interpreters of the world; like all translators, they may have been *tradittori* rather than *traduttori*. When Marx says that, from now on, the object of philosophy should be the transformation of the world, can he still mean *philosophy*? Obviously not. Marx is referring to the new science which will not merely reflect outer reality on inner consciousness (in this process the subject plays a decisive and, therefore, sus-pect role), but will press such photographic imprints on our minds as reproduce reality with absolute faithfulness.

Marx's claim was more sophisticated than that of Condorcet who wrote that philosophy has nothing more to guess, no more hypothetical surmises to make. It is enough, Condorcet felt, to assemble and order the facts and to show the useful truths that can be derived from their corrections and from their totality.[2]

[2] *Sketch for a Historical Picture of the Progress of the Human Mind*, The Noonday Press, New York, 1955, p. 9.

The Positivists went farther: they believed in the existence of one *universal law*, from which all other laws (and *facts*) could be derived. The model for such a universal law was the theory of gravitation which, by its elegance, appealed to the best minds. Saint-Simon, for example, was convinced that Newton's law, enlarged and generalized, would result in a calculus of all subsequent changes in every field of knowledge, since, as he also believed, physical and spiritual phenomena possess the same nature. He proposed the High Committee of Twenty-One Managers for regulating the destinies of Europe, called the Council of Newton, and it was to be invested with authority based on such universal knowledge.

Both Condorcet and Saint-Simon spoke of the importance of facts; they also stressed science as organizer of the totality of facts. To both thinkers, this represented more than a synthesis of all knowledge, past and future; it represented what appeared to them and to their contemporaries to be the distinct possibility of scientifically organizing all departments of human life in accordance with a rational scheme. It bears repeating that the expected result was not only an increased amount of knowledge and a wider intellectual horizon, but also, as Condorcet saw it, the true perfection of mankind. Knowledge, in his mind, was closely associated with moral and political attainments. The philosopher, he felt, is delighted that he has done some lasting good which fate can never destroy by calling back the reign of slavery and prejudice.[3] When Saint-Simon noted the impossibility of instituting a new regime without having first established the new philosophical system to which it should correspond, he was echoing the words of Condorcet who admittedly influenced him and, in turn, Auguste Comte.

The "new science" was supposed to be an *organizational principle*, that is, a substitute for politics. In the first place, this was guarantee that the new society, described in utopian terms by most

---

[3] *Ibid.*, pp. 201–202.

prominent sociologists of the past two centuries, would be managed by the late descendants of the philosopher-kings: industrialists, engineers, scientists, and the like; in the second place, it was a guarantee that the new society was not to be ruled by the caprice of birth and historical movements (recall here the desire to escape the "terror of history"), but that its destinies were to be firmly tied to the sure and controlled march of science. Under such auspices, politics could be considered as definitively excluded from the life of mankind. The science which will govern the world, as the young Renan would have it, is no longer politics but philosophy, the science dedicated to researching the goal and methods of society. The last word of modern science, Renan felt, is the bold yet legitimate claim to organize mankind scientifically.[4]

This was not enough. The new science, as we have seen, was described as the "totality of facts," "universal law," "organizational principle" and, of course, "philosophy," since that traditional term for the "science of sciences" was still in use. "History" was also added to enrich further an already bursting notion. One of Saint-Simon's chief disciples, Armand Bazard, wrote in the Society's paper (*Producteur*, IV, p. 406), that, thanks to the master, history was now able to take its place among the positive sciences and to become superior to the rest; no longer would history have as its object to tell amusing tales or provide illustrations for moralists and philosophers. All at once, history was ethics, politics and philosophy elevated to the rank of one positive science. Elsewhere Bazard continued this train of thought with the assurance that, by discovering the law of social change, history would enable us to determine the trend and the future of the human species in every direction. Furthermore, history would teach our societies how to organize themselves in their march toward their destination.[5]

4 *Cf. L'Avenir de la science*, Vol. III, Calmann-Levy, Paris, 1890, p. 757.
5 Bazard is quoted to this effect in Maxime Leroy, *Histoire des idées sociales en France*, Gallimard NRF, Paris, 1946, Vol. 2, p. 224.

Science Absorbs History

If we may still designate this composite science—a mixture of science, expectations, beliefs and approximations—by the name "philosophy," then we must admit that, with so many cooks preparing it, the broth was certainly heady and also unrecognizable. It was no coincidence that, at the same time, Hegel claimed to have brought philosophy as a discipline to an end by reconciling the tension between individual freedom and communal authority in the Prussian State. It was a strange way to suggest that a problem —What is God's? What belongs to Caesar?—which tried the ingenuity of Socrates, Jesus and St. Augustine and which has erupted with new dramatic impetus in our own times, might be considered closed in an ephemeral creation (the Prussian State, in the form referred to by Hegel, lasted from 1815 to 1871) of the Holy Alliance. Yet, what Hegel meant had an influence that continues today in the belief that philosophical speculation may terminate or cease to be of interest when certain values, cherished by certain philosophers, materialize in some men and in some situations. This is obviously false. After all, there might be—in fact, there *are* —other philosophers who, upon seeing such materialization, would be prompted to speculate about how their own values might also run the same successful course; inevitably there must ensue the clash between the various values and systems and a resurgence of the tension, perhaps in another form. Accordingly, it is more than risky, it is positively naïve to imagine that a philosophical system, that philosophy itself may be abolished simply by the arbitrary assumption that it has "materialized." If nothing else, that very assumption is likely to provoke the resumption of philosophizing.

In the particular climate of modern utopianism, however, it was easy to hold such a belief since, as noted earlier, philosophy was regarded as uncertain knowlege or mere personal opinion, and the utopian thinkers dreamed of possessing not only true knowledge, but a definitive system on which, in Saint-Simon's words, the "new regime" would be based. This is how Engels evaluated the consequences of Hegel's claim: "With Hegel," he wrote in *Ludwig Feuerbach and the End of Classical German Philosophy* (1888), "philosophy comes to an end; on the one hand, because in his system he summed up its whole development in the most splendid fashion; and, on the other hand, because, even though unconsciously, he showed us the way out of the labyrinth of systems to real positive knowledge of the world."

Unconvincing arguments, to say the least, and emotional ones, but Engels revealed, in the same work, the real reasons for his rejoicing:

> The task of philosophy means that we ask of a particular philosopher to bring about what only the whole mankind can do in its gradual development. . . . Today we see the end of philosophy in the sense it has been used. We turn away from all absolute truths . . . and instead we shall seek relative truths, accessible through the positive sciences and the synthesis of their conclusions. With Hegel, philosophy has come to its end.

The "whole mankind"—key words in this quotation—will take the philosopher's place. Engels' assumption, like that of all utopians, is that speculation about "philosophical" subjects is idle and to be tolerated only so long as mankind has not advanced to the stage where factual and certain knowledge becomes available. When that happens, when knowledge will be complete and organized, the task of philosophy will become a generalized science of man and society; in other words, philosophy will cease to be philosophy. This knowledge, or, as we should perhaps call it, this "new science," cannot brook contradiction. Even the exaggeratedly subjective Fichte said that "no man has a right to wander recklessly about in the empty domain of unsettled opinion" since "the individual view is an empty form, for all should and could have the same insight, and not a separate one, arbitrarily arrived at."[6]

In stressing the cognitive side of the new science, Fichte did not speak of it from its perspective as an instrument of power. Yet, that is what Engels and the other utopians had in mind. And long before them, Machiavelli, again like all utopians, aspired to the conquest of Fortuna—chance, incalculability, man's freedom as it manifests itself in history. He was, Leo Strauss writes, the first philosopher to believe that "the coincidence of philosophy and political power can be brought about by propaganda which wins over ever larger multitudes to the new modes and orders and thus transforms the thought of one or a few into the opinion of the public and therewith into public power."[7] "[With historicism] philosophic questions have been transformed into historical questions—or, more precisely, into historical questions of a 'futuristic' character."[8]

Needless to repeat, philosophy thus ceases to exist and becomes identified with public power; it will formulate the objectives of mankind, itself conceived as unanimous. The previous speculative character of philosophy must be abandoned and a new task assigned to it. John Dewey formulated it when he asked:

> Would not the elimination of traditional problems permit philosophy to devote itself to a more fruitful and more needed task? Would it not encourage philosophy to face the great social and moral defects and troubles from which humanity

[6] Quoted in J. L. Talmon, *Political Messianism*, Frederick A. Praeger, Publishers, New York, 1960, pp. 191–192.

[7] *Thoughts on Machiavelli*, Free Press, Glencoe, Illinois, p. 173.

[8] Leo Strauss, *What Is Political Philosophy*, Free Press, Glencoe, Illinois, p. 59.

suffers, to concentrate its attention upon clearing up the causes and exact nature of these evils and upon developing a clear idea of better social possibilities; in short, upon projecting an idea or ideal which, instead of expressing the notion of another world or some far-away unrealizable goal, would be used as a method of understanding and rectifying specific social ills?[9]

It is clear that Dewey means by philosophy what a physician would mean by medicine if he foresaw an end to medical science because of a lack of microbes and sickness. Whether, with Dewey, we speak of society in general (and, in principle, of world society) or, with Machiavelli, of a Renaissance city-State, or Italy itself, philosophy becomes simply a technique in the service of the people. The questions it asks and answers are how to acquire the goods which satisfy the citizens as well as how to acquire power to rule over them. Their philosophy does not even need a style in achieving these objectives: the technique is scientific, that is, self-evident, and acceptance of it must be automatic. If philosophy was once a study of alternatives, the technique into which it has now been changed is unambiguous. If philosophy was once a normative discipline, in its new and definitive version it will be factual, positivistic.

Machiavelli and even John Dewey were in search of a method. The former could make only timid suggestions in favor of a State religion which rewards not the Christian virtues of self-abnegation and withdrawal from the world, but those civic qualities whose object is the glory of the State. Inhibited by other considerations, Dewey refused his disciples' demand, although hesitantly, to elaborate upon the social techniques for reorganizing beliefs and behavior. Writes Prof. Morton White:

[9] *Reconstruction in Philosophy*, New American Library of World Literature, Inc., New York, 1950, p. 107.

The puzzling thing about Dewey's views on this subject is that sometimes he suggests that the fundamental task of philosophy is to build a political technology, and at others he suggests that even the modest theorizing, generalizing, and fixing of ends which technology involves would lead us into rigidity and despotisms. . . . By refusing to formulate ends of social behavior for fear of being saddled with fixed ends, Dewey hardly encouraged systematic political engineering. Those of his students who landed on the left were forced to appeal to the tradition of Marx where they could find more than a methodology of politics.[10]

Not only for the United States of the 1920's and 1930's, but for the sake of the entire "new science," Marx had to complete the task of finding the most radical solution, the abolition of philosophy itself. He recognized early that Feuerbach had applied the same critique *vis-à-vis* philosophy as *vis-à-vis* religion. Feuerbach's first important action, Marx felt, was to prove that philosophy is nothing but religion systematized and elaborated by reflection. It had to be condemned as another form of man's alienation. Let us bear in mind that, for both Feuerbach and Marx, God and religion (that is, the reasons why men worship God) consist of attributes which are potentially those of the human being, but which the human being is forced to project into an ideal being since the conditions here on earth prevent him from truly possessing these attributes. Feuerbach did not go much farther than to express the hope that his contemporaries would recognize this anomalous situation. It was Marx who *explained* why man had been incapable of "reabsorbing" the divine attributes and who *outlined* the method by which men might enter into their possession. When he indicated that he had retrieved philosophy from the false position in which Hegel had left it, Marx meant that the solution must not be

[10] *Social Thought in America*, Beacon Press, Boston, 1957, pp. 244–245.

sought on the level of the spirit, as Hegel imagined, but on that of
the material world, not in the synthesis between the World Spirit
and the individual, but in the transformation of the material world
by collectively organized effort.

With Marx, Science Becomes Praxis (Work)

Now this transformation is called work.[11] If work is to be
radically meaningful, Marx taught, then the entire social system
must change, and the result will be that our perception of nature
will be completely reliable: the mind will not receive mere impressions, that is, reality screened by class control, illusions and
mystifications, but photographic imprints which reproduce reality
with absolute faithfulness. Instead of religion, law, art—all of
which are attempts at presenting a dismal social reality in a
flattering, beautiful and acceptable way—we shall have science
showing us the world as it really is, without false and alluring
embellishments. To the extent that history marches forward and
the struggle of the workers is more clearly outlined, Marx held,
men will not have to learn the sciences; their knowledge will
consist in simply realizing what transpires before them.

The world, as Marx finds it, is in an "unphilosophical condition"
—he really means "unscientific"—because bourgeois-capitalist
mystifications have rendered it unknowable. But it would be
equally wrong for the true philosopher merely to dispel these
illusions which have clouded the minds of men and to work out
a new system of explanations starting from actual data. The
true philosopher must definitively liberate the earth from the
rule of philosophy itself; he must become a positivist, an empirical
scientist, dealing not with images of reality, but with reality itself.[12]

This basic reality is, of course, nature, and when man is en-

[11] Karl Marx, *Nationalökonomie und Philosophie,* Kiepenheuer, Cologne,
1950, pp. 236–237.
[12] On this subject, see Kostas Papaioannou, "La Fondation du Marxisme,"
in the January–February, 1962, issue of *Le Contrat Social.*

gaged in action, he does not so much modify nature from a point external to it as he obeys his own essence. Marx held that man creates objects only insofar as the object-world has created him, and because he, too, is part of nature. Capitalism, which has made work a means of survival and has thereby alienated man from his work, denies this consubstantiality of man and nature; the total reconstruction of "natural man" will be achieved only by the Communist society.

Everything must tend toward this total reconstruction, just as everything must now be subsumed under the category of work. Saint-Simon, in his *Catéchisme des industriels*, held that all spiritual power must be handed over to eminent scientists and artists who would then apply knowledge to satisfy the needs of men. Lenin, in *The State and Revolution*, specified that literature cannot remain an individual activity independent of the proletarian cause. Consequently, down with non-party literature! Literature must become a little wheel in the great social-democratic mechanism, an integral part of organized, methodical and unified work of the party. The 1966 trial of two Russian writers would have been applauded by Lenin.

Totalitarianism is not, therefore, a mere technique of domination invented by the Bolshevik party and applied to the Soviet State; it is a doctrinal necessity inscribed in Marxist theory. Totalitarianism prescribes total domination over man—over all his mental, spiritual, creative and technical endeavors, and its organization of these activities is the *sine qua non* of restoring man to a direct relationship with nature. In the light of this ideal, the present civilization—and every civilization based on exploitation—seems paltry indeed. All institutions must be destroyed since they are nothing but monuments to man's alienation; with them, all spiritual and intellectual achievements will be buried, too, since they remind man of his futile wielding of illusions to break his real chains. It is true that some Marxists—Trotsky was one—believe that, with the sublimation of political struggles, greater opportunity will be available for the struggle "for one's opinion and one's taste," resulting in "constructions which also include art";[13] but the view generally prevails that there will be no need of intellectual activities as we know them today. Alexandre Kojève, for example, writes that, in the Hegelian-Marxist theory, the philosopher is no longer obliged to search for wisdom because wisdom has finally become concretized. Action and contemplation are reconciled; history has reached its end.[14]

A kind of logical chain reaction exists from the abolition of the State to the absorption of all creative and critical activities in work and in what the Marxists call science. Kojève himself points out that when action and contemplation are reconciled, there will be nothing left to do, and the only remaining fear will be the fear of boredom.[14a] Bakunin feels that the State must again become simply "society"; it must dissolve itself into society freely and in accordance with justice. Political relations will yield to social relations freely entered upon, without compulsion by law and based only on needs and natural affinities. Taking the tenth thesis on Feuerbach as a starting point, Prof. Tucker observes that "socialized humanity is not only a classless, but also a stateless, lawless, family-less, religion-less and generally structureless collectivity of complete individuals who live in harmony with themselves, with each other, and with the anthropological nature outside them."[15]

The End of Philosophical Reflection

As certain organs become biologically superfluous, so, under circumstances just described, will the speculative faculty of man be-

[13] Leon Trotsky, *Literature and Revolution*, Russell & Russell, New York, p. 230.
[14] Kojève is quoted in A. Patri, "Dialectique du maître et de l'esclave," in the July–August, 1961, issue of *Le Contrat Social*.
[14a] "Le dernier monde nouveau," *Critique*, Aug.-Sept., 1956.
[15] *Philosophy and Myth in Karl Marx*, Cambridge University Press, 1961, p. 201.

come socially superfluous. According to Trotsky's rapturous description, in the new society's restaurants and schools, and even in its laundries, culture will be absorbed like "albumen and sunshine," while individual egoism will be diverted to the betterment of the human race. But in the entirety of Marxist literature, this betterment is predicated upon the emergence of the *un-problematic man* whose knowledge is absolute and who discards all subtle and subversive value-judgments. Where speculation ends, Marx wrote in *The German Ideology,* real and positive science begins. Empty talk about consciousness ceases, and real knowledge takes its place. When reality is depicted, philosophy as an independent branch of activity loses its medium of existence.

Simply stated, the Marxist philosopher works for abolition of his own branch of activity—speculation. Every step he takes must be directed theoretically to that condition where philosophy will no longer be needed for mankind, just as the Soviet writer is ordered by the party to write novels without those "futile" sentimentalities which supposedly preoccupy only the bourgeois. The greatest philosopher would, presumably, be the one who could demonstrate in one sentence the futility of philosophizing; that same sentence would introduce the ideal science which would show us the real world without the intermediary of thought processes, hypotheses and mental categories.

It would be an error to imagine that Marx rebelled against only the Kantian idealism of his time. He taught positively that the condition for man's transformation is that he become, as it were, one with nature by abolishing anything that may stand between him and reality. For Hegel, the only reality was the Absolute Spirit; for his disciple, who made the Hegelian system "stand on its own two feet," reality was Nature, something that can be more readily manipulated than the Absolute Spirit and, therefore, more useful for a theory of the human condition based on work and science.

How nature serves as a basic substitute for philosophy is shown in the writings of contemporary Marxist philosophers. In fact, it may be said that the division between loyal Communist thinkers and those who have defected lies in the answer to this question: Does philosophy have an authentic existence or not? More so, perhaps, than the issues resulting from the revelations of the Twentieth Party Congress or from even the Budapest insurrection, this issue has engaged the minds and courage of Communist philosophers, and those who opted for the independent *raison d'être* of philosophy usually gave up their party membership.

In Marxist thought there is identity between nature and human nature. Only the historical accident of exploitative economic systems caused human nature to become detached from nature (the "original sin" in Marxist interpretation) and brought it about that an independent meditation on the human condition replaced the happy unity. But there is a second coincidence between nature and the human collectivity; the individual, as such, is meaningless and cannot serve as a measuring rod for the degree of history's accomplishment. Only the collectivity, strictly speaking, has a history, an existence, a meaningful collaboration with nature. Thus the proletariat, or later the Communist society, is the personification of philosophy, or, rather, of its abolition. The proletariat assumes not only the role of the paramount historical personality, but it assumes also the function of thinking! "Communism has solved the enigma of history!" was the triumphant boast of Marx.

What is characteristic in this thought is that it tends toward its own annihilation, or, as the Marxists put it, its "dialectical negation." To be sure, philosophy has a service to render: it must show man to himself and teach the modalities of criticizing the conditions in which he lives and which are responsible for his alienation. The ultimate goal, however, is different. Philosophy will have accomplished its task when it finally negates itself, that is, when it transcends itself in action and yields its function to practical energy.

Henri Lefèbvre, the prominent Marxist theoretician, wrote that philosophy must deny itself in order to materialize, because, if it is sincere, then it wills its own transformation into something else. In itself, criticism, no matter how radical, changes man's real chains of oppression into ideal chains and destroys them in theory only.[15a]

Proletariat Takes the Place of Philosophy

The fate of philosophy as a cognitive instrument is linked with the vicissitudes of historical classes, their conflicts and, ultimately, with the proletariat which is called upon to terminate history and, with it, philosophy as well. Lefèbvre, then, is justified when he speaks interchangeably of communism and of philosophy. He defines communism as a movement and a consciousness of movement toward the highest conceivable form of social organization. It puts an end to quarrels among men, to conflicts between man and nature, existence and essence, reification and self-affirmation, freedom and necessity, individual and species. In theory and in practice, Communism solves all these contradictions, and it is aware that it solves them. Thus, in Lefèbvre's view, philosophy becomes actualized by suppressing itself and by suppressing its problems as well as the terms of these problems. Philosophy becomes the world of reality and ceases to exist as philosophy.

Similar texts proliferate in the writings of Marx and Engels. After he had explained Hegel's dialectical method, Marx noted in *Das Kapital* that in his own method the ideal is nothing else than the material world reflected by the human mind and translated into forms of thought. This is true also of philosophical materialism which disappears not because it is false as materialism, but because it is useless as philosophy. Materialism itself is reabsorbed, as Lefèbvre states, into an anthropology, that is, into an ensemble of

[15a] "Retour à Marx," *Cahiers Internationaux de Sociologie*, 1958.

human sciences. Total man and total society are closely linked concepts, says Lefèbvre, because they have the same content: "total praxis."

This same notion of "total praxis" appears as the conclusion of Soviet philosopher A. Bogdanov's *tectology,* or science of the earth. Bogdanov, like Hegel and, implicitly, Marx, divides history into three stages.

> The third main stage in history is that of the collective self-sufficient economy and the fusion of personal lives into one colossal whole, harmonious in the relations of its parts, systematically grouping all elements for one common struggle— the struggle against the endless spontaneity of nature. . . . It demands the forces not of man but of mankind—and only in working at this task does mankind as such emerge. All ideological forms, including philosophy and the sciences, merge at this stage into one universal organizational science.[16]

Bakunin, it has been noted, believed that, in the society of the future, political relations will dissolve and yield to social relations. In this context, political relations means that society is systematically organized by a class of exploiters according to that image of man which this class finds convenient to propose. Not only are law, police and military forces expressions of this system and servants of its purposes, but so too are art, literature and the churches. Social relations, on the other hand, arrive with the abolition of all systems of government ("structureless collectivity," as Prof. Tucker calls it) and the spontaneous emergence of "natural" relations among men along the lines of their real needs and, as Bakunin wrote, their "natural affinities." Thus the Marxist concept of social relations envisages a society in which philosophy has become superfluous for

16 Quoted in *Revisionism*, Leopold Labedz editor, Frederick A. Praeger, Publishers, New York, 1962, p. 122.

the reason that nature—domesticated nature—will determine relationships between man and his fellows.

In a fully developed communist society all relations between men will be obvious to each, and the social volition will be the organization of all their wills. It will not be a resultant, obtained by elemental accident, independent of the will of the individual, but a consciously organized social decision. ... It will be impossible to observe social phenomena whose effect on the majority of the population will be harmful and ruinous.[17]

The so-called "Marxist revisionism" has not changed the basic commitment of the Marxist philosopher to the abolition of his own discipline. Revisionism started not because Marxists became aware of this contradiction (Pierre Fougeyrollas and Edgar Morin, among others, ceased to be Marxists on detecting this contradiction), but because most of Marx's predictions did not materialize. Among such predictions was the concentration of wealth in the hands of a few super-capitalists and the general pauperization of the working classes. Nor, in later years, did the capitalistic Western powers collapse as a result of war with Nazi Germany—a "civil war among capitalist nations," as Communist writers called it—or under the blows of the Soviet Union and world communism. A readjustment of philosophy became imperative in order to explain, if not the inadequacies of Marxist doctrine in its practical aspects, at least the delay in the timetable of global Communist conquest.

The "revisionist" trend inevitably leads away from the later teachings of the mature Marx (the economist) and back to the young Marx of the so-called "early manuscripts" (1844). Like all reformers, the revisionists want to return to the origins.

[17] N. Bukharin, *Historical Materialism*, International Publishers Co., New York, 1925.

Revisionism, in the concrete, is either pure verbalism or the reaffirmation, in one form or other, of the anti-philosophical position. What the revisionists are attacking is not Marx or the core of Marxist doctrine so much as the present-day party funtionaries, the official guardians of doctrine. In *political* terms this is possibly a healthy and effective movement since it serves to split the ruling orthodoxy—and this despite the fact that within each Communist State the party remains that undisputed font of verity which tolerates no anti- or non-Marxist position. In *philosophical* terms, however, revisionist criticism is irrelevant. It is irrelevant because, whatever the Marxist philosopher's position is *vis-à-vis* the party bureaucracy, the worst he will believe is that Communist society has suffered a temporary setback attributable to the "personality cult," to "tactical errors," to the "anti-party clique" or to Stalin's suppression of "socialist democracy." Marxist philosophers never accepted an invalidating defeat. Whether Communist society materializes tomorrow or in the more distant future is not the critical problem, for assuredly it must one day materialize on the bases explored by Marx and for the reasons he predicted.

The whole position of contemporary Marxist philosophy is perhaps best summarized by the East German thinker, Jürgen Habermas:

Philosophy starts by reflecting on the position in which it finds itself; it proceeds, therefore, from the alienation which it at once experiences and from an awareness of the practical necessity for the alienation to be overcome. This consciousness rises to the level of self-consciousness where philosophy sees itself as an expression of the very situation which has to be annulled and henceforward makes the aim of its critical practice criticism by practice. It knows that it is working toward the abolition of itself *qua* philosophy to the extent that it is endeavoring to realize its own immanent existence. Such criticism leaves . . . the stage of contemplation. It has seen through the façade of its own autonomy by which it has been led to believe that it is able both to prove and to realize itself.[18]

The philosophy of Communism, then, is not meant, like traditional philosophy, to be a perpetual search for the meaning of human destiny, nor is it regarded as a permanent reflection on the condition of man and his relationship to God. Rather, the philosophy of communism is, first, an instrument of victory for the proletariat (and for the classless society) and, secondly, a historical record of the existence and of the abolition of alienation, of the State, and of philosophy itself. The critic of Communist philosophy is thus entitled to say that, insofar as philosophy is considered an instrument, it is not philosophy, but ideology, that is, a "false consciousness," as Engels defined ideology in a letter to Mehring. Insofar as it is an ephemeral activity, coincident with certain stages of economic development but not with other stages, and insofar as it yields to "class-consciousness," Communist philosophy denies itself and abolishes its own universe of discourse.[19]

[18] "Zur philosophischen Diskussion um Marx und den Marxismus," in *Philosophische Rundshau* (1957) as quoted in *Revisionism,* Leopold Labedz editor, Frederick A. Praeger, Publishers, New York, 1962, 347–348.

[19] According to G. Lukacs, the disappearance is marked by the emergence of class-consciousness which takes its place and function.

- PART TWO -

5 - MANKIND'S ONENESS

IN THE foregoing chapters it became increasingly evident that the utopian conception of the world is not so much merely political theorizing as a whole world view from which the political construct of utopia emerges with logical rigor. The search for moral perfection leads to a secularized religion which remains haunted, however, by the idea of God, the God, that is, of the Christian religion as the *ne plus ultra* of a personal divine being. Since he must deny the existence of God as a being radically different from the world, the utopian discovers that his only recourse is to immanentize God and conceive of Him as radically identical with this world, the only being conscious of himself, a "creator" of himself and of his environment, *man*.

Man's imperfections, however, are disturbingly evident and numerous. The utopian's first task, then, is to explain the conditions which have prevented us so far from reaching perfection. His second task is to explain the means of transcending these imperfections: through our aspirations, potentialities and capacity to grow, evolve, amplify and multiply our individual attributes by joining with our fellow men. This discovery authorizes the utopian to project man's actual capacities into a hypothetical future and to describe the biological and historical processes at the end of which a different man—or, rather, mankind—will emerge in full possession of the desired attributes.

Instead of refining the idea of God, as the religious utopian claims he does, it would be more accurate to say that the above schematized process naturally oversimplifies it and makes it grossly anthropomorphic. As I have elsewhere shown, the prototype of the collectivistic ideal is not a being different from man so much as only an enlarged version of what men would like to be.[1] Applied to this anthropomorphic God, Feuerbach's critique is, of course, correct: *this* god is nothing more than the projection of our desire to know, to have power and to be independent of contingencies.

In the preceding chapter the logic of utopianism was shown to demand the abolition not only of meaningful discourse about a personal and transcendental God (theology), but also of philosophy, the meaningful discourse about man in his dependence on God and under the burden of freedom. In the eyes of the utopian, the place of theology is assumed by history and science or by their combination in a kind of generalized theory of historical evolution. Such a new science is supposed to explore the conditions of emergence of man-become-God. It would be, at once, a descriptive and normative science, since it would deal with the data of its subject in a scientific manner and would formulate imperatives on how best to approach the value it proposes to attain. In a similar way, philosophy's place would be taken by a kind of general anthropology from which all elements of uncertainty and speculation would be eliminated. No longer need man scrutinize and interpret God's will and the roots of his own being; he need merely study nature and the course of history attentively, for his destiny would coincide with the indica-

[1] Thomas Molnar, *The Decline of the Intellectual*, Meridian Books, World Publishing Company, Cleveland, Ohio, 1961, p. 340.

tions that these two provide in abundance. Accordingly, it would no longer be a destiny, that is, a course prescribed from outside; it would rather be a royal road to the conscious and scientifically planned completion of super-humanity. Beyond that royal road there could be nothing, nor could there be other possibilities in the form of parallel roads. The end of philosophy would itself be proof that the childhood period was over and adulthood had commenced.

Marx had congratulated Feuerbach for his understanding that philosophy, too, is a form of alienation. Indeed, the utopian is acutely aware of the obstacles which prevent him from reorganizing the world. The main obstacle, the one on which everything else depends, is the existence of God, the guarantor of human freedom. With God eliminated, mankind enters the final phase of its existence which may be called either the stage of freedom from God or the stage of necessity, since nature and history now dictate man's decisions and actions with an absolute authority surpassing that of God. For two reasons the new anthropology does not recognize man's freedom to refuse these dictates: first, because these dictates are proclaimed in the name of nature; secondly, because man is himself part of nature and of history, nothing remains in reference to which he might say "no."

The Utopian Objective: A Coalesced Mankind

A major consequence follows from these considerations. Utopian systems never speak of the individual; they always speak of mankind. It is only on that level that they can broach their gigantic enterprise. Neither the individual, nor groups, nor States tip the scale. It is true that the various fictitious voyages to this utopia describe one particular ideal community, often completely isolated from neighbors, but it does represent mankind. No historical tradition and no geographic or climatic peculiarity set it aside from the rest of men and the world at large. On the contrary, the descriptions of such fictitious voyages are a kind of invitation for others to join in the simple requirement of absolute conformity to the laws which are proclaimed once and for all. The new citizen may start being a "utopian" from the first moment; his past and his preferences do not count, because, upon entering utopia, he has shed all distinctive qualities and has joined a colorless, an *a*historical and non-dimensional existence.

The remaining chapters of this book will deal with the characteristic features of utopia as a political construct. Naturally, the term "political" will have to be properly redefined, if this is possible in the strict sense. Politics derives from the word *polis* (city) in which human beings live out their lives in all their fullness. Politics deals with the many relationships established between people and the groups to which they belong; since these groups are ordered according to a certain hierarchy, tensions arise within them and also within the individual himself who belongs to several of these groups, including the State itself. The concept of politics is, consequently, as rich as the human being who, as Aristotle said, is a political being. The concept of utopia, on the other hand, is narrow since its citizens belong only to one group, the State, and to one order, the communal one. The stress at the beginning of this chapter on the need both to exclude from utopia that God who is radically different from the world and to introduce an immanent God in his place is due to the fact that God always acts like a magnet, attracting to himself a part of man's loyalty. This would disrupt utopia. On the other hand, if mankind, as such, is considered divine, the cohesion of utopia is complete.

The analysis of utopia is not, then, a political analysis, but one which studies the principle of cohesion applied to human beings. It is, by necessity, the study of a mental construct and of the ideal conditions among which it would materialize, if it could materialize.

Cohesion is, of course, a permanent requirement of all societies. Pre-Christian societies often solved the problem by endowing their temporal leader with divine attributes so that he became the center of civic discipline as well as the object of divine worship. The Greek city-states, as well as Rome and the tribes of Africa, meant to satisfy both material and spiritual needs of their citizens, even though the ruler was no longer considered God. However, the ruler was still, as in Rome, *pontifex maximus*, high priest of the State creed. Only the Jewish kingdom and, later, the Christian State achieved the separation of the temporal and spiritual powers, although not without great tensions and conflicts. Each marshalled interminable arguments to prove its own ultimate superiority over the other.

United Mankind as a Permanent Dream

The restoration of unity and cohesion, envisaged for a brief historic moment in the form of the *Respublica Christiana*, remained only a noble aspiration. Elsewhere[2] I outlined the efforts right up to the present to heal the breach and to constitute a world society no longer based on true Christian principles, but on a State religion, or on the universality of reason and science, or on the global necessities of industrial production, or on an ideology acceptable to all mankind. These efforts have so far failed as the Christian *Respublica* failed before them. Yet, such is the attraction of the idea of unity and cohesion that new doctrines arise after the old ones are discarded, and each new doctrine intends to make a radical sweep and prove that a certain new historical factor, detected for the first time, is the long sought key to mankind's oneness.

Interestingly enough, up until the French Revolution the model for cohesion was the pagan world. During the Middle Ages and despite the obviously Catholic inspiration of the Christian *Respublica*, the unity of Rome remained the ideal, one which was to receive fresh emphasis during the Renaissance period when Machiavelli almost overtly recommended that a return to the an-

[2] *Ibid.*, Chapter 1.

cient civic religion of Rome would favor the prince's enterprise of restoring unity to the Italian peninsula.[3] Deploring the dualism that Christianity introduced into the body politic (*Social Contract,* IV, 8) Rousseau pointed out that the division of power between God and Caesar—the medieval doctrine of the "two swords"— which separates the individual from society is an evil. This evil, Rousseau claimed, had come into existence when Jesus Christ came to establish a spiritual kingdom, thereby separating the theological system from the political system and breaking the State in two.

The French Revolution represents a dividing line in mankind's aspiration for unity. Although the terminology and attitudes of the revolutionaries and even of Napoleon's empire were an imitation of ancient Greece and Rome in many respects, the model for utopia was no longer sought in the past but in the future. Utopian thinking, in all its elements and aspirations, forms one whole throughout history; but different events dress it in new garb, re-phrase its terminology and provide it with new ideological instru-ments. Actually it is not wholly accurate to say that the nineteenth-century utopians suddenly turned to the future instead of to the past; more exactly, they no longer needed the historical model of great prestige that was Rome or its pagan religion as a counterpart to Christianity. The completely secular State that made its appearance and its secular philosophy, emancipated from all religious ties, promised better working models and instruments than a historically closed period. After all, Rome had succumbed both as a religion and as a State before a victorious Christianity.

Unity Can Now Be Organized

Accordingly, the idea of mankind's future oneness has been advocated, more and more, as a dominant *leitmotiv* since the

[3] Frederic II, who died in 1250, is reported to have said that if the rulers of Europe accepted his views, he would establish for all nations a system of beliefs and of government vastly preferable to anything past or present.

beginning of the nineteenth century. The conviction has grown that man has entered the "last period"—the period of mankind's maturity—when the concept of God may be discarded and all divine attributes internalized by their legitimate possessor, mankind. This "last phase" was the plenitude of time as Joachim of Flore had seen it at the end of the twelfth century. In his system it was to be the "fourth epoch," the age of the monks and the coming of the Holy Ghost and liberty. The eternal Gospel was to dominate this epoch, but not in its written version: it was to be the spiritual interpretation of the Old and the New Testament. We find similar religious language in the writings of Fr. Teilhard de Chardin, but with a significant difference: the eternal Gospel, in Joachim's mind, will be a spiritual reality, uniting mankind—which has become Christian—in one worshipful body. For Teilhard, the Gospel fulfilment is Point Omega, the pole of evolution, terminal point of maturation of a world finally centered, a finished convergence, the last inward concentration of the Noosphere (cf. *La Centrologie*, pp. 18–19). Teilhard calls this process "hominization," and he defines it as the concentration on itself of terrestrial psychism or, more simply, "increased consciousness." Joachim's spiritualized Gospel and Teilhard's terminal point of maturation are one and the same thing, except that Teilhard expresses himself in the language of evolution and is unable, therefore, to distinguish clearly four or, for that matter, any number of epochs. As earlier noted, this is an advantage for Teilhard. Whereas Joachim gives dates for his epochs (the fourth was to begin in 1260, about fifty years after his death) and could be proved wrong in his predictions, Teilhard cannot be pinned down. Rather than tell us at what point we stand in the hominization process, Teilhard tells us only that we are "on the way" to Point Omega.[4] Hominization, at any rate, has not ended with *homo sapiens:* in 1950, Teilhard (*Le Coeur de la*

[4] The utopian's enthusiasm once got the better of Teilhard de Chardin when he assigned 1957—First International Geophysical Year—as the first year of the Noosphere.

matière) greeted the fantastic spectacle of *collective thought* ascending rapidly at the rhythm of an increasingly unitary organization.

"Organization" is the keyword of the contemporary utopians. It suffices for the materialist because his ideal for mankind is power over nature: nature's capriciousness and spontaneity must be organized and its enormous potentialities placed at the service of mankind. What was, for Joachim de Flore, the fourth epoch is, for Soviet philosopher A. Bogdanov, the third main stage of history, that of the collective, self-sufficient economy. He describes this third stage as the fusion of personal lives into one colossal whole, harmonious in the relation of part to part, a systematic grouping of all elements for the common struggle against nature's endless spontaneity. This third stage demands the forces of all mankind because only by working at this task does mankind, as such, emerge.

For the non-materialist utopian, however, "organization" is clearly an incomplete principle of cohesion. God is not merely an organizer of matter and nature, but He is also a creator whose qualities, in turn, permeate creation. Such a utopian feels compelled, therefore, to transfer such qualities as goodness, love and harmony to mankind. Consequently, the language used to describe future mankind is a strange mixture of emotional and scientific terms, that is, expressions denoting generosity, endearment and encouragement which invite one to follow now reason, now the heart.

Marx wanted to situate mankind in those ideal conditions where he would find the fulfillment of every aspiration in concrete reality. In this way, mankind need never again invent such systems of mystification as religion, art and philosophy. The socialists, whom Marx called utopians, insisted that the ideal conditions include also a development of sentiments. Saint-Simon, the most clear-sighted among them, actually envisaged the restoration of Christianity in some radically new form. And the Romantic Schleiermacher spoke of affinity as the basis of all ties uniting mankind. Generally speaking, however, from the Saint-Simonians to the anarchists, all agreed that in the most favorable conditions men would also develop their affectivity, their sense of submission to and adoration of universal harmony. The Saint-Simonian periodical, *Le Producteur*, predicted that the earth will belong to one people united through the ties of industry, science and a feeling of kindness. And Bakunin, while holding that unity is the goal toward which mankind ceaselessly moves, also noted that the new organization will have no other basis than the natural needs, inclinations and endeavors of men.[5]

Love and Science Cement Unity

But love and affection are still not sufficient. The "theology" of man-God is couched in a mystical language similar to that of all religious mystics. While this language is different in that it does not celebrate the union of the soul with God, yet it does serve to stir up enthusiasm for a collective project which has difficulty in getting started by its own efforts. The enthusiasts stand around this project's altar, encouraging themselves with imprecise references to the expected rewards, and they try to achieve by incantation what is unwarranted by reason and experience. In view of what has been said about the nineteenth-century socialists and the climate of literary romanticism in which they lived and wrote, it should be mentioned that their language is not necessarily romantic or lyrical. Saint-Simon, Comte, Proudhon and Bakunin were in many respects down-to-earth realists, efficient organizers and lucid stylists exactly as were those other utopian thinkers, before and after them, who were prominent in scientific or political activities. At the same time, when a certain chord in their

[5] *Fédéralisme, socialisme, et anti-théologisme*, p. 16.

intellectual-emotional makeup was struck, they did not hesitate to use the language of utopia. Twentieth-century utopians, as will presently be indicated, use the same language as the medieval heretic or the nineteenth-century socialists, that curious mixture of emotionalism and science so suited to utopian thought.

Because love and affections only partly guarantee the desired cohesion of mankind, the laws by which these effusions are correctly channeled must be discovered. Fourrier claimed the simultaneous discovery of cosmic truth and social truth which, like the truth of geometry and physics, is independent of people and places and is universally valid. If there is unity and harmony among all parts of the universe, Fourrier taught, there must be a similar cohesion among each of its constituting parts. Society must then be linked with the universe rather than follow independent laws of its own. Consequently, Fourrier could speak of a "destiny of mankind . . . to be fulfilled when mankind, as a whole, has fully grasped the meaning of its calling and the phases through which it enters the true and final phase of its history, universal harmony linking the efforts of all men."[6]

The utopian usually begins by exalting the beauty and nobility of universal love. But he soon discovers that, to make love universal, one must legislate it, establish the laws of loving the right objects in the right way: he introduces organization into love. The many "ifs" in utopian texts are very quickly converted into "musts." Fourrier believed that mankind's essence is love because he was convinced that all the parts of the universe are held together by some sort of love or harmony. Yet he was impatient for this love to become explicit and to assume an active role in bringing about unity. Sooner or later, mankind must grasp the profounder meaning of its calling, the sign that it has reached the stage of fusion between reason and love. Then all will be perfect, that is, as Fichte said, all will be "absolutely identical." "If all men could be perfect,

6 Cf. J. L. Talmon, *Political Messianism*, Frederick A. Praeger, Publishers, New York, 1960, p. 138.

if all could attain their supreme final goal, they would all be absolutely identical; they would be one. The ultimate goal of society is the fusion of all, the unanimity of all the possible members . . . the unanimity of all in their practical conviction."[6a]

At this point, *cohesion*, explained both by natural affinity and reason, becomes *uniformity*; more than that, it becomes *coalescence* into one indistinguishable mass. Substituted for the alleged defense of the individual against the spontaneity of nature and against crushing political forces is mankind's defense against the spontaneity and freedom of the individual. The evil is diagnosed as the split that religion, particularly Christianity, effected in man's mind and loyalties, so that, in order to heal the split, the loss of individual freedom is chalked up as mankind's gain. All the suffering inherent in the human situation is ascribed to freedom, and freedom is described as a state of childhood. Maturity must bring about renunciation of individual freedom in favor of mankind's freedom to fulfill its destiny.

This is, in general, the message of those whom Talmon calls the nineteenth-century "prophets."

[These men] took upon themselves the mission of re-establishing the unity of life which they claimed had been broken by the Christian teachings on the fall of man and the eternal enmity between spirit and matter. . . . The Messianic thinkers triumphantly claimed . . . that man's freedom was commensurate with the advance of social cohesion. . . . They believed that conditions were maturing before their eyes for a complete harmonization of all the elements of the social framework. They considered it their mission to impart to their fellow-men the life-giving awareness of being agents within a progressive and purposeful Unity across time and place.[7]

[6a] *Ibid.*, p. 186.
[7] *Ibid.*, pp. 506–507.

One may, perhaps, properly speak here of an idea gone mad, namely, the idea of unity. However, this is the peculiar madness of the utopian who confuses unity with actual oneness. And the reasons for the madness are these: all the energies of an immanentized God are now supposed to work for a goal which, for the first time in man's existence, is said to be clearly recognized; the veil that so long hid man's true destiny from his eyes is now torn away, and all the passion and adoration previously claimed as God's due is directed to mankind. No expression is strong enough to celebrate the coalescence of all men. The freedom of insufficiently socialized man appears to Fr. Teilhard (*L'Avenir de l'homme vu par un paléontologiste*) as still rudimentary. Man's fundamental choice—which seems to have been, in the eyes of Teilhard (cf. *La Grande Option*), the choice to be an individual—will yield to the common choice of the human mass.

So much for the religious utopian. Yet, the agnostic utopian sees the same fundamental option. In *Caliban*, Renan expressed the opinion that in the indeterminable future everything will become one single center of consciousness in which all human beings will participate and which will give a meaning to all their sacrifices. In the same way as mankind has emerged from animality, Renan continues, the divinity will emerge from mankind. In their turn, the superhuman gods will become one single god.

The language of biology, religion, sciences of every sort, even electronic communications, are all fused into one language to describe this god. Let there be no mistake, however, for this god is nothing other than mankind; mankind, in turn, is a diffuse, amorphous being about which only the vaguest notions can be entertained. Any precise statement regarding this being must be at once suspect, since the very value of coalescence is its perpetual becoming and diffusion. Precise statements imply limitations on the endless possibilities. For the very same reason, precise questions, requests for clarification, let alone reasonable expressions of doubt, are also considered as sabotaging the future. Since the future is, in spite of the utopian's visions and predictions, shrouded in layers of clouds, the question "How do you know that this will happen?" elicits the utopian's counter-question "How do you know it will *not* happen?" In the utopian's eyes, the world as well as mankind are supposed to be continuously expanding and enriching themselves, becoming ever more marvelous. Therefore anything may happen, the accepted rules of logic and experience notwithstanding.

The utopian is unquestionably an irrational man. In his mind the supreme equation is this: "Everything is equal with everything else." This is not only political truth for the utopian, the truth of total democracy, but it is chiefly an ontological truth (pantheism). In his marvelously precise way, Chesterton gave the best comment on the utopian mind when he wrote of Mrs. Besant and her theosophy:

> According to Mrs. Besant the universal Church is simply the universal self. It is the doctrine that we are really all one person; that there are no real walls of individuality between man and man. If I may put it so, she does not tell us to love our neighbor; she tells us to be our neighbors. . . . The intellectual abyss between Buddhism and Christianity is that, for the Buddhist or theosophist, personality is the fall of man, for the Christian it is the purpose of God, the whole point of his cosmic idea.[7a]

Teilhard's Noosphere

The walls of individuality, mentioned by Chesterton, are torn down in various ways, spiritual or material. It is easy for the utopian to assume that all contemporary movements, inventions

[7a] *Orthodoxy*, Dodd, Mead and Company, New York, 1927, pp. 244–45.

and phenomena tend essentially in the same direction, that what he morally approves is advanced by evolution on the plane of scientific discoveries, and vice versa. Thus the utopian sees relationships and harmonies where such do not exist. However, since all of these are immersed in the evolutionary stream, the utopian is supremely confident that others will agree with him when they catch up—as they eventually must—with the wave he rides. The breakdown of individualities—or their fusion, which amounts to the same thing—is announced, from the utopian's viewpoint, by spiritual and material portents, that is, by everything happening around us. In this connection, Teilhard de Chardin (*Esquisse d'une dialectique de l'esprit*) claimed that, in order to be alpha and omega, the Christ himself must, without losing his human dimension, become co-extensive with the physical immensities of Space and Time. Teilhard's assertion at least forecasts an objective, although, in typical utopian style, the author uses the verb "must," meaning expected fulfillment, instead of a term to indicate the merely desirable. Yet even this semblance of forecast disappears in another passage where it is said that nothing can be foreseen with any degree of probability. None of this, however, deters Fr. Teilhard from certitude in detecting converging tendencies between Christ, who becomes coextensive with the material universe, and mankind, which becomes a super-organism and collective thought-machine. We are assured that the super-evolution of mankind is actually taking place. It would be vain to predict its concrete forms, but one may indicate the axis of the metamorphosis. Our species tends to constitute itself into a closed system, a veritable super-organism in which individual reflexes will be grouped and will reinforce themselves in the act of one simple unanimous thought. Mankind, it is asserted by Teilhard (see Fr. Henri de Lubac's *La Pensée religieuse du Père Teilhard de Chardin*) is advancing toward a phase of collective and superior thought, the critical point of socialization and co-thinking.

As should be apparent by now, it is more and more difficult to

derive rational statements from utopian writers engulfed in the orgy
of their visions. One no longer knows whether the texts describe
a machine, a human being of tremendous dimensions, a materially
coalesced group—that is, a mass of human flesh—a super-Christ,
or an infinitely perfected network of telecommunications. When
Teilhard speaks of Christ, his language resembles some of the
crude medieval texts in their description of the Virgin's milk
or some saint's miraculous powers. On the other hand, some
utopian writers ignore the coalescence of consciousness while exploring the social effects of mechanical communication. In *The
Last and First Men* by Olaf Stapledon and *The Last Prophet* by
Haldane, communication by telepathy results in a social super-
organism. Electronic waves convey the social consensus at all
moments of life, so that the members of the community act automatically in the common interest. Similarly, Julian Huxley attributes the growth of mental substance to the improvement of
communication and to the numerical increase of men: "Mankind
as a whole will achieve more intense, more complex and more
integrated mental activity which can guide the human species up
the path of progress to higher levels of hominization."[8] Mixing
his own terms and insights with those of Teilhard, Huxley then
points out that the earth is now in the process of becoming cephal-
ized, that is, of acquiring a brain: "the incipient development of
mankind into a single psycho-social unit, with a single noosystem,
or common pool of thought, is providing the evolutionary process
with the rudiments of a head."[9]

As earlier noted, Fr. Teilhard has no intention of being left
behind in proposing such a rudimentary "head" for mankind. His
original contribution consists of the fervent images which remain
just as unimaginable and inconceivable as Huxley's crude ones. Yet,
one cannot dismiss Teilhard simply by saying that he is a mere

[8] Cf. Preface to *The Phenomenon of Man*, Harper & Row, New York,
1959, p. 17.
[9] *Ibid.*, p. 20.

visionary. In many instances he is quite specific, although his details are as consistently irrelevant to the real world as are his perfervid generalizations. He writes, for example:

> The noosphere tends to constitute a single closed system in which each element sees, feels, desires and suffers for itself the same things as all the others at the same time. . . . We are faced with a harmonized collectivity of consciousness equivalent to a sort of super-consciousness. The idea is that of the earth not only becoming covered by myriads of grains of thought, but becoming enclosed in a single thinking envelope so as to form, functionally, no more than a single vast grain of thought on the sidereal scale, the plurality of individual reflections grouping themselves together and reinforcing one another in the act of a single unanimous reflection.[10]

After such a chain of absurdities, one may ask what Fr. de Lubac meant when he wrote in his defense of his brother Jesuit that Teilhard has only contempt and disgust for the "pitiful millenarians," of so many ideologies where we see on the horizon the flat profile of a golden age. He accuses more than one neo-humanist, Fr. de Lubac[11] goes on, of confusing the great idea of human maturation with these miserable dreams.

Soviet and Chinese Examples of Enforced Unanimity

Fathers de Lubac and Teilhard are both right in denouncing the "flatness" of so many millennial dreams about a golden age. It must be admitted that many "pitiful millenarians" do describe purely material satisfactions and/or grotesque achievements which merely show that man's desire to dominate the forces of the universe

[10] *Ibid.*, p. 251.
[11] *Op. cit.*, p. 54.

includes also a playful element. But we should not be misled by the dividing line that Fr. Teilhard and Fr. de Lubac, who seems to agree, draw between these platitudinous constructs and the great idea of human maturation. The line is artificial because one and the same utopian will unites the two, even though the religious or spiritualist utopian of the Teilhard type eludes the charges by projecting his images not merely into a hypothetical future still within the context of history, but into a biological, psycho-biological, even cosmic future that is at a safe distance from all possible verification or approximation. Hence his ample use of such expressions as "the noosphere tends to" and "the idea is of the earth becoming. . . ."

The important thing is to understand that Teilhard falls into the category of the millenarians he so rightly despises. In spite of his daring images and astrobiological anticipations, Teilhard, like all utopians, is apprehensive about human freedom and insists on reducing it to strict, planned order. In harmony with other utopians, he recommends eugenic measures to discipline the human race. When the utopian finds that mankind, as constituted, does not fit in with his future scheme of things, he abandons the idea of political regimentation and directs his attention to medical intervention. To put it more precisely, in every instance the utopian regards political regimentation as the last resort to administer biological changes. As in certain German concentration camps, total power permits medical experimentation in view of what is euphemistically called "improving the quality of the race." Writes Teilhard:

> So far we have certainly allowed our race to develop at random, and we have given too little thought to the question of what medical and moral factors must replace the crude forces of natural selection, should one suppress them. In the course of the coming centuries it is indispensable that a nobly human

form of eugenics, on a standard worthy of our personalities, should be discovered and developed.[12]

It is important to deal at length with Teilhard's writings on this matter because they represent what is meant to be the theological guarantee of utopia. It would be an error, however, to think that Teilhard's notions about mankind's coming oneness are separable from the utopian manifestations of today's totalitarian ideologies and empires. Teilhard merely seems to set the problem of man, as the utopian sees it, on lofty heights; yet, his terminology, which mixes archeology, sociology, biology, astronomy and a vulgarized theology, can, in fact, be translated at every turn into the language of collectivism and of totalitarian policies.

Léon Emery pointed out that nothing in the name and policies of the Soviet State applies officially to a particular territory or is circumscribed by geographical and historical precision. The new era, he writes, happened to begin in one particular area of the world, but other Soviet societies will naturally join as they come into existence. The borders of the new society are, therefore, not fixed; they will remain temporary borders until the time when they will coincide with those of the globe. The same may also be said of Soviet man; when he declares himself a Communist, he is rid of the heredity which alienated him and becomes integrated in the great community of workers.[13]

The Soviet writer V. Ilenkov expressed the same thought in his novel, *The Highway*. Commenting on the uniformity of thought that, through Soviet society, had become a reality for the first time in history, Ilenkov observed that people have suffered for thousands

---

[12] *The Phenomenon of Man*, p. 282. Furthermore, the odious part here is that Teilhard de Chardin would use this "nobly human form" of eugenics to prepare the "super-mankind" for its meeting with the equally emerging "super-Christ."

[13] "Les Nations et la Supra-Nation," in *Le Contrat Social*, March–April, 1962, p. 81.

of years because they did not think alike. Soviet men have now, for the first time, come to understand each other, thinking identically about the principal things of life. Because Soviet men are strong by ties of ideological unity, they are superior to all other people who are torn and divided by the pluralism of their thought.

In practice as well as in official proclamations, the Chinese communists have until now gone farthest in trying to extirpate the natural sentiments of private man and to replace them with enforced public sentiments. One may argue that such compulsion has a twofold motivation; first, it is necessary to counterbalance the natural individualism of the Chinese by pressuring them to devote more attention to collective aims; secondly, the celebrated family loyalty among the Chinese is an obstacle to the amount of collective work which Communist leaders have assigned their subjects. The fact remains, nevertheless, that the texts of the proclamations, manifestoes and allegedly genuine personal statements reflect the will, imposed from above with incredible ruthlessness, toward complete submersion of the individual in the collectivity and the collectivity's total coalescence. Love or any sort of solid attachment for another person may not be isolated from political attributes. In fact, whoever is not politically motivated in his attachments and shows no interest in the collectivity does not really love. If, on the other hand, love is based on the correct socialist criteria, then even physical separation from the loved one ceases to be painful.

In a magazine published for the women of Red China, a letter from a young Communist girl is quoted. She tells of a message just received from her boy friend to the effect that he has enrolled in the work force at Lake Tungking. Far from being disappointed at his departure, the young girl is especially happy, she writes, because she knows that her Lao Tong is taking part in the collective effort to build socialism.

The same issue of this magazine holds up the example of a Mrs.

Chou. In her letter to the editor she tells of counseling her sons and daughters-in-law about the paramount importance of the group and the relative unimportance of the family, about the satisfaction which comes from obedience to party discipline and from devoting even leisure hours to party aims. The article lays special stress on the teaching that love of the group and adequate participation in collective production imply the necessity of putting one's family life on a rational basis. Production, it is made clear, will suffer if family life is not properly organized.[14]

Utopian Order and the Order of Freedom

The evidence is overwhelming that such an outlook on the relationship between individual and collectivity is unnatural. This kind of attitude can exist only in minds devoted exclusively to abstract constructs and in the will of a class which tolerates no opposition in its absolute thirst for power. It is beside the point here to consider the examples of religious orders, fanatical sects, self-sacrificing élite groups and even Japanese kamikaze (suicide) pilots because the individual in all these examples *freely* abandons a part or even the totality of his right to privacy and to life, and freely submits himself to discipline and sacrifice. The utopian argues that such willingness to sacrifice for the community ("socialization") is not only to be found in the hearts of all men, but, as Teilhard and others claim, evolution and history make this willingness increasingly natural and necessary. According to the utopians, order must then emerge out of the present chaos (the chaos of history is equal to the random decisions of men; the chaos of nature is equal to the crude forces which have not yet been dominated), and this order will be characterized by mankind's oneness in thought, intention, and action.

[14] Both of these letters appeared in Paul Hollander's "La Vie privée en Chine," in *Le Contrat Social,* January–February, 1964, p. 40.

However, the questions that should be addressed to the utopian are these: Is not order the coordination of several elements without loss of their specific natures? Is not human order the coordination of persons without loss of their individual natures? We use the term natures—the plural—since a human being is not merely the abstract element of a potential order, but a rich and complex reality, existing on many equally precious planes whose coordination may be desirable. St. Thomas Aquinas' concept of order contradicts the utopian's insistence that there is only one order which the individual is not free to reject because it is historically and/or biologically necessary. According to Aquinas, order is that sum total of a being's relationships by which it is enabled to realize the perfection of its nature. Relating this to man, it must be borne in mind that his nature is a composite; order, then, is multiple. Man's nature is *social*, so that man is meant to be coordinated with society; but his nature is also *rational*, so that he is intended to understand the universe of which he is part; man's nature is also *creatural*, whereby he must strive so to order his life that he may reach God as his natural end.

The foregoing is anarchy and disorder to the utopian because he sees no guarantee that these various orders can be integrated in view of a supreme efficiency. The utopian assumes mankind's goal to be the perfection of the collectivity; accordingly, he holds that this goal will be attained in the most efficient and fastest way only when all men work together on this common assignment. All talk, then, of the integration of different orders found in the complexity of human nature is a waste of time and energy to the utopian, and serves to confound his unique insight into the destination of the universe.

In the practical order—in fact, especially in the practical order—the utopian's drive toward community perfection invariably leads to dismal failure. Although cooperation among members of society is highly desirable, there is no escaping the inevitability of antagonisms. The scarcity of industrial products before the Industrial Revolution created no more conflict among individuals and communities than the current abundance of such merchandise. It was Charles Maurras who observed that even in the midst of universal plenty there will always be the matter of good and bad quality. And when every elementary need will have been satisfied, there will always arise other appetites in need of satisfaction.[15]

In this very effort to show the practical utility of utopian drives, the utopian feels he sees the reason why a mass society, in which everybody is equal and thinks only of executing the community-approved projects, is the form best suited for the era of abundance. When distribution of abundance is well organized, he points out, conflicts among individuals are eliminated, as are wars among national communities. The ensuing permanent peace may then be further organized with a view toward leisure, culture and general happiness. The facts of life, however, show that mass societies are even more oppressive and militant than societies in which a certain elite (oligarchy or aristocracy, for example) exercises considerable prudence simply to remain in power. On the other hand, the pressures exerted on the populations of mass societies make them only more brutal; in fact, the more equal the individuals are, the less are they subject to moral discipline or responsibility and the more evident becomes the basic primitiveness and absence of control in their behavior. The call to collective accomplishments, the endless regimentation, lead not to pacifism, but to a militaristic psychology. Even pacifist groups and others who call for disarmament are arrayed in morose battalions, shouting their bloodthirsty slogans: War on Tyrants! Death to Warmongers!

Mankind's attempts at total, utopian integration will manage to move forward only on that day when artificial sentiments support artificial objectives, when natural sentiments are torn out by the roots and replaced by false feelings and aspirations. The utopian

[15] *Mes idées politiques,* Préface, Fayard, Paris, 1937.

assumes that the vistas he exposes to mankind are so glorious that we can show adequate tribute only in a permanent state of enthusiasm. Although enthusiasm usually manifests itself in loudly voiced approval, it is, basically, a constant affirmation of unity and pledge of participation.[16] Yet, as Lord Percy of Newcastle notes in *The Heresy of Democracy,* the hectic search for unity must entail mob violence and legalized terror; it lies in the more fundamental fact that a people, thus summoned to demonstrate its unity as the pre-condition of its liberty, must regard enthusiasm as the first duty of citizenship.

[16] Typical examples of such enthusiasm are to be found in the Chinese letters and reviews noted above. In them, the more than a century-old description of Fourrier's Phalansters becomes a gruesome reality. "We could see in the early dawn about thirty industrious groups leaving, in parade formation, the Palace of the Phalanster. They were dispersing in the fields and workshops, waving their flags with shouts of triumph and impatience." Quoted by Raymond Ruyer, *L'Utopie et les Utopies,* Presses Universitaires de France, 1950, p. 220.

6 - PASSAGE TO
UTOPIA

IN THE FACE of any delay in the process, impatience is to be expected on the part of those for whom mankind must one day coalesce. The fact of emerging unity is beyond dispute, but how it will come about is somewhat problematical. If only a system could be found, say the utopians, to gather together the forces of nature and the determinations of men to replace the present dispersal and disunity, the process would be immeasurably accelerated. Given such a system, the results would be so overwhelming that, from that point onward, only scattered opposition would manifest itself, and with decreasing frequency and vigor.

As is always true of utopians, one particular moment, situation or institution is considered the decisive target: the abolition of a particular institution, the introduction and universalization of one certain attitude, or "one last effort on the part of mankind" is singled out as the decisive event meant to bring about the desired transformation. Understandably, then, utopian thinkers spend considerable time in studying the *period of transformation* as they severally see or predict it.

The Utopian's Will to Power

Utopians, as earlier and frequently indicated, consider individual freedom as the stumbling block on which the grandiose idea of mankind's totalization may flounder. Granted that the utopian may not condemn human freedom as such, granted also that he may even attach great value to it—provided guarantees in man's material, psychological or spiritual make-up are found to insure this freedom's integration with other freedoms for the common goal— still eventually there comes the choice between freedom and cohesion. The utopian opts for the latter either because, as Hilaire Belloc writes, "the human and organic complexity which is the color of any vital society offends him by its infinite differentiation"[1] or because he assigns to mankind a sort of cosmic adventure. In the first instance—again in Belloc's eloquent words—"the prospect of a vast bureaucracy wherein the whole of life shall be scheduled and appointed to certain simple schemes . . . gives his small stomach a final satisfaction." In the second instance he visualizes the globe as having become one powerful dynamo from the integration of all its natural and human potentials and launched upon the conquest of other globes, planets, solar systems—and God himself. The pettiness of the first scheme and the fantastic character of the second should not lead to the belief that the two schemes lack a common source: *power* over things and men—the will to be God—is the ultimate objective of both. Observed H. G. Wells in *A Modern Utopia*:

> The Utopia of a modern dreamer must needs differ in one fundamental aspect from the Nowheres and Utopias men planned before Darwin quickened the thought of the world.

[1] Hilaire Belloc, *The Servile State*, Henry Holt and Company, New York, 1946, p. 127.

Those were all perfect and static States, a balance of happiness won forever against the forces of unrest and disorder that inhere in things. But the Modern Utopia must be not static but kinetic, must take shape not as a permanent state but as a hopeful stage, leading to a long ascent of stages.

To understand, with the utopian, that human freedom jeopardizes these prospects, these states of happiness and this long ascent of stages injects incalculability into the march of things and accounts for the differences between one man and another, is also to understand why it is of relatively little importance for the utopian to deprive mankind of the instruments of freedom. The transition period toward utopia is, then, the process of removing and abolishing certain of these instruments of freedom. Granted, in every age these instruments change and the utopian, child of his age, concentrates on those which in his eyes are the most obstructive of common happiness, yet, even though some of these instruments are permanent, they are still denounced with passion or by cold logic throughout the pages of utopian literature.

The Stumbling Blocks: Government and Property

The instruments through which human freedom most importantly manifests itself in the practical order of things are government—institutions in general—and property. The study of why utopians denounce institutions belongs to a later chapter; attention will here be given to the process of abolishing property and money—money being the means of converting one form of property into another. Economic analysis exclusively will not suffice, and for the reason that property is no mere personal satisfaction that may be inherited or purchased at current prices; property is also *a means of domination as well as a means of resisting domination*. Those who have an inordinate amount of property tend to dominate those who have less; furthermore, those who do have property have the means to withstand pressures or positively to exert influence on those who hold powerful political means. Therefore, private property at once introduces the problem of power and power relationship, whereas collective property represents ideally a state of equilibrium. Property can be maintained in collective ownership by collective acceptance of an ideal which temporarily supersedes the desire by private individuals to distribute it or it can be maintained by superior force against private individuals. In the second case, as Aristotle said in his criticism of Plato (*Politics*, Book II), collective property is either neglected or else it is fought for; on the other hand, the aspiration to own property privately is a natural form of self-love and also a form of self-defense. This was recognized by Marx when he argued, in the *Critique of Political Economy*, that the essence of ownership is the right to command others, that is, a relationship of domination and subordination. It is reasonable, then, to say that the best way of altogether abolishing or, at least, extenuating such relationships would be to secure for everyone such a reasonable amount of property as would enable each individual to lighten the burden of his subordination in society. It is just as obvious that the Marxists play on words when they pretend that the problem of domination and subordination is solved when the State, or collectivity, concentrates all property in its hands—the play on words being found in their position that nobody owns this property. This is simply not true because the State owns it, that is, the most powerful possible social entity owns it, a power over which none may exercise control and from the hands of which none may wring concessions.[2]

Socialists customarily argue against even such forms of private ownership as shareholding. Strachey,[3] for example, charges

[2] It is, of course, a further aggravating circumstance that the abstract collectivity is, in reality, a political class whose power is the more unlimited as it hides behind the veil of "collective ownership."

[3] *Contemporary Capitalism,* Random House Inc., New York, 1956, pp. 231–232.

rather hypocritically—since he is against private ownership anyway —that shareholding, because it is impersonal, contradicts the concept of private property as enunciated by Locke. But our basic argument holds against Strachey: even in this impersonal form, when most shareholders never even set eyes on the actual plant or business in whose ownership they share, property rights are respected by managers, banks and delegates of the shareholders, so that property represents power in shareholding, no matter how minimal.

And not only power in some naked form, but also the reasonably free exercise of one's faculties to take care of himself, to initiate and carry out plans, to create. The Catholic Church formulates this possibility of free exercise of one's functions and responsibilities as the principle of *subsidiarity*. Popes Pius XI[4] and John XXIII[5] stressed emphatically the need to create those social conditions which permit each man to decide and act whenever he can do so on his own initiative and according to his own means. The principle of subsidiarity thus recognizes the inherent right of each inferior order (in the ascending order of individual, family, group, institution, government) to initiate and undertake anything within its capacity and ends; concurrently it enjoins on each superior order not to intervene or assume control until it is ascertained that the former canot fulfill a given task. Socialist arguments against this principle amounts to a gradual takeover of all tasks by the highest superior order—the State—with the result that all inferior orders become paralyzed and atrophied. The entire society is thereby turned into a monstrous public assistance system and is members are reduced to the status of children.[6]

Because of this close relationship between the right to property

---

[4] *Quadragesimo Anno.*

[5] *Mater et Magistra.*

[6] Alexis de Tocqueville foresaw in the new society "a multitude of similar and equal individuals . . . working to procure themselves petty and vulgar satisfactions. Above these men there rears a monstrous tutelary power who provides for their security, foresees and supplies their necessities, directs their industry, regulates the descent of property, and subdivides their inheritances: what remains but to spare them all the care of thinking and all the

and the elementary freedoms, utopians naturally have never ceased to denounce individual ownership, free exchange of goods, and the existence of money. Second-century Christians devised equalitarian utopias, basing them on their mistaken concept of God's justice: "only the laws of men," they argued "have created inequality and injustice by the institution of private property, thus violating natural law." In the same vein, the Pelagians proclaimed that since we may only use the property which God, its owner, has loaned to us, then all goods must be returned to the Church for redistribution.

Similarly with more modern utopias. In Icaria, the ideal republic along Communist lines described by Etienne Cabet (1840), the visiting Lord Carisdall notes that nobody pays his fare either on the boat or on the tramways. He learns the reason: everything belongs to the Sovereign, the beautiful and good Republic, exclusive entrepreneur and universal provider. Edward Bellamy's *Looking Backward* tells that, in the year 2000, money will not exist because, the author explains, money is important only where it is needed as a means of exchange. As soon as the State becomes the sole producer and distributor, exchange among private individuals ceases. Bellamy displays horror, so typical of the utopian, at the thought of any kind of trade which he views as immoral, as incompatible with mutual good will, as essentially anti-social. Bellamy also forbids putting money aside in savings; in his utopia the government discourages such a practice because the citizens need no reserve; the State guarantees complete security to everyone. Because the State is sole investor, it may use any part of the national labor force for whatever purpose it decides; again, therefore, there is no need of private savings or private capital.

Utopia's theoreticians are necessarily antagonistic to money and all its functions (trade, savings, investment) because possession

---

troubles of living?" (*Democracy in America*, Vintage Edition, Random House, Inc., New York, 1954, p. 119).

of money allows for individual choice which, in turn, confuses centralized planning. A typical example of this thinking is J. K. Galbraith's well-known *The Affluent Society*. It is Galbraith's thesis that, in an affluent society, reasonably well-to-do individuals purchase and invest in superfluities, status symbols and silly luxuries, the symbol of which is the automobile's tailfin. As remedy for this intolerable situation, Galbraith suggests that, by curtailing the individual's purchasing power, funds will become available for such communal projects to be determined by the government as roads, schools, hospitals, cultural centers and the like. In other words, the private individual is ignorant, unreliable, selfish; government is wise and acts in the interests of all, even when it advises citizens on what they *should* want.

The economy of the affluent society is far more complex and sophisticated in its requirements than an economy of scarcity. In Thomas More's *Utopia* is found nothing like the collective investment possibilities of which Galbraith speaks; we find, instead, general storehouses supplying the needs of all. The city, writes More, is divided into four equal districts, in the center of which is a market which provides the necessities of existence. Each family brings to this central market the products of its work, and each household head takes home whatever his family needs for sustenance. He neither pays nor barters, yet he is refused nothing, since nobody in Utopia asks for more than he needs. And, More adds with a disarming, but significantly dangerous naïveté, "Why, indeed, would a person, who knows that he will never lack anything, seek to possess more than what is necessary?"[7]

[7] As I noted earlier, such honesty and unselfishness may exist in such small communities as a religious order or a kibbutz, communities of a voluntary nature, or it may be found in temporary arrangements where the initial burst of enthusiasm remains strong. At the outbreak of the Spanish Civil War, for example, some Andalusian villages sent all their money to Madrid to help the government, and they distributed milk and food among members of the community in accordance with the size of the families.

For present purposes it is sufficient to see why utopians must and do denounce free enterprise, private property and money: to remove all resistance to domination by a vast, all-powerful central command. Two positive steps will bring this domination about: either the many will yield their power and resources to the few on a voluntary basis; or the latter will take matters into their own hands, through violence if necessary. Saint-Simon opts for persuasion rather than violence for the reason that it is ridiculous to assume despotism will ever be founded on science.[8] Until his time, Saint-Simon felt, people exerted only individual and isolated efforts on nature. A large part of individual enterprise was destructive, he said, because one faction devoted its forces to domination of the other, while the other consumed much of its skill in resisting the domination. Yet, in spite of this enormous loss of energy, the human species in the most civilized countries, has achieved a remarkable degree of well-being and prosperity. Here Saint-Simon wonders to what heights people could actually soar if there were no efforts wasted, if people—and nations—stopped trying to dominate one another and organized themselves.[9]

Apparently it never occurred to Saint-Simon to ask whether the remarkable degree of prosperity which he saw around him might not be due precisely to free enterprise and whether what he considered "waste" might not be an essential part of all human enterprises. Nor did Saint-Simon ask, as did his younger contemporary Tocqueville, whether the new system might not create a "nation within each nation," a "monstrous tutelary power" above the rest which "foresees and supplies their necessities, directs their industry, regulates the descent of property and subdivides inheritance" and spares them "all the care of thinking and all troubles of living."[10]

Unwittingly accepting the fallacy that State-owned property is

[8] *Textes Choisis*, Editions Sociales, 1951, pp. 83–84.
[9] *Ibid.*, p. 128.
[10] Tocqueville, *op. cit.*, p. 119. (See above for full quotation.)

property owned by no one, Saint-Simon believed that the establishment of economic well-being would assure the disappearance of power and domination among men. This assumption is to be found as well in Strachey:

> Contemporary democracy is the diffusion of power throughout the community. And the diffusion of power pushed further and further points, in turn, towards the elimination of power. For if everyone could have exactly equal power, no one, clearly, would have any power over his fellows. That, of course, is for us a distant ideal; it is the ideal of perfect cooperation in perfect liberty.[11]

We have earlier remarked on the nature of utopian systems that they all assume that their dreams could materialize *if* moral insights could catch up with historical forces and *if* differences among men could be abolished. Marx's thought should be regarded as superior to that of other utopians because he did establish a mechanism by which transformations can be effected, and he based his predictions on a historical analysis of previous transformations when the same mechanism had been at work. Nonetheless, this fact does not justify Marxism's claim to be scientific.

The Transition Period According to Marx

Wells' statement that modern utopias are kinetic applies, first of all, to Marx who contended that all history is but a continuous transformation of human nature, that is, of all social relationships at any given time; social relationships, in turn, are the transitory creations of productive forces and, consequently, must give way to new social forms under the impact of the newly developing productive forces. Social classes are necessary only when productivity

[11] Strachey, *op. cit.,* p. 217.

is feebly developed. But at the present phase, Marx concluded, productive forces allowed for the dictatorship of the immense majority for the benefit of the immense majority. Between capitalist and Communist societies, he said, lies the period of revolutionary transformation of the one into the other and, corresponding to this, there is also a political transition period in which the State can be nothing but the revolutionary dictatorship of the proletariat.

Regardless of what various disciples of Marx may have added to or taken away from his system, they all agree on the necessity both of class struggle and of the dictatorship of the proletariat. As late as September 28, 1962, the Tenth Plenary Session of the Chinese Communist Central Committee emphasized in its communiqué that class struggle marks the period of proletarian revolution and proletarian dictatorship and will continue throughout the historical period of transition from capitalism to communism—a transition that will last scores of years or even longer.

Marx regarded the transition as beginning with the armed insurrection of the entire proletariat, the majority of the people, which would overpower the bourgeois State—its police, armed forces and governmental apparatus. Commenting on the events of the Paris Commune, Marx stated that when the majority of the people overpower their oppressors, there is no longer need of professional forces of repression. In proportion as the functions of State authority are exercised by the totality of the people, the less need is there of State authority, and the State has already begun to disappear. Lenin follows this analysis in *The State and Revolution*, and he concludes from the example of the Commune that these functions of State authority will be so simple to perform and so modestly remunerated (Marx had noted that the Commune paid no official more than an ordinary worker's wages) that all of them may be entrusted to men and women who know the four operations of arithmetic. Hence, the functionaries themselves will be interchangeable and will never think of constituting a separate class of privileged bureaucrats. With this step the State ceases to be a State in the proper sense of the term. Engels wrote in a letter to Bebel that, with the establishment of a socialist regime, the State dissolves itself and disappears. Then, while noting that the Marxist and the anarchist converge on a common goal, Lenin takes up the matter of how the Marxist will proceed. All instruments, means and procedures of State power will be brought to bear against the exploiters. The former process will be reversed when the new, temporary function of the State (which has been conquered by the proletariat) will be to repress the bourgeoisie.

Decades later—in the current era of Communist compromises at least in practice, if not in doctrine—the transition period is described in less brutal terms, and the main instrument of transition is conceived as cooperation with all revolutionary, democratic and progressive elements in any given situation. It is Henri Lefèbvre's recommendation to the "left," in general, that it must aim at the deepening and not at the elimination of democracy. It cannot oppose socialism and, consequently, communism without destroying its own essence. The role of the "left," he explains, is to act efficaciously on the modalities of the transition to socialism and communism, so that this transition may take place with the least possible damage and violence. Disagreements with the socialists or the communists cannot concern either the short-range or long-range goals of the movement, but only the rhythm and modalities of the transition period.[12]

Welfare State as Transition to Utopia

This dilution of the properly revolutionary element of the passage to socialism from Marx and Lenin to Lefèbvre was made possi-

[12] Henri Lefèbvre, *La Somme et le reste*, La Nef de Paris, 1958, I, p. 221.

ble by the intervening evolution of the centralized Welfare State designed to take the wind out of the sails of the revolution. The question is: Does the Welfare State tame and organize the revolutionary idea, or does it merely serve the ultimate objectives of the revolution by adjusting people's attitudes to the post-revolutionary world? The fact is that the concept of the State (or the community), completely dominating and regulating the lives of its citizens, has been, by and large, accepted in the second half of the twentieth century. Although there is still considerable discussion, largely theoretical and irrelevant, about what Lefèbvre calls the "rhythm and modalities" of the transition, the debate of the past several decades has been merely whether the State, the race, the ideological Empire or World Government will stage-manage the last acts of the passage to a coalescing mankind. Whichever prevails, the trend has been unmistakable for a long time now: the mechanism is in place; small, concrete decisions are made daily; only the theoretical measures are still discussed.

As early as 1891, Chauncey Thomas outlined the general process in his utopian novel *The Crystal Button*. The community is described as living in the Year of Peace 4872 (1372 years after 3500 years spent under the calendar of *Anno Domini*). The novel's characters refer to the end of the nineteenth century as almost a prehistoric date when certain signs already indicated the shape of things to come. The Professor tells Paul Prognosis, the Bostonian who dreams of the future.

> Even in your day it was one of the signs of the times that small interests were beginning to be absorbed by corporations, and those by giant monopolies. By slow and peaceful steps, the same movement progressed until the government itself came into possession of such industries as were of peculiarly public interest, including all means of communication and transportation, and life and fire insurance; and the land question was settled in the same manner.

Ever since Chauncey Thomas wrote these lines, the trends he detected have become immeasurably stronger. The Welfare State is an accepted fact; two ideological empires exist; and both the Welfare State and the ideological empires resemble each other increasingly in the techniques they utilize and even in some fundamental thinking. The world government is still only a distant image, but many highly regarded statesmen speak about it as a distinct possibility.[13] In his own way, Adolf Hitler also believed that larger units than states were emerging and that the transition needed the skill of political minds of his own cast. This is what he told Herman Rauschning:

> The conception of the nation has become meaningless. We have to get rid of this false conception and set in its place the conception of race. The New Order cannot be conceived in terms of the national boundaries of the peoples with an historic past, but in terms of race that transcend these boundaries. . . . I know perfectly well that in the scientific sense there is no such thing as race. But you, as a farmer, cannot get your breeding right without the conception of race. And I, as a politician, need a conception which enables the order that has hitherto existed on an historic basis to be abolished, and an entirely new and anti-historic order enforced and given an intellectual basis.[14]

Less nebulous and romantic, and still influenced by the concept of the Roman State, Mussolini wrote that the people should be viewed qualitatively and, therefore, they may be represented in the will of a few or even one. In this respect, judgment belongs not to

[13] When India suffered under the invasion by the Red Chinese in 1962, Indian politicians consulted Nehru regarding his intentions. He simply told them that, by the year 2000, border conflicts would be a thing of the past since all countries would be provinces of a one-world organization.

[14] Quoted in A. Bullock, *Hitler,* Harper & Bros., New York, 1952, pp. 363–364.

the individual, but to the State, because the State is all citizens, and its formation is the formation of a consciousness of its individuals in the masses. Hence the need of the Party and of all the instruments of propaganda and education which Fascism uses to make the thought and will of the Duce the thought and will of the masses (cf. *The Encyclopedia Italiana,* Vol. XIV). Rather obviously, Mussolini's mind, untrained in theory and formed by only a few writings of prominent socialist doctrinaires, was struggling with incompatible concepts: masses, individual rights ("the Fascist State organizes the nation but leaves a sufficient margin afterward to the individual"), Party and absolute leader. But the twentieth-century utopian *leitmotiv* is present: individuals have value only when coalesced in the whole: "For the Fascist," writes Mussolini, "all is comprised in the State and nothing spiritual or human exists—much less has any value—outside the State. . . . The Fascist State—the unification and synthesis of every value—interprets, develops and potentiates the whole life of the people."

The Function of Education in the Transition

The transition period to Utopia, according to the utopian authors themselves, will occur as a revolution after the evolutionary mechanism has become exhausted, or as a cataclysmic event or when mankind has achieved a state of sufficient maturity. Education has been, however, the most obvious step in the direction of utopia since, with every new generation, a new potential comes into existence. The utopian does not believe in a permanent human nature; if he did, he could not hope to accomplish a complete break in the long line of generations; too, he would know that each generation might go through a similar and ever-repeating evolution from childhood with its fantasies to old age with its resignation, creating in the midstream of life something new which, nevertheless, resembles things old. Yet, unless human nature is permanant, we cannot speak of civilization, of the lessons of the past, or of minds communicating across the ages.

Yet the utopian never ceases his efforts to create, at a given moment in history, an educational system which will transform not only his contemporaries, but all future men as well. One essential precondition of this educational system favored passionately and advocated by all utopians is the necessity of removing children from the care of parents. One wonders at the inconsistency. Granted that this is a necessity *once,* when the great break between old and new is effected; but if the new product is reliable from the point of view of utopian cohesion, then the parents of the future should be trusted to bring up their offspring in the new spirit in which they were themselves educated. The utopian betrays himself because, deep in his heart, he knows that the old Adam is present in the parents—that is, in the adults—in spite of the new educational system. And the meaning is clear: utopia is impossible because the work of cohesion must be done anew at every turn, at the birth of every generation.

Let us simply note, then, that the utopians prefer to work with the young. The old people of Plato's ideal republic had been sent off to the fields. The French Communist exiles' draft (London, 1840) stated that children of five in the new society must be taken away from their parents because the parents make them selfish by inculcating ideas which clash by their heterogeneity. In other words, the child must be as homogeneous a product as possible and, for this reason, he must be brought up not in divisive religion, but in the feeling of human fraternity and, incidentally, without books that praise the pre-1789 regime (*ancien régime*). In Cabet's Icaria children may remain in the family home; however, mother and father will make special efforts to avoid giving their children such false ideas, errors and prejudices as those formerly suggested by servants and ill-bred peasants.

Even where utopian societies were actually attempted, as at

Oneida, N.Y., particular care was taken to supervise family relationships because, observes Raymond Ruyer,[15] exclusiveness is a threat to communal solidarity. Among the Hutterites the family was the channel through which capitalism seeped into the community. The Perfectionists of Oneida hoped to offset this same danger to the collective solidarity by discouraging exclusive attachments.

It should not be surprising that many contemporary utopians hold the teachings of Zen in such high regard. To attain the *satori* (awakening), writes G. Renondeau, a person must expel from his mind everything which ties him to this world and its structure; next, he must concentrate on abstract problems in order to uproot the routine of life and abolish the rules of logic. The ultimate objective of these efforts is to make the mind free of educational, philosophical and religious principles learned since childhood.

Once the child is removed from the family circle and the disintegration of the family is achieved, the fabrication of the new man may begin. The first matter, of course, is the teaching of the new subjects. In Louis Sebastien Mercier's utopian work—his *Memoirs of the year 2500,* published in Paris, 1770—the traveler, after asking his guide whether the children are taught Greek and Latin, is told that there are more important things for children to learn. Where once children were taught the dead languages because it was imagined that they contained every sort of science, the fact is that such education gave the children no idea about the people with whom they were to live. In the new society, continues the guide, children learn the national language and they are even permitted to modify it after their own taste; for not grammarians, but men of eloquence are wanted. Little history is taught because history is the disgrace of humanity, its every page crowded with crimes and follies.

15 *L'Utopie et les Utopies,* Presses Universitaires de France, Paris, 1950, p. 49.

In addition to new subjects to be taught, new methods are also elaborated. In Cabet's Icaria, each child will be taught as much as possible and through a methodology which will make every subject easy, quickly learned and satisfying. Every lesson should be a game, and every game a lesson. All the inventive powers of the members of the Committee are exhausted in efforts to devise and to multiply such methods and, whenever experience leads to the discovery of a new technique, it is quickly adopted. The beauty, the facilities and convenience of Icaria's schools, the patience, gentleness and competence of the instructors, the appealing simplicity of methods, the clarity of demonstrations, the mixture of study and games— all these combine to achieve Cabet's dream.

The New Man

The real objective, however, is situated beyond subject-matter and method: it is the creation of a new human being. Much has been written, in both utopian and anti-utopian literature, about the ideal man of the future. In the past he was pictured either as a disciplined, hard-working and unimaginative fellow who, when the day's compulsory work hours were completed, turned his attention to "leisure and play" with equal zeal and an austere spirit; or he was pictured as a *bon vivant* like the residents of Thélème in Rabelais' utopia, late-rising, hard-drinking, and woman-chasing, who generally did what he pleased according to the watchword, *"Fais ce que voudras."*

Contemporary anti-utopian literature has a new mood which displaces the gaiety of Rabelais and the gloomy regimentation of Cabet, Fourrier and Mercier. In this century the ideologies of Marxism, mass democracy, national socialism and revolutionary socialism have taken utopia out of the books and constructed it in the market place. The mass-man and robot-regime have frightened writers who would normally be expected to be enthusiastic advocates of utopia. As a result, for some time now the fashion has been to write utopian texts in reverse, centered about totalitarian regimes and their depressing techniques. Kafka and Nabokov (*Invitation to a Beheading* and *Bend Sinister*) have added imagination to the stark, mainly political critique of an Orwell and the social critique of a Huxley.

These writers generated a natural and healthy reaction against the utopian elements in our twentieth-century life as well as for twenty-first-century prospects, by stressing the grotesque and deformed aspects. However, modern utopianism is not interested in creating goose-stepping paramilitary organizations or clownish Führers; these may be by-products of temporary growth of power in the hands of party officials or scientists, urged on by a chorus of utopian intellectuals. Modern utopianism, as Wells said, is kinetic: it dreams of mankind on the way to becoming God; it envisions individuals as indefinitely mobile, expanding, cosmic and godlike.

It is characteristic of utopians that they do not want to transform the schools merely into centers of indoctrination and conditioning; they expect that the new mentality will be shaped by the entire social climate, itself permeated by goodness, rationality and mobility. Since our entire existence would be one uninterrupted process of education, it follows that we must so shape institutions and culture that they, in turn, should inspire us only with the most generous motives.

What product is expected to emerge from this educational process? The answer deserves to be examined. While the utopian claims that he wants to populate his utopia with exceptional people —those of all-absorbing intelligence and great virtue—in reality he mistrusts individuals, particularly the exceptionally gifted ones; yet he aims at endowing the collectivity with sublime qualities. While the utopian may speak of education as an institution which encourages and produces talent, he does not really mean this literally because he wants to exclude excellence as an individual goal and to regiment individuals until they fuse their personalities in the common mass. What the individual loses, reasons the utopian, he really gains, for now his particular talents will not endanger the collective march of humanity toward a bright future.

The Communist Babeuf, who was executed in the backlash of the French Revolution, denounced excellence in violent terms. The superiority of talent and diligence, said Babeuf, is mere illusion which ensnares those who plot against the equality and happiness of men. It is absurd and unjust to reward those whose work demands higher intelligence for the simple reason that they cannot eat more than the others. If one person can work as much as four others, should he receive the wages of four people? No, answers Babeuf, such a person would in effect, be a conspirator against society, would destroy its equilibrium and equality, should be suppressed by his associates as a social curse, and should at least be compelled to do the work of one man only and for one man's compensation.[16]

Passion for equality blinds the utopian to the fact that society, as a whole, is based on inequality among men in two respects: the inventor, the innovator, the exceptional man creates something new and insures continuous progress; the others emulate his work or merely improve their own lot by benefiting from his creativity. Now, to deny to this exceptional man the extra compensation— higher salary, honors, prestige and more responsibility—is to extirpate his inventiveness. The sorry state of socialist regimes shows that no amount of officially stimulated collective enthusiasm for the artificially defined common good is a substitute for individual incentive and reward. It is significant that in Communist societies "capitalist" advantages are granted to the few on whom rest the regime's spectacular achievements, such as space technology and aircraft production. These scientists live in great luxury; they have

[16] Cf. Maxime Leroy, *Histoire des idées sociales en France*, Gallimard NRF, Paris, 1946, pp. 75–76.

private villas, chauffeur-driven cars and special stores for their purchases. Yet the utopian insists on forging the collective enthusiasm and hopes that the new man will be integrated in the collective excellence.

The kinetic concept of utopia demands that the new man should not have such static qualities as knowledge, culture, virtues, convictions and principles, but "dynamic" or mobile qualities; he should be adaptable to the global and possibly cosmic adventure of mankind; he should possess dispositions satisfied with something nebulous in content and located in some vague future. Youth should be given an education, urged pedagogue Gaston Berger,[17] an education whose principles, spirit and content are still to be discovered. Men must not remain fixed in any attitude; they must be flexible and learn to be happy in mobility.

In the October, 1961, issue of *Prospective,* a pedagogical series initiated by Prof. Berger, the objectives of the new pedagogy are further elaborated. Individuals must be physically healthy, balanced and globally developed; they must be able to make quick decisions even on very important matters, although they must also show patience and moderation in the face of complications; they must be able to summon at will their intellectual, emotional, imaginative and aesthetic faculties; they must be optimistic, generous and profoundly sociable; finally, they must be cultured, have a lively curiosity, specialized knowledge and a taste for general ideas. It is the conclusion of the contributors to *Prospective* that children must accept the modern world with optimism, but that the adolescent develops anguish the moment he really encounters the world and discovers its absurdity. However, the authors triumphantly explain, this is because the education which the adolescent receives is exaggeratedly preoccupied with the past.

The past must be abolished since utopia—man come-of-age, coalesced mankind—is ahead of us; and—the utopian always stresses

[17] *Cahiers Pédagogiques,* No. 32, January, 1962, pp. 55–56.

this—mankind, not its individual members, has now reached the point where it is able to choose its own destiny. "The advanced industrial civilization," Dr. Lawrence K. Frank wrote, "cannot function according to the unmotivated choices and decisions of uninformed individuals." The latter should act under the "education and persuasion of counseling and orientation services." But to enact such new and far-reaching changes in societal relationships, Dr. Frank suggests that the schools should be utilized because they are "the institutional pivots where the transformation of the social order" will take place. The education given there "has now, apparently for the first time, the difficult duty to help students un-learn —that is, to liberate them from the traditional and outmoded folklore, beliefs and postulates."[18]

Whether Zen Buddhism wants to create a *tabula rasa* of things learned, or Mercier and the Chinese Communists take children away from their families, or Prof. Frank assigns to schools the task of unlearning traditions—in all events the utopians end up powerless and unimaginative when they want to fill up the container now left empty. The greatest embarrassment always comes to them when they have run to the end of the imaginary line—that is, to the end of the passage to utopia—and find that nothing concrete and positive takes place. How does one teach "mobility"? How does one create a *tabula rasa* in the human mind and soul? How does one remove children from their families without letting the very basis of social coexistence—family solidarity and individual incentive— collapse? What does one teach adolescents when no principles, no convictions and no knowledge may be fixed in their minds and personalities?

Thus the passage to utopia is destined always to remain a passage—a corridor leading nowhere.

[18] *Esprit,* January, 1959: a symposium on American social sciences.

7 - EVIL
GOVERNMENT

THE PASSAGE to utopia leads nowhere, but, then, neither does sin. Yet there are sinners in far greater number than saints. Man is free in the use of his body and mind; as he is able to sully his body, he is far more able to let his intellect wander freely along strange imaginary paths, along even dead-end streets.

In the political realm, man's imagination is powerfully assisted by his *libido dominandi,* so that he is challenged not only through his intellect, but he is literally dazzled by the limitless possibilities of power. The result is that man is perfectly capable of committing violence on nature, using this simple reasoning: "If I can do it, why should I not do it"? It is always easier to let one's instincts and imagination run loose than to overcome them by imposing restraints. Restraint implies a superior authority in whose name man submits to moderation; if he denies superior authority, then only the secular version of the golden rule—John Stuart Mill's liberalism—remains to remind him of limitations: "One man's sphere of action should be limited by the sphere of others." At this point, a new temptation arises, one we shall call the utilitarian temptation. Why not in-

157

crease the happiness of the greatest number, even though this may lead to the unhappiness of the few, the minority? Then follows the utopian temptation: Why not make everybody happy through their absolute cooperation with one another, so that all shall partake of the infinite mass of available happiness? This is no longer Mill's tolerant, although vague, liberalism, but the utopian totalism of an Erich Fromm in *The Sane Society,* the promise that alienation will end with the attainment of the "experience of union with another person, with all men, and with nature under the condition of retaining one's sense of integrity and independence."[1]

Natural Men Would Live in Fraternity

As Prof. Dante Germino points out, Fromm is in agreement with Fourrier and many others in holding that by proper social organization—the grouping of men into "communities of work"—the disparities between rulers and ruled can be terminated and man made fully autonomous.[2] The Marxist and utopian-socialist bias permeates Fromm's pages because he makes equalization of labor the principal condition of equality and because man-to-man contact in labor is his guarantee that the workers will be mutually enriched and made "autonomous." It is important to understand the fundamental principle which motivates Fromm, Fourrier and all the other utopians. Because we still live in the era of socialism—a reaction to unbridled industrialization—work is the great fetish which, in its organization, we expect to determine all our other endeavors and perspectives. The "worker" will be loyal in a different way, will love in a different way and will enjoy life in a different way—so say the socialists. Yet, if we discard the socialist view of man as essentially "the worker," a transformer of nature, a consumer of his products, then we discover a far more basic concept which is the substance of utopian motivation.

[1] Published by Holt, Rinehart and Winston, New York, 1955, p. 32.
[2] Cf. "Eric Voegelin's Contribution to Contemporary Political Theory," *The Review of Politics,* July, 1964.

Even if sophisticated economic and sociological doctrines are woven around the idea, the "fraternity of workers" is merely another way of saying that men love each other when allowed to face each other in their human nakedness. The "worker" is the nineteenth- and twentieth-century notion of *man as he is*—man, stripped by the fundamental experience of work and contact with nature of all the social, cultural and religious accretions with which society has encumbered him; he is natural man, Marxists would say; he is the second Adam, as Christian utopians would say and then conveniently add that Jesus was a worker,—one who abandoned his workman's status only for a divine status.

What of the term, "fraternity"? Contrary to the Christian belief which stresses the salvation of individual man, utopians believe in the salvation of mankind as a collectivity. Nobody may be left out, since God is really "all mankind"; if even one individual were not saved, an element of division would be introduced into the total spiritualization (utopians prefer this term to "salvation") of the world substance. The result would then be God minus one—a scandal for the utopian who does not believe in sin and damnation. Fraternity, then, refers to a principle of cohesion—or of coalescence, in the more impatient utopian texts—which elevates men to a state where the mere manifestation of their perfect humanity replaces all other previous and imperfect relationships. When this state is reached, man's communion with man will be so obviously complete that he will need no social intermediaries, institutions or even voluntarily formed groups by which to communicate with others and, in a sense, with himself. Prof. Tucker is accordingly justified in saying that Marx's "socialized humanity is not only classless, but also a stateless, lawless, family-less, religion-less and generally structureless collectivity of complete individuals who live in harmony with themselves, with each other, and with the anthropological nature outside them."[3]

[3] Robert Tucker, *Philosophy and Myth in Karl Marx*, Cambridge University Press, 1961, p. 201.

Only Imperfect Men Need Government

The utopian principle on which this is based is that when mankind reaches sufficient perfection or maturity, it will do away with government as evil and the symptom of evil. We need government, says the utopian, only insofar as we are imperfect. Perfect man is his own government, says the humanist, when he realizes that he is the measure of things and therefore responsible for his own behavior. The disappearance of political power—power of man over man—is the ideal, and it will come about by evolution or, perhaps, by revolution, in the course of which, as Marx wrote in his essay on the Jewish question, the individual will reabsorb in himself the abstract citizen of the State. He will still have social power and, in fact, an increased amount of it, but he will not allow it to be separated from himself in the form of political power; he will not allow its institutionalization. Proudhon expressed this associative principle in its purest form when he reasoned that, in making a contract, each one is his own master. If he could make that contract with everyone and if every group of citizens, every commune, canton, department, corporation and company formed by such a contract and considered as a moral person, could deal with each other, it would be exactly as if each one's will was repeated *ad infinitum*. The laws would be the laws of each one and, if this new order of things were called government, it would be each one's government in the regime of contracts substituted for the regime of laws. It is difficult to see how "contractual society" would be different from a society regulated by laws. It seems obvious that violators of the contract would place themselves outside the contractual system and would have to be dealt with by laws.

The central concept on which atheistic and religious utopians all agree is the need for the individual to reabsorb the citizen, the need to be redeemed following his fall as a political animal. In a way, this is more than a central concept: it is the natural religion of mankind, just as its philosophical corrolary, Pantheism, is "the permanent natural bent of the human mind."[4] Now it is perfectly natural for any man to say, "I am under constant pressure from the government, its courts, police, army, tax departments and the like. I want to be left alone. If all people were like me, society would be better. I don't want to hurt anybody, and nobody should want to hurt me. We could all live in peace if only the officials left us alone." Yet, if the individual thinks a little further, he soon realizes the impossibility of being left alone, an impossibility which has its roots in his very soul. Nevertheless, there is no doubt that part of communism's enormous appeal in theory is its promise, brutally broken and contradicted by the Communist State, that the presence of government and officialdom will be lifted from men's shoulders.

Denunciation of the Political Principle

Predominant in utopian literature is the denunciation of the political principle. In this, both atheistic and religious utopianism concur as they do in most other respects. After all, they both feel that an irresistible current carries them in the right direction. They are as two ships riding side by side on the river; the goal is the ocean; meanwhile the crews hope to persuade each other in a dialogue conducted from the decks.

They agree on the following points:

1) The religious utopian regards the mere fact that there are man-made institutions as proof of man's fall and his blindness to God's bright light. In the atheist's language this means that external conditions prevent mankind from satisfying its natural aspirations.[5]

---

[4] C. S. Lewis, *Miracles, A Preliminary Study,* The Macmillan Company, New York, 1947, p. 85.

[5] A classical formulation of this conviction is found in *De l'Esprit* by Helvetius (1758). The vices of men do not derive from their individual

2) There should be no man-made laws, says the religious utopian; we should all live under God's direct kingship. The atheist holds that when all men will accept Reason as their connecting link, they will live in harmony.

3) The religious utopian holds that since the divine essence is slow in penetrating those who are too immersed in matter or who fall away from God for some other reason, then the elected few—the pure—must lead the majority to salvation. In the language of atheism, old structures and prejudices still present tremendous obstacles, so that the planners of utopia have the duty to cure, re-educate and guide the recalcitrant elements.

The first two points concern the problem of evil government, the concern of this chapter; the third point has to do with good government, or total utopia (theocracy) to be examined in Chapter 8.

According to popular understanding, error is at the opposite pole from truth. In reality, they are very close to each other. Error has all the elements of truth except one, but this privation has enormous consequences. Truth and error may be imagined as two pairs of rails; a train is driven along one pair of rails until, at one point, a faulty switch sends it in an altogether different direction. For a while the train runs along a landscape familiar to the engineer; only later does he realize that the slide of an inch at the start now represents hundreds of miles, and that the two lines keep steadily diverging. In the same way, ideologies always stem from a real cause, an intolerable situation, a threat, a grievance general enough to affect a multitude of people. Then someone elaborates a theory in the center of which is found the correction of the situation, a redress of the grievance. However, the theory concentrates so ex-

---

tendencies, but from the contradictions which exist between these tendencies and the laws and institutions of the country where they live. In order to change man, one must first change the laws. "It is evident," Helvetius adds, "that ethics is a superficial [*frivole*] science unless identified with politics and lawmaking."

clusively on the originating cause that it becomes one-sided, only obliquely relevant to the entirety of man's situation. Because our mentality has a weakness for systems (the *esprit géometrique* of the seventeenth century), it seeks further to render the theory coherent and invulnerable, with little regard for the consequences, namely, a gradual neglect of human needs which originally were never affected by the threat or grievance. By this time, ideology has acquired the momentum of a train, but a train which runs on the wrong pair of rails and arrives at the unscheduled terminal of utopia.

It is true, for example, that the medieval rules and mores of many monasteries and convents left much to be desired, that severity and asceticism perhaps played an exaggerated part in the daily lives of monks and nuns. But Rabelais' Abbey of Thélème is a rather tedious opposite picture: no walls, no clocks regulating life and prayer and, above all, no rules. But Rabelais does not stop here: the Thélèmites, both men and women members of this new monastic order, must be handsome; their triple vow is "marriage, wealth and freedom"; their way of life is soft luxury. Their entire life is divorced from laws, statutes and rules, and they live as they choose. Regulations are useless for free and honest people, Rabelais informs us, because such people possess by nature an instinct and a sense of direction by which they commit virtuous acts and refrain from vice.

In Louis Sabastien Mercier's projection of the year 2440, religion and theology no longer exist, and there are no more "fanatics." Monks have become volunteers for all sorts of painful tasks. They have given up their "stupid vows" of not ever being men, and have taken for wives those cooing pigeons who always sighed after a less saintly and more agreeable status.

Another example. British law courts were extremely harsh even in the eighteenth and nineteenth centuries until a certain amount of mercy tempered western man's moral vision. Pickpockets had formerly been hanged, minor criminals were deported for life, and the famous Debtors' Prison was the exemplar of filth, vice and corruption. A reasonable criticism of prison conditions was certainly called for, and Jeremy Bentham, for one, devoted many years to it. But, in an outburst of utopianism, William Godwin wrote: "If juries might at length cease to decide and be contented to invite, if force might probably be withdrawn and reason trusted alone, shall we not one day find that juries themselves and every other species of public institution may be laid aside as unnecessary?"[6]

Impatience with the Human Situation

These examples show that very often the utopian design stems from a real situation improperly analyzed. The lack or failure of the analysis is not due to the temperament of the author, or to his impatience; generally speaking, these utopian works are produced over a lifetime. The utopian writer is, of course, impatient, but not with a particular situation so much as with the human condition as such. He believes he has found the key by which the human condition may be transformed. Raymond Ruyer[7] is right when he describes the reasoning of the utopian as an unwarranted passage from social situation A to social situation B. Between A and B there are many intermediate phases, each demanding attention, each capable of disconcerting us from the pursuit of B, each a possible point of departure for C and D and E. The utopian limits himself to the preaching of B, without stopping to worry about the existence of society at the intermediary stages.

It is precisely these intermediary stages which represent continuity, including institutional continuity, without which the life of societies is inconceivable. By neglecting them or even suspecting them of disrupting the élan toward the perfect state, the utopian displays the core of his thinking. He plays God who says "Fiat,"

[6] *An Enquiry Concerning Political Justice*, 1793.
[7] *L'Utopie et les Utopies*, Presses Universitaires de France, Paris, 1950, p. 63.

and things spring into existence. Or he plays the sorcerer in the children's tale, the possessor of the magic word through which gates open and empty tables are covered with magnificent dishes and rich food. One reason why it is so difficult to unmask the utopian is that he is deceptively individualistic. His fundamental preference for the collectivistic solution becomes manifest only in what was listed above as the third point of agreement among all utopians—compulsion of the majority by a minority—and even then he can say that his good will is thwarted, that, although his love of man has not changed, he must now use new and coercive methods against so much indolence and resistance. Therefore, as the utopian explains it, there is a deep and unbridgeable gap between the individual and society *in their unredeemed state*. The individual is simple and free; society is complex and chained at every articulation. By definition, then—but with circuitous reasoning—the utopian cracks the difficulty: only free individuals, those liberated from the claims and complications of society A, may form a free society B. Bakunin expressed this thought along his own anarchist line when he taught that political legislation, whether it is based on a ruler's will or on the votes of representatives chosen by universal suffrage, can never correspond to the laws of nature. Such legislation, he said, is always hostile to the liberty of the masses, if only because it forces upon them a system of external and, therefore, despotic laws.[8]

Rejection of External Law

If laws imposed from outside—and how else can laws be imposed?—are necessarily despotic, then only internal laws are acceptable because they alone express the freedom of the individual. The utopian stops only for a moment at this contradiction: if each individual has his own internal law, then society will have no law,

---

[8] *Dieu et l'Etat*, Geneva, 1882, p. 27.

for otherwise individual laws would clash. Therefore, says the utopian impatiently, individuals must live under those evidently valid laws which God himself—or Historical Necessity—has imprinted on individual souls, laws which are not man-made. In his *Le Dilemme de Marc Sangnier,* Maurras tells that the French Christian-Socialist Marc Sangnier believed that all mankind's efforts, aided and sustained by the inner forces of Christianity, must aim at ridding the people of carnal tyranny and elevating them to spiritual liberation.

But do we know these laws in their precise formulation? Are they so evident that they cover the entire human situation and render contradiction impossible? Are we in such complete communication with God, or can we interpret the "decrees" of history so completely, that we may live by these evident laws alone? Since we cannot penetrate God's ultimate design, and since we have but a limited view of history, should not law be regarded as an imperfect hypothesis which facilitates the coexistence of people? In the Aristotelian system, politics and laws fall into the category of practical philosophy in which man can hope only for probability, not certainty. Today we speak of "political *science*" because such philosophers as Descartes and Hobbes wanted to emancipate the political realm from practical philosophy in order to assign it a scientific character similar to that of the natural sciences. Utopians are not necessarily Cartesians or Hobbesians; in fact, most of them would be repulsed by the "geometrization" of politics, but only because they reject the political principle as such, because they deplore the need of redeemed human beings to have institutions which falsify and distort direct contact with God and among themselves. While the modern political scientist would oversimplify political life by subordinating it to formulae, the utopian oversimplifies it by scorning anything which is not spontaneous.

The truth lies somewhere in the middle. As B. Roland-Gosselin writes in connection with Augustine's political doctrine, there is no doubt that the individual soul of every man is the sole substantial value in humanity. But there is such human solidarity in good and evil, such an interchange of ideas, sentiments and influences that it is impossible not to consider each man as forming part of a social whole that transcends the individual. St. Thomas taught, following Aristotle, that man is a social animal by nature. Therefore, in the state of innocence, regardless of the Fall, men would have lived in society. But a common social life could not exist without someone to control common efforts for the common good. Such a person or persons need not be despotic, for it is evident that the members of even the smallest social unit, the family, have various functions to perform, and someone must delegate the work to the individual members. In wider societies, the enforcement of the accepted rules, defense against outsiders, the teaching of the young, and other responsibilities must be entrusted to different agencies or institutions which specialize in their respective tasks to develop competence in these special functions. Therefore, such agencies contribute to everybody's well-being and increase the citizens' freedom and happiness rather than diminish them. As Lagarde notes, the social fact enters in the economy of divine providence not as a consequence of the weakness caused by the Fall, but as a requirement of human nature wanted by God for the beauty of His work.[9]

Doctrines Rejecting Institutions

Yet the religious utopians in every age try to interpret the Gospel literally and to use it as a leaven of rebellion and anarchy. Under the guise of universal liberty and charity, and in the name of Jesus, they condemn all social hierarchies, every organization devoted to the service of justice, all private projects, any display of force even in the service of right, and, of course, the State. Heretics in the early

[9] Georges de Lagarde, *La Naissance de l'esprit laique*, Ed. Nauwelaerts, Louvain, 1956, Vol. II, pp. 68–69.

Church accepted the State as a pagan institution, but they rejected
it for Christians on the basis that perfect men, as they considered
themselves to be, do not need the State. The ideas of Marc Sangnier
typify this illusion. For Sangnier the reform of the individual had
become the goal of social organization. He favored those institutions which provided the least support for people, because, he said
the more the individual lacks protection from these quarters, the
more must he rely on internal support, his faith in Christ.[10] Heretical utopians reject Church institutions, then the institutionalized
Church and, finally, the Church itself; utopians, in general, reject
the State; both reject the need of organizing certain aspects of social
existence. Writes Msgr. Knox:

> The denial of an institutional Church, if it is pressed by
> ardent thinkers, leads to a denial of all validity of human
> institutions. The Anabaptists recognized no relation to the
> State as such. The State, in their opinion, belonged to the
> realm of darkness with which the brethren had nothing in
> common. . . . The Lollards maintained that it is not lawful
> for a Christian man to bear office or rule in the Common-
> wealth; that no man's laws ought to be obeyed . . . that all
> things be common, and nothing several.[11]

Whether before or after the Reformation, heretical utopian
movements in the Church display a remarkable similarity in their
approach to the political principle and its institutional manifestations. They all deny the validity of man-made institutions and elaborate a new hierarchy depending on the purer or less pure vision
that their members have of God. In this way they may claim to live
under God's immediate authority and to be entitled to ignore mediating institutions. In every one of their actions, they argue, God's

[10] *Ibid.*, pp. 64–65.
[11] *Enthusiasm*, Clarendon Press, Oxford, 1950, pp. 122–123.

will is manifest, and this is the supreme guarantee for being on the right path. These heresies must advocate a theocratic system in which, naturally, there are no institutional safeguards for the majority. The elect communicate directly with God and, in some cases, even partake of His essence; the non-elect, the impure, suffer their subordinate position by a kind of divine predestination.

It was indicated earlier in the present volume that the Gnostics took great care to prove that God is infinitely far off and, consequently, unsullied by creation of the material world. A series of eons (from the Greek word *aion,* eternal) intervenes between God and the actual creator who handled matter. In the same way, say the Gnostics, men are also divided into categories: the Gnostics themselves who possess the highest degree of spirituality; the ordinary Christians in whom matter and spirit balance each other; finally, the pagans, or "material ones," or "hylics" (from the Greek word *hylos,* matter) in whose constitution matter prevails.

The Manicheans believed that man was defeated by Satan, the eternal principle of evil, and that man, in consequence, bears the marks of this defeat. Some men are able to free themselves and to efface those marks, but not all of these succeed to the same extent. Those who do succeed are the elect and they are distinguished by the triple seal: on the lips, the hands and the breast. Those who do not succeed are "auditors."

In the eastern part of the Mediterranean which was under Greek influence, heresies as well as Orthodox theology were interested chiefly in the philosophical aspect of the doctrine; in the West, however, Roman legal preoccupations tended to prevail. In consequence, it was the western heresies which turned to political considerations. The Albigensians, for example, were violently anti-clerical, anti-militarist, anarchistic and communistic. They distinguished between the elect and the simple believers. They emphasized their scorn for the impurity of life by practicing continence and by considering suicide the highest ideal of sanctity.

The principal Reformers considered man as almost totally depraved, but they drew opposing conclusions from this conviction. J. W. Allen is of the opinion that Luther had no theory of the State at all, that in the duty owed to the magistrate Luther really saw only a duty owed to God. On the oher hand, Luther wanted "of man-made law as little as possible. We all know what is right, and where we cannot see clearly, the scriptures will guide us. Love needs no law, and if we were all truly Christians, we should need neither law nor Prince."[12]

Calvin, on the other hand, had only scorn for people who asserted that all coercive power was evil: "they would that men should live pell-mell like rats in straw." He was impatient with men like Luther who thought that, in a society of true Christians, no law was needed. What a foolish dream, he declared. Therefore, "to reject government as needless is an inhuman barbarism. Coercive government is no less necessary to man's well-being than food and water, sun and air."[13] Carefully considered, this view, although it acknowledges the need of government and laws, is contiguous with the basic utopian thesis: the social fact is a punishment, an evil. Other systems consider man too good to live under laws; Calvin considers him too evil not to need coercion.

All Reformers after Luther and Calvin insisted on placing government "under Christ," arguing that no human being is worthy to rule over others. At the end of the sixteenth century, Robert Brown declared that the Church consisted of true Christians united into a company whose members placed themselves directly under the government of God and Christ. Insofar as these doctrines con-

---

[12] J. W. Allen, *A History of Political Thought in the Sixteenth Century,* University Paperbacks, London, 1960, p. 23. This is borne out by the study that Fr. Yves Congar makes of Luther and Protestantism. "The Church is nothing but Christ's community formed among men by faith. The true Church is that of the true believers, that is, of sinning men who put all their trust in Christ and profess to be saved exclusively by faith in Him." *Vraie et fausse réforme dans l'Eglise,* Editions du Cerf, Paris, 1950, p. 386.

[13] *Ibid.,* p. 60.

tributed immediately to the weakening of royal authority, they prepared the way for Rousseau, for the concept of popular sovereignty and for democracy. The German Calvinist Althusius announced at the beginning of the seventeenth century that "the compact of the citizens is the cause of political action."

Nevertheless, while democracy and varieties of the social-contract theory found their way into the domain of political action and planned their own institutions, there continued within religious thought a utopian rejection of society's institutional fabric. Pietism provides an example. A contemporary of the Pietists, the Lutheran theologian Valentin Loscher, criticized Pietist teaching on seven counts: its doctrinal indifference masked as piety; contempt for sacraments and appeal to personal inspiration; millenaristic tendencies; destruction of the aid of religion and recourse to individual inspiration; indulgence toward illuminist sects; perfection, or the demand to abolish the old Adam while recommending that Christian life consist of a growing internal faith; disdain for the Church, and a desire to found it again with the help of the regenerated.

Exclusive Reliance on Individual Resources

All these teachings, from the Albigensians to Marc Sangnier, may be summed up as an inordinate reliance on the individual by rejection of external support, and on his inner resources of faith, inspiration and ability to rise to perfection, to be "reborn." There is an exact parallel between the religious and the secular or even atheistic utopian here too. The religious utopian hides his pride behind the mask of humility; he recognizes God alone; he does not recognize ministers or the sacraments since he puts himself in the place of both: he ministers to his own religious needs and he consecrates his inner self as a place of worship more worthy of receiving God than the churches and temples. Secondly, he substitutes his own sentiments and emotions for doctrine because, in his estimation, doctrines are man-made speculations unable to comprehend God's essence; in his feelings, however, God is more evidently present than in reasoning. Thirdly, the religious utopian considers the sacramental, ceremonial and generally institutional aspects of religion as rigid and expendable molds which are adequate for the unthinking who need strong sensations and impressions to sustain their faith and to permeate their moments of worship. He, on the other hand, places his trust in his own individual inspiration, strengthens his faith through direct and permanent contact with the divine and so rises as a pure spirit to the level of a "truer" religion.[14] Since he retains from God only what is acceptable to his pride, his "truer religion" has very little in common with the traditional faith from which he started out. He will still call his state "religion," but, in reality, it is a personal religion.

The secular utopian also displays excessive pride. He believes that societies of the past were based on error since they yielded to the political principle of organization and hierarchy. That organization and hierarchy are inseparable from any society is the last thing that enters the utopian mind. Rousseau himself confessed that the state of nature, which he posits as an unspoiled origin, may very well never have existed at all in historical actuality; yet he assumes its theoretical existence as the counterpart of what now exists. The goal of the utopian as of Rousseau, then, is to create a society in its pristine purity, as it were, unsullied by laws and

---

[14] "The patient," writes Screwtape to his nephew Wormwood, referring to a man who must be seduced for the devil, "may be persuaded to aim [in his prayers] at something entirely spontaneous, inward, informal, and unregularized; and what this will actually mean to a beginner will be an effort to produce in himself a vaguely devotional *mood* in which real concentration of will and intelligence have no part . . . This is exactly the sort of prayer we want . . . [and by which] lazy patients can be taken in for quite a long time. At the very least, they can be persuaded that the bodily position makes no difference to their prayers; for they constantly forget . . . that they are animals and that whatever their bodies do affects their souls." C. S. Lewis, *The Screwtape Letters*, The Macmillan Company, New York, 1962, p. 20.

magistrates, functioning through its members' natural good will and cooperativeness. Laws, institutions, symbols, flags, armies, discipline, patriotic encouragement and the like will all be abolished both because, for pure social beings, the inner motivation of social living—"togetherness"—is quite sufficient and because they would serve to anchor the citizens, bodily and emotionally, in the soil and reality of the State just as pomp and ceremony, rules and institutions anchor the faithful in religion. The utopian needs only the exaltation generated by reason which tells him that the new society, without government, will represent a higher expression of individual and, therefore, social conscience.

Political Messianism: Abolition of the State

Politics is expressly excluded from the Phalanstery of Fourrier; it is therefore assumed that there can be no disorders therein. In the eyes of the pre-1848 socialists, writes Talmon, "the State is nothing but a body of measures designed to prevent the masses from voicing their wishes and gaining satisfaction for their grievances."[15] In Germany, Fichte agreed that the goal of all government is to make itself superfluous since the desirable objective is that all should freely obey the moral law. The same insistence is found in England where Godwin writes in his *Enquiry:* "We should not forget that government is, abstractly taken, an evil, a usurpation upon the private judgment and individual conscience of mankind."

While the nineteenth century became increasingly emancipated from religion and religious doctrine and modernism was claiming men's minds, a certain vague religious spirit, compounded of moralism and sentiment, was on the move both to fill in the religious gap and to undermine further the political principle. This was not the

---

[15] *Political Messianism*, Frederick A. Praeger, Publishers, New York, 1960, p. 159.

religion of St. Thomas and Bossuet, of Pius IX, or Newman, but rather the "new Christianity" of Saint-Simon, Lamennais' concept of alliance between Pope and proletariat. It influenced almost all who were not out-and-out materialists. Thus, Emile Zola, in one of his novels, gives a lyrical summary of a book written by his main character, the young Abbé Pierre Froment, called *La Rome Nouvelle*. The inspiration for this book, which is threatened with the Index, came from the abbé's study of "contemporary socialism," and it shows that underneath the evolution of religion there always hides an economic question, the eternal struggle between rich and poor. Jesus, writes the Abbé Froment, came to announce to the poor the hatred of the rich, the Golden Age, democracy, socialism and communism.

The abbé goes on to say that the Roman Empire fell because its officials became corrupt and its bankers and financiers were concerned only with profit. Unless the modern world regenerates itself through a return to socialism and anarchy preached by the prophets, including Jesus, it too will collapse.

Prof. Talmon has pointed out that, in this new syncretism to which the teaching of Saint-Simon contributed the largest share, Jewish influence was also a prominent factor. After all, Jewish influence had played an important part in the elaboration of Saint-Simon's general teaching. Several of Saint-Simon's closest friends and advisors on industrial and banking organization were of the Jewish faith. Saint-Simon himself said that the Jews had always perceived the incompleteness of the doctrine elaborated by the Church Fathers, because this doctrine stressed spiritual power without an attempt to include action by the temporal power as well. A true and universal religion should be able to regulate both. One of Saint-Simon's most loyal disciples, Rodrigues, also a Jew, spoke of the reconciliation of Christians and Jews in a more universal Christianity. The consensus of the Saint-Simonians was that Christianity must be revitalized as a synthesis of knowledge, science, social ideals and reforms.

Jews welcomed enthusiastically, Talmon finds, the Saint-Simonist doctrine with its "messianistic creed, offering salvation also from the special ailings of the Jew in the gentile world."[16] Their own messianism to which the suffering of centuries had added a sense of immediacy, now that traditional society was crumbling, fitted admirably in the general utopian climate. It continues to be heard in Martin Buber's social philosophy. Revolution, Buber holds, should be an affirmation of society *vis-à-vis* the State. Like so many utopians, Buber makes the decisive error of believing that the private associations, established by early Communist Russia, became corrupt because the political principle of the State infiltrated them and modified their structure. Again, like most disappointed sympathizers with the Russian Revolution, Buber urges a greater vigilance when the next and final revolution occurs. The establishment of a non-political society is vital, he writes, but it much be preceded by peace on earth. To avoid a new and gigantic centralization, we must "not hand the work of planetary management over to the political principle."[17]

Buber, and others like him, conceive the political principle differently from its traditional meaning. Their understanding of the political principle came into being with the modern democratic State, ultimately, however, with the French Revolution. Since their concept of political power is associated with the sprawling modern State, they view the political principle as a substance which can enter into and corrupt any association. In the past, political power took the form of the magistrate, the tax collector, the feudal lord and his haughty hunting companions. They were flesh-and-blood individuals, and the citizens merely wished to be rid of them. Today, however, the presence of authority is felt everywhere. The modern utopian, then, is more likely to see in power an "essence" attached to some forms of human associations, but not to others. It does not occur to him that politics is created by the mere fact of association,

[16] *Ibid.*, p. 81.
[17] *Paths in Utopia*, Beacon Press, Boston, 1949, p. 133.

since association means structuralization and division of functions, which in turn imposes the regulation of relationships, inequality of power, authority and subordination.

Contemporary utopian thought is, then, particularly preoccupied with the problem of government since it recognizes in the State a power-concentration greater than any time before in history. We will see in another chapter why modern utopians believe, nevertheless, that the State is withering away and that today there is a better chance than ever for the associative principle to conquer the political one. After all, even the Marxists believed that the proletariat only needed the conquest of the State in order first to make use of all its, now totalitarian, power, and then to dissolve it from within. Like the other utopians, they did not understand that power is generated by association and that it cannot be dissolved. Engels maintained, not unlike Buber, Tillich and other religious socialists, that person-to-person relationships may replace institutions. In the final outcome, he writes in *Socialism: Utopian and Scientific,* after the proletariat has abolished itself as proletariat, the State "becomes the real representative of the whole society, it renders itself unnecessary. . . . State interference in social relations becomes, in one domain after another, superfluous, and then dies out of itself." As it has not existed from all eternity, Engels continues in *The Origin of the Family, Private Property and the State* (1884), the State will disappear because it will become a positive hindrance to production. "The society that will organize production on the basis of a free and equal association of the producers will put the whole machinery of State where it will then belong: into the museum of antiquities, by the side of the spinning wheel and the bronze ax."[18]

---

[18] The irony is that even Stalin seems to have believed it. Milovan Djilas notes that "Stalin thought that the State would disappear by having all the citizenry rise to the State's level and take charge of its affairs." *The New Class,* Frederick A. Praeger, Publishers, New York, 1959, p. 87.

8 - THEOCRACY

AS NOTED in the preceding chapter, the logic of the utopian endeavor in clash with human realities results in the following situation: the political principle, discredited and abolished by the utopians, remains obstinately present in the new association of equals. Recalcitrant individuals remain; in fact, they actually constitute a majority usually referred to, however, as a backward, unregenerate minority by which the rest may be influenced, seduced or bribed. For this reason, the minority of regenerates must temporarily take command for the ultimate redemption of all. Their first task is to define who are the candidates for regeneration—that is, who show the required obedience and zeal—and who are to remain excluded from the community. This guarantees the indefinite perpetuation of the absolute and ruthless rule by the minority which conducts the purge and which decides when regeneration has been achieved.

Diffusion of Power Leads to Concentration

In all utopias, fictional or actually attempted, we therefore find that the political principle is not only present, but it is present in an

177

exacerbated form. This fact is masked in the following way: all utopias aim at the enthroning of a type of man called perfect. The minority, which believes that it embodies this ideal, is convinced also that its presence and blueprint for the future are guarantees that utopia will materialize and that the obstacles are only temporary. For all intents and purposes, therefore, the desired results will soon be achieved, and whatever the ruling minority decides and does will result in the removal of additional roadblocks. The increasingly greater power of the minority exalts its members with the conviction that the ultimate objective is in sight; their interventions in public affairs, therefore, invariably assume the character of quasi-divine decrees. Thus, while the utopian's primary contention that the associative principle must prevail over the political one is given theoretical satisfaction with the abolition of institutions and intermediary bodies, nonetheless the associative principle itself is strangled in its infancy. Fear and suspicion prevent people from associating outside the ritual association permitted and strictly supervised by the minority; in fact, the minority interferes, at every step, with even the ordinary processes of society. Since the minority (Party, State) now controls all relationships (whether informal relationships or Proudhon's "contracts"), the very act of controlling, as Karl Popper[1] notes, creates new relationships. The political principle is fully restored and immeasurably strengthened.

These dismal consequences are not avoidable chance developments; they are inscribed in the utopian assumption itself which insists on the exclusiveness of the associative principle. Theoretically, Strachey is right when he describes democracy as "the diffusion of power throughout the community." However, Strachey is wholly unrealistic in his observation that "the diffusion of power pushed further points, in turn, towards the elimination of power. For if everyone could have exactly equal power, no one, clearly, would have any power over his fellows. That, of course, is for us a distant

[1] *The Open Society and Its Enemies,* Harper & Row, New York, 1962.

ideal; it is the ideal of perfect cooperation in perfect liberty."² First
of all, that people are equal in political rights does not mean that
they are equal in talent, ambition, thirst for power and the like. A
state of equality is hardly, therefore, one of stable equilibrium because the more ambitious or the more talented men easily find
channels to get ahead of their fellows. In the second place, equality
is a challenge to form associations such as parties and pressure
groups which, on becoming strong, attract others and exploit the
explosive potential in their equal rights as citizens. This is why
Maritain is right in pointing out that "from transmutation to transmutation, the Rousseauist principle [each is born free and should
obey only himself] ends, by way of an almost continuous series,
in communist sociolatry, or, through a reactive backward movement, in totalitarian statolatry."³

Diffused power does not remain diffused unless it is concentrated
in institutions as well as in the hands of individuals, and while the
two are balanced. They cannot, of course, be balanced when the
institutions are imposed from above as permanent molds and when
the individuals are considered not as free agents, but chips from the
monolithic block of the collectivity. Jacques Maritain makes this
distinction between the human person and the Marxist party member: "The person whom Marx strives to liberate is conceived as
purely immanent in the group. Hence the only emancipation which
communism could achieve would be that of the collective man, not
of the individual person."⁴

The utopian emphatically disagrees. In the first place, the term
"collective man" makes no sense to him. He regards the human
being as a bundle of identifiable needs, partly work and partly play.
Whatever remains is a kind of craving (spiritual, religious) created

² John Strachey, *Contemporary Capitalism,* Random House, New York,
p. 217.
³ *Scholasticism and Politics,* The Macmillan Company, New York, 1960, p. 97.
⁴ *The Person and the Common Good,* Scribner's Sons, New York, 1947,
p. 83.

precisely by dissatisfaction on the level of normal requirements. When the requirements have been satisfied, the cravings will disappear, or, in the language of the religious utopian, the state of satisfaction will include a state of permanent enthusiasm and face-to-face dwelling with the source of spirituality.

Utopia Leads to Fixity

In the second place, the utopian objects to such criticism by pointing out that he never speaks of a static situation, but of one which evolves: both the individuals and the collectivity continue to grow and mature in consciousness. Therefore, Maritain's reference to the individual as "purely immanent in the group" makes no sense to the utopian. With the advance toward the universal human community, new and unimaginable perspectives will open up: the "new man" will share in freedom undreamed of, in health, mobility and happiness in proportion as he submits to the collectivity and absorbs its objectives. Thus, what the critic would attack as the fundamental fallacy in the utopian vision becomes, in the utopian's defense of this vision, the fundamental virtue, the pivot of all perfection and the guarantee of all happiness. When it is urged that society without government is unrealistic, the utopian retorts that not only is such a society possible, but it is the only possible one; in fact, every society which has preceded it was merely a groping in the dark. Here is a passage from Chauncey Thomas' *The Crystal Button,* an excellent example of this reasoning:

> "But," exclaimed Paul excitedly, "if you make no new laws, you have no law-makers, and no need of them; and if no law-makers, then no legislative bodies; and if no legislatures, then no elections, no voting, no parties, no politics, no politicians!"
> "Your deductions are correct," said the Professor, smiling; "and you may extend your list of defunct officials by adding generals, admirals, custom-house inspectors, kings, emperors,

or even presidents; for, in the ancient sense, there are now no well-defined boundaries for official domain other than municipal."

"You do not add," said Paul, "that you no longer have any governments, although I almost expected to hear you append that to your list of outlived institutions. Please tell me, have you a government or not?"

The Professor smiled, and then, after a short pause that lent emphasis to what followed, he added seriously: "Yes, Mr. Prognosis, we indeed have a government—the simplest, the strongest, the most effective, the most enduring government that the world had thus far known, which has been slowly evolved out of the needs of the people. Yet if you should seek for its head, in the person of a single man, you would find none, for there is none. This is a government of established forms. These forms time has fixed inflexibly in the minds and consciences of the people. All the methods of administration have been carefully considered and gradually shorn of objectionable features; and, so far as human wisdom can provide, they are the best possible forms suitable to existing circumstances. To distinguish it from all predecessors, this is called 'The Government of Settled Forms.'

"The Government of Settled Forms is very simple and needs no tinkering. It is universal, having been accepted by all nations. It knows nothing of the uncertainties of law-making, and I am glad to tell you that it knows very little of law-breaking, for law-breaking is no longer amusing or profitable —no longer honorable. There can be no general disturbance of the public in these days for the simple reason that education of an advanced type is now universal, all men and women are usefully employed, and there is no school of poverty or vice for developing a discontented class. Moreover, the population has again become homogeneous, with common customs, needs, language, religion, aims, ambitions. If we were called upon now to trust the decision of momentous questions to the nod of majorities, we could safely do so; but there is no longer any such need. The initial questions have been determined in the stormy past. We are now enjoying the results and peacefully developing details.

"I have explained the workings of the Department of Justice. The other elements of our government may be classed as the departments of Education, Public Health, Agriculture, Meteorology and Public Works. These are general in character, and the sub-departments are local in their operation but under the direction of Division Councils, who, in turn, are guided by the decisions of the Grand Council of the World.

"The duties of the Department of Education are obvious and need no explanation. That of Public Health has absolute control of everything pertaining to the sanitary condition of the people, such as the purification of rivers, water supply, disposition of refuse and its useful employments, and the location and character of all places of habitation.

"The Department of Agriculture determines the amount of seed to be sown each year, and the number of animals to be raised, to meet the requirements of the world. This department maintains the food conservatories of which I have already spoken, which are always amply supplied with a surplus to compensate for short crops. In short, its duty is to see that the world has plenty to eat.

"The Department of Meteorology determines the proportion of forest growth to tillage land and indicates to the Department of Public Works means of improving the climate and, to some extent, of equalizing the rainfall."[5]

Perhaps the strongest appeal is offered by the utopians when they present their otherwise dreary communities as cemented together

[5] Chauncey Thomas, *The Crystal Button;* cf. *The Quest for Utopia*, Doubleday & Co., Inc., New York, 1962.

by *love*. For the unsuspecting, even the frightening aspect of social symmetry, uniformity, regimentation and even despotism are allayed by assurances that these do not exclude the reign of love, that, indeed, they presuppose it! Christian utopians fully exploited this theme, and also in pagan times many utopias, Plato's excepted, were similarly conceived. Although these utopians did not place love at the center of their organizing principle, they did place there what they conceived as closest to love: wisdom.

In the course of his attack on Plato's *Republic,* the Stoic Zeno envisages a community of wise men. The perfection of their moral conduct renders social machinery superfluous. In a curious anticipation of Marxism, Zeno throws the entire apparatus of civilization overboard in the same way as the perfect classless society would discard religion, art and literature. The liberal arts vanish from Zeno's utopia together with family, institutions and social classes; the only real relative of the wise man and his only true fellow citizen is another wise man. The slate has been wiped clean: religious ceremonies, temples and clergy have been suppressed as have law courts and armies, trade and currency.

The Stoics were the first to introduce to the Greek world the concept of cosmopolitanism, the historical concomitant of Alexander's empire and of the extension of Greek civilization to the entire Mediterranean area and deep into Asia. Much like today, the sudden increase in communications and contacts among formerly isolated parts of the world brought about a universalist craving in intellectual circles. While in one small corner of the Mediterranean world a little-known State was preparing the subjection of the world, the Stoic philosophers began to indulge in utopian dreams.

Norman Cohn mentions two extant works written under strong Stoic influence. One was written a century before Christ; the other, a century after Christ. The first text describes the seven islands of the blessed which are inhabited by the Heliopolians, the sun men. The craving for uniformity is obvious throughout the text. The days and nights are of equal length and the summer is eternal. The population of each island is divided into four tribes, each tribe having four hundred members. All citizens are perfectly healthy and beautiful and work for the State at such tasks as hunting and fishing, something later to be echoed by Marx. All land and tools are common property, and so are the women. Children are brought up by the tribe, but in such a way that mothers are unable to recognize their own. Therefore, there is no heritage, inheritance laws or competition among heirs. There is but one law, the law of Nature, and it secures complete concord. When the Heliopolians die, invariably at 150 years of age, they do so voluntarily and in peace.

The other work is associated, perhaps erroneously, with a Gnostic sect, the Carpocratians. Here, too, we have an equalitarian doctrine illustrated by the impartiality of the sun which shines on all. God's justice is similarly a "community in equality," but it was destroyed by man-made laws which introduced the notion of private property—hence, of crime. Men have also ignored God's command that all should mate freely "as animals do."

These descriptions show a confusion between *love* and *uniformity*, a typical confusion of the utopian mind. This mind holds that love discourages the partners in love from pursuing divisive excellence. Conversely it holds that habitual exposure to the experience of uniformity creates a sense of security which, in turn, is equated with love. Much of contemporary psychology and modern educational methodology also stress "conformism" for the sake of reducing individual differences and promoting sociability, their special jargon for love.[6] The confusion figures in Campanella's *City of the Sun:* "The majority of the boys, since they are conceived under the same constellation [judged to be favorable by the supervisors of mating], are of the same age and resemble one another in strength, manner and appearance. This gives rise to much lasting

---

[6] Some current trends in education pursue mediocrity as an ideal. They do so in the name of democracy which is itself conceived along vague, sentimental lines. In fact, in some English schools good pupils are not promoted lest they cause a trauma in those who are held back.

concord in the State, for they treat each other lovingly and help-fully."[7]

Love, then, is the guarantee that the utopian community will not fall apart and will successfully check its eventual centrifugal forces. At this stage the utopian still hopes that a purely *inner transformation* will bring about the attitudes of self-abnegation and unselfish-ness needed for uniformity. Hence, at this stage the religious or spiritual utopian still has the upper hand, so to speak, because no coercion is envisaged to implement regimentation. When Marc Sangnier outlined, at the turn of the century, the aspiration of his *Sillon* movement to create a Christian democracy, he used the lan-guage of religious utopia and stressed Christ's direct help in achieving it. In order to make democracy possible he held men must have such a strong love for the common good, such a clear concept of social justice and such an overpowering desire to create a true democracy that anything which would work against democ-racy will be regarded as a personal injury. Democracy will be possi-ble, Sangnier said, when selfishness is destroyed.

Proponents of this plan place their hopes in education but not education of the traditional kind. Education would be the relentless work of instilling all the proper sentiments in people's hearts, of arousing an unquenchable desire for democracy and of teaching an unmistakable doctrine of what constitutes the good of all. Saint-Simon had already elaborated a scheme for an "academy of senti-ments" which would be staffed by teachers of morality, lawyers, theologians, poets and painters. It was their work to inspire the right kind of sentiments. He also proposed a National Catechism, a "general doctrine" and a "universal science." The result of these efforts would be, according to Saint-Simon, the disappearance of all present evils: arbitrariness, incompetence, and intrigue. Order would easily be maintained in the reformed society because people would be convinced of the full competence of their superiors and

[7] This, like other references to Campanella's work, is my translation from *La Cité du Soleil*, Vrin, Paris, 1950.

follow them naturally. Families, cities and nations will form one single human family, and in this single city founded on the only correct doctrine everyone will be brother to everyone. The leader will not issue from an election box, but will himself be a living law. Saint-Simon believed that the first two leaders were Moses, who revealed the law, and Jesus, who revealed love; he, Saint-Simon, was the third and final leader who would crown their work by revealing progress.

In the kind of doubletalk (or newspeak) popularized by George Orwell's *1984*, Saint-Simon added that freedom, as past ages understood it, consisted of servitude and fatalism; however, the reign of authority which he and his disciples were announcing, would be the rule of liberty and Providence. He concluded, as would Sangnier a century later, that civic obedience will be voluntary because the State will use education instead of force.

Saint-Simon's national catechism is reflected in another utopian work, Conde Pallen's *Crucible Island* (New York, 1919). As soon as they are capable of learning, children are taught the socialist catechism.

Q. By whom were you begotten?
A. By the Sovereign State.
Q. Why were you begotten?
A. That I might know, love, and serve the Sovereign State always.
Q. What is the Sovereign State?
A. The Sovereign State is Humanity in composite and perfect being.
Q. Why is the State supreme?
A. The State is supreme because it is my Creator and Conserver in which I am and move and have my being and without which I am nothing.
Q. What is the individual?

A. The individual is only a part of the whole, and made for the whole, and finds his complete and perfect expression in the Sovereign State. Individuals are made for cooperation only, like feet, like hands, like eyelids, like the rows of the upper and lower teeth.

At this point, love, noble sentiments, enthusiasm and religion are still mixed and there is an impatience to prepare the human material for the expected transformation. But love is soon shed, and the utopian slips by degrees into limitless undisguised adulation of uniformity and symmetry. For example, the gentle Bishop Fénelon, famous for his sinuous style, lost debates with Bossuet and friendship with Mme. Guyon, protector of the Pietist sect in France. Yet that same gentle prelate becomes as austere as Thomas More, Bacon or Campanella when he writes in his didactic work, *Télémaque,* of the legislator in his ideal republic. All luxury is proscribed; the law-giver will determine in minute detail how much land a family may own, what decorations may be used in the home, how much and what kind of furniture may be owned. The State must suppress all manifestations of individualism. And Fénelon, a bishop of the Catholic Church, takes the position that children belong to the Republic rather than to their parents.

In Plato's *Laws* the organization of an imaginary settlement or colony is the subject of conversation. The population is fixed at 5,040 and divided into four classes. The capital city is at the center of the settlements, and the Acropolis at the center of the city. Twelve districts are distributed around the main square. The homes, situated on the periphery, are arranged in the form of a circle, and they touch one another so as to form a protective wall. Each citizen's land is divided in two; one plot is close to the center of the city and the other is situated farther out, so that every citizen owns a city home and a country home.

The Voyages and Adventures of Jacques Massé, by Tyssot de

Patot (1710) has, as its narrative cadre, an island discovered by survivors of a shipwreck. They come ashore to find a country where everything is symmetrical and geometrical; even the houses and gardens are square in shape. The people who inhabit this island live a very simple existence, strictly regulated in time and space, with but few motivations to stir their robot-like character. Raymond Ruyer quite justly remarks that Plato's Republic, the capital of Atlantis, More's Utopia, the City of the Sun and the capital of Icaria are all symmetrical.[8] Because the utopian author imagines himself in the role of supreme and all-powerful lawgiver, any spontaneous thought or action on the part of his imaginary citizens would upset his calculations, twist the threads which meet in his hands. Both Friedrich Hayek and Karl Popper have pointed out that the utopian planner must simplify his problems by eliminating individual differences and by reducing to absolute uniformity all beliefs and interests. This can be achieved only by education and propaganda until that ideal moment comes when the interests, the beliefs and thoughts of all will be identical.

At this point the utopian writers cease to speak of inner transformation, and the religious-spiritual tone fades out; they increasingly stress the necessity of behavioral conformity. This is necessarily the case because behavior is easier to supervise and control. Obviously this presents no problem since the inhabitants of utopia have "internalized" the common good, that is, the robot has "absorbed" the political animal. But even here uniformity is the only available guarantee that the laws remain permanent and that they have become habits. In analyzing the planner's holistic approach to human affairs, Karl Popper notes that such a "scientific" control of human nature leads to social suicide. Holistic control, which ostensibly seeks the equalization of human rights,

---

[8] *L'Utopie et les Utopies*, Presses Universitaires de France, Paris, 1950, p. 42.

"leads to the equalization of human minds and thus to the end of progress."[9]

For two reasons, however, the utopian does not feel that progress depends on the individual's aspiration and free search for excellence; first, he believes that individuals can be adequately motivated only when they have been absorbed into the collectivity; secondly, he holds that unsupervised excellence is too high a price to pay for any progess it might accomplish. In fact, the utopian feels, it is better that the collectivity not benefit by certain breakthroughs in, say, science and art, rather than risk the loss of its uniformity and blue-print existence. For example, during its half century of efforts to collectivize agriculture, the Soviet leadership has had ample chance to return to individual ownership of the land and thereby solve the problem of feeding its industrial population. If ever statistical data were reliable, they are in this case: they demonstrate irrefutably—and the Soviet leaders admit it—that the small plots accorded to the individual farmer and cultivated in the few hours a month that can be stolen from the *kolkhoze* or the *sovkhoze* contribute more than half of the country's food supply. Yet, the Soviet leaders would never dream of admitting the failure of their system or of changing it. Instead, they persist in saying that the failure of the food supply is attributable to the still lagging spirit of "socialist consciousness."

Utopia Must Use Constraint

Uniformity, therefore, is an essential, built-in element of utopian existence, and it is no less important that this uniformity remain permanent. The resulting system is a far cry from what had been claimed: free association and the elimination of the political principle. Increasingly greater guarantees are needed to maintain regimentation on a permanent basis: as *love* is abandoned as the

[9] Karl R. Popper, *The Poverty of Historicism*, Beacon Press, Boston, 1957, p. 159.

cement of social cohesion, *force* is introduced. This cannot be stressed too strongly, and it serves to underline the indispensable part which leadership plays in holding utopia together.

The utopian, in his turn, is just as vehement in his denial regarding the use of force and the role of leadership. And understandably so, because the division of society into leaders and followers reveals the reappearance of the political principle. Utopians then resort to every kind of subterfuge. They will say with Saint-Simon, Comte, Engels and others that, while the old State was characterized by the need to *govern people*, utopia will know only the *administration of things*, as if "things" were not created, moved and consumed by people whose relationship to one another is determined partly by their relationship to these "things." Or the utopians will say with the communists that a socialist country is, by definition, *owned by the people*, so that nobody really rules except as the people's appointee—which brings us back to Lord Newcastle's diagnosis that the concept of "the people" is subject to endless manipulation: for example when Communist leaders claim to be the people's appointees, "people" means the party which these leaders dominate in the most absolute way. Again, other utopians will say that the alleged leadership class is appointed by God to lead mankind to happiness and to salvation. This is theocracy (or, in its secularized version, the rule of historical necessity) in which the divine sanction—divine, therefore unquestioned—authorizes the most ruthless and cruel reintroduction of the political principle through those leaders who interpret the divine commandment. Finally, the utopian may simply adopt a double standard such as that illustrated by Cabet. After his Icarian guide has described the total regimentation of the population of Icaria from the waking hours to curfew, the visitor asks him whether such a law is not tyrannical. The guide glibly explains that such a law would be intolerable if promulgated by a tyrant, whereas it is the most reasonable and useful of laws when adopted by the people as a whole in the interests of their own health and working conditions.

Rule of the Elect

The four utopian circumlocutions just enumerated have one common characteristic: they all take it for granted that the leaders *love* those under their care. This love is not to be confused with a sense of responsibility or even with love in the ordinary sense of the word. The leaders of utopia are not supposed to be ordinary men: they are the Elect, the Pure; they are closer to God than other mortals and more in the stream of History than their groping fellow men; they possess more of the distinguishing substance, whether it be "spirit" or the understanding of Marxist dialectics. Small wonder, then, that the ordinary man's love of his utopian leader transcends personal and civic loyalty and even admiration for the carrier of a historic mission; his feeling for his leader is worship because the utopian leader is the guarantor of salvation—or, in earthly terms, complete security. He lifts responsibility from the shoulders of others; in a kind of secularized incarnation he assumes the burden of thinking, of deciding and of planning for the future. The utopian leader possesses more than sacerdotal powers because his solicitude embraces both the spiritual and the temporal well-being of the ordinary utopian citizen.

Compatible in every way with the utopian leader's love of the common citizen is his utter ruthlessness and use of force. With but slight variations, this feature is to be noted all through the history of utopias. Although, generally speaking, utopias present a dreary and monotonous picture, they manifest at least a certain air of serenity about them, the result of their citizens' final acquiescence to the concept of happiness imposed by a gentle force. The truth is different, for a careful reading of utopian texts reveals the same features of life as does the reading of reports from Communist societies, whether of the religious or Soviet brand. In their enthusiasm and naïveté, utopian authors unwittingly allow revealing passages to slip into their encomia much as the speeches by Soviet leaders are revealing in between-the-lines reading. Resistance to utopian rule and way of life, and suppression of that resistance is invariably disclosed.

The reasoning of the religious utopian is that neither institutions nor ceremonies are necessary because the true Church (which coincides with the good society) will be governed only by the invisible word of God. This is what the Anabaptists *taught*.[9a] However, the actual evolving of this teaching was in dramatic contrast to their professed humility before God, and the Anabaptist high command under Thomas Münzer was nothing but a band of cruel despots who had to be reduced by similar cruelty. Münzer's associates were not only raving madmen who instituted a reign of terror in the city of Münster, but they even considered themselves authorized by their status of Elects to commit immoral acts, to keep concubines, to give full vent to their sensuality. In this they are not alone in the long history of heretical sects and utopian movements whose exalting of absolute moral purity and condemning of things carnal have led them to unrestrained sensual indulgence. The Carpocratian sect of Christian antiquity drew the conclusion, logical for utopians, that whoever purified himself, as did the members of that sect, need fear sin no longer, for the pure cannot be sullied. In fact, some sects went so far as to proclaim that the promiscuous sex lives of the Elect are proof that sin and the mark of sin cannot touch them. The founder of Pietism, Fr. Molinos, taught in his *Spiritual Guide* (1675) that man's soul should be so absorbed in God (and thereby acquire quietude) and become so indifferent even to desiring Heaven that he may indulge in sin and still remain essentially good (or, rather, "quiet"). Because man's will, absorbed in God, does not give consent to sin, his soul remains spotless.

[9a] Not only the Anabaptists, but, as Fr. Yves Congar shows, the Reformers generally. "What is our link to Christ? Wyclif, Hus, Zwingli answer: predestination; they end up with an invisible Church. And Luther concluded: What links us to Christ is the Word, the Word alone." *Op. cit.*, p. 417.

The Cult of Utopian Rulers

The Elect, or the utopian leaders, consider themselves pure or, at any rate, above those standards by which the rest of humanity is judged. In his attempt to systematize utopian leadership, Saint-Simon believed that politics would soon become an exact science to be manipulated by experts only, an oligarchy of scholars to be called the Council of Newton. Saint-Simon was fascinated with religion because, in contrast to his more starry-eyed contemporary utopians, he correctly judged that social cohesion cannot be based on the "scientific view" alone. In this respect, Saint-Simon was far in advance of such prominent twentieth-century utopians as Bertrand Russell or Julian Huxley. Not only was Saint-Simon fascinated by the possibilities of subjecting religion in general to the service of the industrial utopia, but he selected Christianity, or, rather, "New Christianity" for this role. Formally Catholic terminology is common in his writings, and in *Mémoire sur la Science de l'Homme*, Saint-Simon even expressed the hope that the oligarchy of scholars would elect a pope dedicated to the "new scientific theory."

The Council of Newton was to consist of twenty-one carefully selected geniuses, a mixture of scholars and priests. The Council would direct the new religion. Newton would be in the center of the new cult, and people would come to worship in temples erected in his honor. The dogmas of the new cult allowed for neither doubt nor questioning, and a special catechism expounding these beliefs would be taught in the schools. Saint-Simon admitted that he found the model for his new clergy in the Egyptian and Indian sacerdotal castes which monopolized power as well as the corps of scientific knowledge.

Auguste Comte, a leading disciple of Saint-Simon, subscribed even more fully to a leadership along sacerdotal lines. The dogmas on which future social cohesion would rest, said Comte, must be elaborated by competent authorities whose love for the people would be unquestionable because no other interests would absorb them. In Comte's view, the masses would not be intelligent enough to understand the dogmas, yet they would be unshakable in their conviction regarding need to believe the dogmas. Accordingly, the ordinary people will confess to their leaders, assured that their leaders have only their good at heart.

Throughout the nineteenth century, thanks to the realization that industrialization presented some serious problems and social conflicts, utopian ideals began to assume more concrete form. Industrial organization served as a model for modern versions of utopia. The utopian writers wanted both to continue the industrialization process and, at the same time, to eliminate the abuses created by that process. Utopian regimentation would take the form of industrial discipline. Taking into account the nineteenth-century fear that this discipline might one day break down, utopians sought to devise new motives for social cohesion to keep the industrial society of the future together. It was evident to them that the self-interest of both workers and managers called for safeguards for the continuation of the process, but they would not believe that the two self-interests, momentarily in conflict, could be harmonized by a politically free climate. They believed, therefore, that only some combination of love and force could guarantee social coexistence, and the Saint-Simonist leader, Enfantin, exulted "in the yoke of common conviction and in the power which would drive men on to progress."

Illustrations from Communist History

As the nineteenth century advanced, so did the impatience of utopians. This was due, in part, to the growing contradiction that existed between the high productivity of the new factories, machines and methods, and the misery of the masses, that is, of the immediate producers. Marx, learning from Ricardo, built his reputation on his so-called scientific analysis of the inexorability of this contradiction, which he proclaimed to be inherent in the capitalist mode of production. In fact, there was no contradiction at all, because the standard of living of the masses was steadily improving, but the general betterment was obscured because of the new work forces thrown on the labor market and by the occasional economic crises which created unemployment, without adequate social legislation to cushion the shock.

With characteristic disregard for facts and for the actual forces at work, the utopian thinkers continued to envisage a final solution, or, rather, they expressed their eternal desire for a final solution in contemporary terms. These terms now included "revolution," "organization of Europe," "capital," "social utility," and the like, just as in other ages they were "the reign of Christ" or the "rule of the Elect." They all expected the coming of the millennium, the glory of science and organization. The "leaders" had to be ready to usher in the golden age, men who, said Bakunin, must be devoted, energetic and talented, men who, above all, would love the people without ambition and vanity. A hundred revolutionists, firmly and seriously bound together, he said, would be enough for the international organization of all Europe.[10]

[10] *Statuts Secrets de l'Alliance*, p. 132. Let us note here that even the anarchist Bakunin whom his violent views made one of the foremost utopians of the last century, received a salutary shock when confronted with the ruthlessness of Marxist theory and with Marx himself. In 1873 he published *The State and Anarchy*, in which he indignantly revealed the Marxist plans in all their brutality. "From the realization that the social insurrection and reconstruction must be based on sociological science [the Marxists] conclude that the commanding minority should be a small elite trained in this science. . . . The so-called popular State will thus be a very despotic rule over the masses by a new aristocracy of real or self-defined scholars. Since the masses possess no erudition, they will be freed from the burden of governing, and will be corralled in the government's stables." We have seen, however, that Saint-Simon's teaching was based on the same idea. A more objective, less utopian Bakunin could have attacked the whole trend of utopian socialist thought. If he singled out Marxism, it was because at the meeting of the First International he clashed with Marx in person.

The separation of leaders from the masses whom they were supposed to lead to scientific happiness continued according to the laws of utopian thinking. Saint-Simon distinguished a *national party*, those who understood and promoted progress, and an *anti-national party* of retrogrades and parasites. In the national party would be those who engage in socially useful work, those who provide the producers with necessities and, finally, the investors and managers; in the anti-national party would be those who consume without producing, those who are not engaged in socially useful work, and those whose political views harm production and the prestige of the producers. The threat against the "anti-national party" is very thinly disguised here, in fact, not disguised at all in light of Saint-Simon's general theory of society. But the philosopher Max Stirner was more specific. To bring about great change, he believed that a certain number of men must first undergo an inner change, that is, they must recognize their own welfare as their highest law. Afterwards they can force all the others and promote, by force, the outward change: the abrogation of law, State, and property.

These illustrations of utopian logic show the return of the political principle to utopia, but in excessive form, so that now the gap between leaders and ordinary people is wholly unbridgeable. What is not immediately apparent in utopia, however, is the fact that it is catastrophic to belong to any but the leadership class, because the rest are held, as Bakunin realized, in the "regime's stable." What starts out as a society of equals enjoying free associations becomes one of morose beasts trying to crush one another in a horrible scramble to get nearer this unique source of power.

This power will never be diffused throughout the social body as the utopian has predicted. The class of leaders sees to it that the qualifications of the Elect are more and more narrowly defined, with the result that the greater and greater numbers are forever excluded, while, at the same time, those who are inside the leadership circle may be purged in the name of some new doctrinal formulation. An ex-leader of the Chinese Communist Youth described the process of the naked power struggle. He explained that in totalitarian regimes there is but one way for the individual to assert himself and that is through the central power. Unless one becomes the latter's agent, he must remain a pariah. The risk is incalculable for the individual whether he opts for servility to the leadership or for his status as a pariah. There is no alternative.[10a]

Communist societies, or, to be more exact, societies under Communist regimes, display in a particularly striking fashion the utopian fallacy, namely the reintroduction of the political principle while those who accumulate the new and excessive power in their hands keep postponing the passage to a society based on the associative principle. Prof. Leonard Shapiro, analyzing the Communist Party Program of 1961, remarks that the Soviet State is still very far from withering away.[11] The Party, which, after all, was supposed to abolish itself, "will not only survive, but will have an especially important role to play in leading society towards communism." The "government of men" is, thus, not ready to yield to the "administration of things," and, as the Programme admits between the lines, there are plenty of tensions in a society supposedly inhabited by spontaneously self-administered, happy people.

These tensions (sabotage, under-production, huge wage differences, bureaucratic abuse, famine, scarcity of goods, high crime rate) are so real that the Soviet leaders must continually threaten with reprisals and punishments. In a speech before the plenary session of the Central Committee, November, 1962, Mr. Khrushchev said—or rather threatened—that if all Party, Komsomol and trade union members were put to work inspecting and controlling Soviet society, not even a mosquito could take wing without being detected. This is, of course, the habitual attitude of tyrannies, but

[10a] Suzanne Labin, *La Condition humaine en Chine communiste*, La Table Ronde, Paris, 1959, pp. 252–253.
[11] "From Utopia towards Realism," article by Leonard Shapiro, *Encounter*, Aug., 1962.

in this case the utopian structure doubly reveals itself: in the first place, the citizens are supposed to live in harmony so that any sign to the contrary is considered an aberration, an anomaly; in the second place, Khrushchev, like all utopian leaders, took it for granted that the members of the group of Elect possess an absolute right to control the activities of the non-Elect. One might say that his brutal way of asserting this right is characteristic of his usually unpolished mode of expression, but we find that almost all utopian writers express themselves with similar violence when speaking of the punishments meted out to non-conformists.

Within the confines of utopian logic Khrushchev was, of course, right to assume complete social harmony, pretend astonishment at not finding it everywhere and threaten with penalties. What gave him this right was the utopian assumption of *unanimity* which, whether it exists or not, ideally *does* exist (Rousseau's general will), and of which he is the embodiment. The utopian leader, as we said before, does not expect this unanimity to include the whole population: he can always restrict the *real* population precisely to those who adopt the views on which unanimity is supposed to be established. Even if he alone holds the "correct view," the fact of unanimity is unquestioned. As Professor George L. Kline points out, Soviet spokesmen actually "insist, in the face of the evidence, that under socialism *moral* norms (in contrast to *legal* norms which are sanctioned by State power) find their sanction in a 'public opinion' which would unanimously condemn inaction [in a citizen]." He then goes on in a very interesting passage: "The sanction of moral norms is supposed to become increasingly internalized as Soviet society approaches full communism: the external voice of public opinion is to give way to the 'inner voice' of conscience or 'Communist consciousness.' Khrushchev himself has said: 'Our task is to transform the new moral demands into an inner need of all Soviet citizens.' "[12]

[12] "Philosophy, Ideology and Policy in the Soviet Union," *The Review of Politics,* April, 1964.

Regimented Behavior and Punishment in Utopia

The issue of "internalization" of external pressure is a very important one, and we dealt with it in other chapters. Here is the place to point out, however, that when the citizenry of utopia is expected to internalize the correct way of thinking about public and private matters, the non-conformers can and must be punished under one of these three headings: indolence, sabotage or actual resistance. In fact, they can and must be punished for mere external conformism too (that is, if the leaders want to indict them for any reason known only to them, they may use "external conformism" or opportunism, or lukewarmness—these are then synonymous—as the manifest charges). The truth of utopia's official ideal is so evident that only a perverted will may prevent its internalization. To what extent the demand in this direction may go, is shown by examples given in Paul Hollander's article on private life in Red China.

Hollander quotes a certain Won Tshih-pou whose article in *Youth of China* appeared under the title of "On the ideal life of revolutionary youth." The article puts a young woman on the pillory of shame for expressing hopes of a quiet life with her husband —after, of course, all the revolutionary goals had been achieved. These hopes are modest and humble, but in Communist parlance they are described as "bourgeois." She mentions an apartment with bookshelves and radio, quiet evenings at home after the day's work, the weekly visit each Sunday by their little daughter who lives in a children's center. She does not aspire to the frivolous life of the bourgeoisie, the young woman writes, yet she is criticized, along with her husband, for the hopes they entertain. . . . It is true, the woman writes, that the revolution and the building of socialism should serve the people and its future, but they should give present satisfaction, too.[13]

[13] Hollander, "La Vie privée en Chine," *Le Contrat Social*, Jan.–Feb., 1964, pp. 38–39.

Unanimity is assumed on the most minute matters, including renunciation of the most legitimate aspirations. The above example shows that "public opinion," that is, the internalized commands of the leadership class, cut as deeply as possible into people's private life. The latter are also required to accept and even enthusiastically and unanimously to recommend measures directed against themselves. The Red Chinese law on labor unions, promulgated on June 29, 1950, states that the union's duty is to instruct and organize the masses of workers and cadres that they should support the laws and projects of the People's Government; they should also execute the latter's decisions in order to strengthen its power, since the power of the People's Government belongs to the working class. What were the laws which, under compulsion, were supported by the unions and the resolutions they "spontaneously" passed in the period 1950-1954? Reduction of wages in view of aiding the country's economy; various voluntary contributions to the State; renunciation of the yearly bonus; numerous campaigns of socialist emulation against laziness in the factories and against unmotivated absences.

Under the "commune" system, the Chinese communists interfered most brutally with married life in its most intimate aspects. Couples were separated and lodged in men's and women's dormitories; on appointed days they were authorized to mate, and on such occasions the husbands had to line up to have access to their wives. However shocking this sounds, it is again in absolute conformity with utopian thinking. In *The City of the Sun,* Campanella would regulate the relationship of the sexes: "If any man is seized with a violent love for a woman, he and she are permitted to converse and joke together, bestow garlands of flowers or leaves on each other, and make verses for each other. But if the function of breeding is endangered [we saw earlier that breeding was to be performed at appointed times under the supervision of astrologers], under no condition is intercourse permitted them unless the woman is already pregnant or sterile. But love consisting of eager desire is scarcely known among them; it generally consists only of friendship." The inhabitants of Cyrano de Bergerac's utopia push these rigid measures to a grotesque extreme: a law regulates the number of sexual acts between husband and wife. "Every night the neighborhood physician visits the homes, examines the couples, and indicates according to their state of health how many times they may embrace one another."

Since all this is done in order to change the nature of man, extirpate his selfishness and instill collective conscience, the acts of renunciation and obedience are supposed to express the associative principle in a higher, perfected form. The utopian leadership always claims that its function is merely to facilitate association among equal citizens, including among members of a family—or, in the religious utopian language, communication between them and God. Under such a claim, the citizen shows his virtuousness to the extent that he abandons the socially divisive attitude of looking out for his own and his family's interests, and, with a complete and loyal candor, trusts the leadership class to take care of his needs, including his need for affection. Thus, within its own system of utopian logic, the leadership class can always legitimately claim that confidence in its ability to lead people to happiness—an ability bolstered by love for the people—is not only reasonable, but also virtuous. Conversely, doubt in, and resistance to, this ability (and love) show stupidity, obstinacy and viciousness: doubters and resisters must be punished.

But such is the utopian view of man and society, that they are not punished as simple derelicts or criminals: since they contradict the associative principle and break unanimity, doubters and resisters must first be excluded from the membership of utopia's citizenry, hence from membership in the human race. The utopian who has scorned and "abolished" the coercive power of the State, with its police, laws, courts and executioners, proceeds to restore them in the most matter-of-fact way, since, as Cabet wrote, the same thing done by a "tyrant" or "adopted by an entire People" is not the same thing. Speaking of the "ultrasupernaturalist," Msgr. Knox remarked: "So long as he is living within the confines of a state governed by worldly men according to the dictates of carnal wisdom, the ultrasupernaturalist outlaws himself, usually, from its constitution. When once a theocratic state is set up, under a 'perfect' ruler, or an army is in the field marshalled by 'perfect' generals, there is danger that he will be not less but more bloodthirsty than is the common wont of men."[14]

On the extermination of resisters to utopia all utopian writers are in agreement. We saw in an earlier chapter that the medieval "Revolutionary" prophesied the coming of the "Emperor" who, once a year, would issue a decree for the purpose of unmasking sin, would encourage sinners to confess their sins voluntarily and urge others to inform against them. The judges will punish all sin —for what is mercy toward sinners if not a crime against the community as a whole?

Similar attitude and justification may be found among Puritans, whether in Geneva, Scotland or early America. They punished sinners with the understanding that these sinners were enemies of virtue, hence unsaved, and deprived of the common rights of humanity. In Icaria, too, society plans and directs everything, subjects to its command and discipline the will and action of people. In the face of triumphant communism, Cabet writes, any blind passion for liberty will be considered an error and a vice, meaningless under the new dispensation. In the new condition of society without government, writes also W. Godwin, "not a sword will need to be drawn, not a finger to be lifted up in purposes of violence. The adversaries will be too few and too feeble to be able to entertain a serious thought of resistance against the universal sense of mankind."[15]

14 Knox, *op. cit.*, Clarendon Press, Oxford, 1950, p. 132.
15 Godwin, *op. cit.*, pp. 222–223.

So much abuse is heaped on the non-conformer that we are not astonished to find that some utopian writers look at him as abnormal. Obviously, since in proportion as the glory of utopia becomes more shining, the resister becomes less understandable; should he not be judged sick and insane for his opposition to so evident a truth, to such a complete happiness? In *The Crystal Button* this conclusion is actually reached: "In the hospital," the visitor is told, "there are [among others] those who are morally deranged . . . we simply treat them as persons morally deranged or ailing! 'But how do you punish them?' 'We know no such thing as punishment in their case. We confine them, partly for their own good.' " Even more systematic is J. M. Brown (writing under the pseudonym of Godfrey Sweven) in his *Limanora,* The Island of Progress (New York, 1903): "Whenever a Limanoran child became afflicted with an evil or retrogressive passion, he was hurried off to the ethical laboratory, and the nerve centers of his emotional and moral nature were microscopically photographed. . . . An ethical sanatorium [was established] for obstinate moral diseases . . . and moral physicians and nurses . . . applied their therapeutic power to the center that was diseased."

9 - CONTEMPORARY
UTOPIANISM

THROUGHOUT this book is the recurring theme that a common thread runs through all utopian systems, whether they be Church heresies, fictional discoveries of islands of happiness, Marxism, or the spiritual evolutionism of Teilhard de Chardin. When the intellectual climate or external circumstances are favorable, this type of thinking is almost bound to come forward. Utopian thinking in our own time, then, is not an aberration peculiar to the modern mind. After all, heretics and utopians do deal with the great problems of existence, just as authentic philosophers do; they respond, however, to only a certain kind of problem. Nothing is more natural than the interest this age takes in the possibilities which earlier utopian thinkers indicated as desirable; in fact, the contemporary utopian is able to depict a plausible utopia which is almost ready to materialize, so that he will dismiss all counter-arguments as unrealistic.

Yet, not even this feature that utopia is within grasp is new or original. In every age the utopian has found ample evidence for belief that his age was a penultimate phase ready to usher in the last and definitive transformation. Since utopian systems are essentially illusory patterns of thought with their own logic, expectations, and interpretive mechanism, real data do not substantially influence the utopian thinker: he is able to fit the data on the Procrustean bed of his desires and to find encouragement even in the most unfavorable events. Contempt for the present as well as for those points in time which separate mankind from the desired end marks the utopian's outlook. He chooses to concentrate on arrival itself and scorns all questions about the means of arrival. The world is worth consideration only in view of the final station, and history is but a preparation, in itself indifferent, for the last act. The last act itself is to be heralded by highly dramatic events or intolerable conditions, as if all the forces standing in the way of utopia had gathered for the ultimate resistance. This particular belief enables the utopian to ignore warnings that world circumstances do not seem conducive to utopia. He calls, instead, for a new vision of the situation, a bold anticipation, an enthusiastic will. He dismisses realistic appraisals as emanating from the "poor in spirit, the sceptics, the pessimists, the sad of heart, the weary, the immobilists . . . and generally from those who are against Progress."[1] He remains indifferent, even callous, before the world's suffering because he sees in it a new proof that things are coming to a point of critical maturity. Contemporary evil, in his eyes, is the last manifestation of the Antichrist and necessary in the economy of utopian salvation. Consequently, evil is not even real: if it were, its existence cannot affect the new world on the threshhold of which men stand. There is a parallel here with those heretics who believe that the purity of the soul is unaffected by the immorality in which the body indulges; in fact, such heretics may actually engage in immoral acts so as to emphasize the distance between soul and body, to show the divine stamp on the soul and the abjectness of the body. Similarly, the utopian often rejoices over the existence of evil because he believes

[1] Teilhard de Chardin, *The Future of Man*, Harper & Row, New York, 1964, pp. 72 and 117.

that it helps us to grasp better the emerging contours of a perfect state of affairs.[2]

Whether our century has had more than its share of horrors must remain an undecided question. Certainly we may say without exaggeration that it has had its fair share of suffering, injustice and crushed illusions. It has even invented such new forms of evil, as genocide, concentration camps, brainwashing techniques and psychological warfare. Although these evils may seem incommensurable with anything in the past, actually they are only quantitatively new. Technological advances have spread these evils to all parts of the world and have also enabled small groups of people to terrorize majorities even entire nations and continents—as has never before been feasible.

Viewing such horrors, the contemporary utopian sees in them signs of imminent general happiness. First of all, he interprets the very intensity of evil as a promise of radical improvement; secondly, he is encouraged by the planetary diffusion of evil because he is convinced that the thorough and ultimate remedy may be secured only if all mankind partakes in the renewal of moral conscience. It is reasonable, then, to say that the only new element in contemporary utopian thought is that it takes technology into account.

Technology: New Element in Utopian Thinking

How will this be done, how can a tool—even a formidable tool like modern technology—bring about internal transformation? The utopian does not deny that technology, by itself, is a blind force usable indiscriminately for good and evil; yet, by the fact that it also represents a measuring rod of the progress of science, it is a force of progress, particularly in view of planetary unity and the cohesion of mankind. Its additional role is to quicken the desired

[2] Teilhard de Chardin holds that the totalitarian regimes of the twentieth century have been imperfect efforts of the all-governing evolutionary forces to bring about ultimately a perfected form of "totalization" on our planet.

evolution, partly because it imposes the necessity of immediate decisions, partly because it has already unleashed evil forces that must be brought urgently under control. Therefore, the utopian enthusiastically greets the fact of technology which brings about in short order the human cohesion.

We saw that all utopians agree on the necessity of subjugating nature, and that the process of subjugation must be a task for all men, in common effort; well, technology represents just such a collective effort, and, moreover, it suppresses nature's spontaneity against which utopians warn.

This suppression of natural spontaneity presents man to himself as divine, creator of a new and improved nature. Gnostic doctrines and utopian-heretic ones rebelled against creation, accusing it of being full of flaws, of accepting the existence of evil. But the new nature, originated by mankind in a series of conscious acts, will be flawless insofar as it corrects existing ills and responds to future needs.

Even if left to itself, the guiding hand of necessity would so organize the new technological inventions as to favor and eventually bring about universal cooperation. This is the inherent meaning of technology. But technology also offers the unique opportunity of establishing a world organization under whose authority the whole technologized planet would be placed. Not merely the nuclear weapons, but also space travel, various large-scale projects of industrial, agricultural and medical (for example, eugenics and birth control) nature are to be brought under such a control.

The two phenomena: technology and world organization (world government) would tend, in fact, to strengthen each other, thereby guaranteeing that there will be in the future neither technological retrogression nor political division. The need of servicing a planet-wide technology would impose cohesion, and, *vice versa,* the need to maintain mankind's unity would continuously activate and perfect the technical means.

Contemporary Faith in Knowledge and Power

Encouraged by reckless ideologies, drunk with technical power and at the same time fearful of the forces he has called into existence, modern man is tempted to explore the limits of his possibilities, and even to push beyond. Paul Valéry saw the essence of modernism in the mind's ambition to advance ever farther and leave even knowledge behind for the sake of power. In contemporary art, science, literature, politics and war, an irresistible urge to explore whatever imagination conjures up is everywhere evident. The distance between traditional standards and the adventure of the mind is ceaselessly growing, with the result that contemporary civilization is no longer a system of correcting and softening the impact of nature without and within us: rather, as Valéry remarks, civilization is *antiphysis,* a counter-nature in which we see the paradox of civilization crushing the civilized man and thereby collapsing. Intelligence engenders stupidity and lends arms to brutality. By becoming less enslaved to nature, says Valéry, modern man has become the slave of anti-nature.[3]

Contemporary man, therefore, has a well developed utopian consciousness just as his ancestors had an eschatological or millenaristic consciousness. He knows as unquestionable fact that mankind is nearer than ever, indeed decisively near, the end of evolution. Not only can he now envisage the future course of evolution, but he can also predict its unilinear development and even take a hand in shaping it. Contemporary utopians believe that mankind now possesses the inner drive and resources for self-salvation.

Technological inventions, the predictability of social and economic developments, perfected communications media, a more mature understanding of the psyche and the discovery that evil has

---

[3] Valéry is quoted by P. Roulin in Vol. 28 of the French magazine *Cahiers,* 1964, in "Paul Valéry, témoin et juge du monde moderne."

reached limits beyond which mankind may not go without self-immolation have all altered the data of the human condition. Man has reached that point for which the entire preceding existence of the universe and the prior history of man have been but one long period of preparation and maturation. Up to this point the forces of the universe, of man and of historical communities have been *dispersed,* although for romantic and sentimental reasons dispersion was called "freedom." From now on, the orientation of these forces will be toward *unification:* large political units, gradually approaching the World State; ideological consensus resulting in a universal secular religion organized around and in the name of mankind's almightiness; and a growing cosmic consciousness whose objective cannot as yet be defined, but toward which men must passionately concentrate their efforts, since it is the very essence of evolution.

In all this it is easy to recognize the traditional tenets of utopianism as described in preceding chapters. Illustrative of this is Teilhard de Chardin's 1948 view (*Trois choses que je vois*) that before the Christ could appear on earth it was necessary that, in conformity with the general processes of evolution, human kind could be anatomically constituted and socially advanced to a certain point of collective consciousness. Granted this, he said, why not take one more step and imagine that, for the second and last coming, Christ is waiting for a new mankind—a collectivity so fully developed in its potentialities that it should be capable of receiving from Him the supernatural consummation?

It could, of course, also be argued that for the arrival of Julius Caesar (or of Pericles, Alexander the Great or Aristotle) it was necessary for the human race to exist anatomically and to possess political awareness; in other words, Teilhard's statement merely amounts to saying that for Christ to become man it was indispensable that human beings should exist in the first place. Teilhard's first sentence is a redundancy, and his second is pure imagination. Yet, to utopians, the Teilhardian statement has not only the value of something better than a fact, but it serves also as a guarantee that the historical events which they are witnessing have a deeper meaning which is clear only to them as members of a new dispensation, of a new race. They persuade themselves that they are the participators in the final mutation, not merely anatomical, but intellectual, moral and spiritual as well. In the framework of the Teilhardian vision, the present is simple to understand since it is regarded as already past; it is known in retrospect, from the point of view and with the knowledge of someone who is reading the last chapters of evolution.

Illusion of Diffused Power

Confidence in man's growing and improving faculties and virtues is confidence simultaneously in such contemporary political and social formations as seem to conform with mankind's supposed evolution and seem to promote its goals. As a consequence, although the anarchistic element remains at the core of utopianism, nonetheless the revolutionary and/or welfare State and its institutions are clearly glorified. And the reason is this: the political formations which emerged from the revolutions of the past several decades are not considered political, but, says the utopian, transitional to a new associative organization of mankind. This amounts to a complete re-evaluation of the idea of the State. The nineteenth-century Liberals distrusted its accumulation of power and sought to secure for the individual citizen every sort of safeguard against State encroachments on his rights. Today, under the utopian impact, those who still call themselves Liberals would grant colossal powers to the State, and even to a Super-State with authority over the entire planet. What has happened in the meantime is that there has been apparent headway toward the utopian ideal of the association of equal citizens living in a classless and stateless society: the State no longer appears frightening because, in the welfare States of the

West, power seems to be distributed ever more evenly, while, in Communist countries, power seems to be held and controlled by the workers, that is, by every citizen.[4]

From a feared and distrusted Leviathan the State has suddenly become a performer of miracles, a distributor of benefits, an equalizer of the human condition. According to the crude arithmetic of the collectivist, the amount of satisfaction given to the poor through welfare legislation exceeds the amount of discontent of the rich from whom the corresponding sum is taken away. This is the rock-bottom justification of the welfare State. In the eyes of philosophically subtle utopians, the New State or the New Society is virtuous because it prefigures the final unity of mankind awaiting its next cosmic-divine adventure. Monistic thinking is unmistakable in all this. Writes Prof. Talmon:

> The Messianic trends [of the nineteenth century] considered Christianity as an arch-enemy. Their own message of salvation was utterly incompatible with the basic Christian doctrine, that of original sin, with its vision of history as the story of the Fall, and its denial of man's power to attain salvation by his own exertions. The dichotomies of soul and body, etc., stood condemned before the majesty of the oneness of Life and oneness of History, and the vision of a just and harmonious society at the end of the days.[5]

---

[4] In the free world's welfare or semi-welfare States the impression of evenly distributed power is created by progressive taxation and other equalizing fiscal measures: everybody is taxed for everybody else's benefit. In Communist countries power and financial benefits are very unequally distributed, but the State does not permit the questioning of official ideology of the "worker state." Yet "before as well as after the revolution there are distinct social groups; the problem is to know in whose favor does the ruling minority work." Raymond Aron, *La Lutte de classes*, Collection *Idées*, Gallimard, Paris, 1964, p. 110.

[5] *Political Messianism*, Frederick A. Praeger, Publishers, New York, 1960, pp. 25–26.

Illusion of Growing Moral Consciousness

Contemporary statolatry, then, is the expression of utopian man's confidence that the world is converging toward larger units of total and beneficial power. Thus our integration with the State and society and the world community does not appear as a frightening process, but, first, a natural, and, secondly, a desirable one. In the eyes of some, State power still appears as a questionable good; they are worried by images of future society as painted by George Orwell and Aldous Huxley. But they are reassured when told that a simultaneously growing moral consciousness and democratization will dispel the danger. If we willingly immerse ourselves in the stream of the evolutionary process and grow with it, then our collective destiny will coincide with our individual aspirations. It is never made clear how this will happen, how one can eat his cake and have it. Teilhard quite brutally admits that our freedom may be considerably curtailed if his dreams come true:

A convergent world, whatever sacrifice of freedom it may seem to demand of us, is the only one which can preserve the dignity and the aspirations of the living being. Therefore *it must be true* [Teilhard's emphasis]. If we are to avoid total anarchy, the source and the sign of universal death, we can do no other than plunge resolutely forward, even though something in us perish, into the melting pot of socialization.[6]

The utopian Teilhard blows hot and cold. On the one hand, he declares that man has achieved a high degree of spiritual maturity, and because he has come into full possession of his sphere of action, his strength, his maturity and unity, he will at last have become an adult being. On the other hand, Teilhard declares that these new and more complete human beings must give up their freedom and

---

[6] *The Future of Man,* Harper & Row, New York, 1964, p. 52.

purposefully bring to life a common soul in the vast body of coalesced world society. He even resorts to threats against those "who do not believe in progress":

> Despite the compressive and unifying conditions to which we are subject, Mankind is still made up of terribly heterogeneous parts, unequally matured, whose democratization can be effected only with the use of imagination and suppleness.[7]

Like other utopians, Fr. Teilhard creates an artificial separation between two imaginary categories of men. He does not call them "pure" and "impure" or by any of the labels used in Gnostic, Manichean and Marxist literature; he calls them "those who believe in progress" and "those who do not."

> The profound cleavage in every kind of social group (families, countries, professions, creeds) which during the past century has become manifest in the form of two increasingly distinct and irreconcilable human types, those who believe in progress and those who do not—what does this portend except the separation and birth of a new stratum in the biosphere?[8]

There is nothing new in invoking some authority whether it be God, history, evolution or science, in order to separate mankind into "good" and "evil." "Progress" and "anti-progress" are not even new categories, and Fr. Teilhard's contribution to contemporary evolutionary utopianism is merely the addition of some holy water, or, rather, of some undefinable and intangible substance which he variously calls "consummated human Thought," "social concentration," "synthetic organization" or simply " a passionate longing to grow and to be." In all this, the essential thing for the utopian is that "enforced coalescence" (another Teilhardian term) is expected

7 *Ibid.*, p. 243.
8 *Ibid.*, p. 117.

to produce the benefits for which no price is high enough: permanent peace, universal consensus, and everlasting happiness. What has been so far outlined in this chapter is the theoretical basis of contemporary utopianism. We have remarked that due to the emergence and ubiquity of technical instruments and of the communications network covering the globe, ideas spread quickly, although superficially, to virtually all people. As a result, utopian notions and ideals enjoy a greater popularity and have a larger following than in other ages. Due to the enthusiasm of utopian proponents, the impression is created that we are on the threshold of the Golden Age. This is not pictured as Fr. Teilhard's Noosphere, but, as with all popular and popularized notions, as an answer to various contemporary preoccupations.

Abolition of War

The abolition of war and the establishment of a world government are the two main themes of contemporary utopianism. These objectives are as old as utopian thought itself. As noted earlier, new elements are technology and the sense of urgency created by global wars and the atomic bomb. To large segments of the population we are living now in the time of the Grand Option (Teilhard's term) and they are convinced that what is *good* today is already the sign of the Grand Option, whereas what is *bad* is the sign of an imperfect groping for correct solutions. This is why so many regard enslavement of individuals and whole countries by communism and other horrors as merely temporary misfortunes which are ultimately in the general line of evolution.

Utopian approaches to the abolition of war are various and contradictory, except that all agree on man's natural goodness and consider wars as the consequence of conspiracy (by politicians, the military, ammunition manufacturers), misunderstanding, lack of the right kind of education, and so on. In his *Travel in the Moon*, Cyrano de Bergerac resorted to ridiculing war (as did Rabelais and

Swift); he declared that all victory is unjust because it is the fruit of chance. In order to diminish the role of chance, the Selenians arranged their battlelines so that cripples opposed cripples, giants opposed giants and weaklings opposed weaklings. After battle, they counted the dead, the wounded, and the prisoners; if the numbers balanced each other, they cast lots to determine the victor. In *The Coming Race* (1871) Bulwer-Lytton writes that since each citizen possesses the"vril" (a form of energy), the possibility of mutual annihilation eliminates warfare.

In the face of a universal holocaust today, there are those who would avert it through equalization of atomic power and those who see universal disarmament as the only answer. No matter which of the two positions prevail, they say, peace can be preserved only by a supranational agency, ultimately a world government.[9] Disarmament, then, would serve as merely the first phase toward the permanent utopian objective of universal harmony. Contemporary utopian hope lies also in the belief that space exploration will soon divert mankind's attention from terrestrial rivalries and warfare and unite its members for spatial and interplanetary exploits. Viewed from outer space, the earth will appear as a little province of the universe, and all men living there as compatriots. The notion that men will merely carry their competitive spirit into space (as European explorers carried their dissensions to the four corners of the globe) is given no thought at all.

Planetary Unity

The real driving force of contemporary utopianism remains, then, the search for planetary unity of which both space travels and the

---

[9] "We believe in a League system in which the whole world should be ranged against an aggressor. If it is shown that someone is proposing to break the peace, let us bring the whole world opinion against her. . . . We do not think that you can deal with national armaments by piling up national armaments in other countries." From Clement Attlee's speech, March 11, 1935.

Teilhardian Noosphere are projected images as well as guarantees in the philosophical and technological order.[10] However, the very idea of planetary unity assumes the existence of a new and mature mankind which is capable of transcending all evils which used to mark old mankind. This "new man" derives not from religious turmoil, as had the "pure" among the medieval heretics, but from political turmoil. Although this turmoil is often identified with the French Revolution, it is more usually referred to as the "revolutions of our time" whose events extend from 1789 right up to the present. In this sense we may speak of a "revolutionary spirit" sweeping over the globe and feeding the enthusiasm of utopians. In this sense, too, Jean de Fabrègues uses the term when he denounces those who believe that the Revolution will solve all problems, not only in the political-economic sphere, but also in the private domain of morality and sex.[11]

Boredom, Alexander Kojève points out, is not the least threat to the private life of the integrated, complete man of Utopia, and the same may be said of his public life—if one is permitted to distinguish between private and public life in Utopia—when all progress has come to a standstill.[12] Talk of this sort in no way discourages the utopian since he is irresistibly attracted by a total vision, not its details. As Jacques Maritain remarks in his *Meaning of Contemporary Atheism,* the Messianic myth of "the Revolution"

[10] In the August 27, 1963, issue of the French newspaper, *Le Monde,* appears a letter from M. Alfred Nahon, prominent in various peace movements and disarmament proposals. Among other things, Nahon wrote: "Mankind's survival will not be guaranteed until material and moral disarmament will not be the responsibility of a world authority. . . . The era of national defense is gone forever; the defense of global mankind has begun. . . ." (Translation mine.)

[11] Cf. *La Revolte ou la foi,* Desclée et Cie., Tournai, Belgium, 1957, p. 64.

[12] In an interview in *Le Figaro* (Aug. 24, 1963), the Israeli writer, Maurice Politi, made some interesting comments about life and mentality in a kibbutz. He speaks of the utopian organization and regulated, eventless existence: "same people, same problems, same conversations: boredom. This freely accepted work is harder and more implacable than the most tyrannical military service. . . . In a kibbutz everybody is obligatorily happy."

is so absolutistic in its quasi-religious demands that it inhibits genuine reform movements of a truly progressive character, the kind which will have to continue until the end of human history. The Messianic myth is of the very essence of contemporary utopianism in both halves of the present world, one half under regimes which are nominally utopian, the other half strongly, but far from exclusively, influenced by utopian thought. Despite the fact that the ideologies of the two halves are apparently in conflict, still a common utopian foundation is found in both, even though, for various reasons, the explicit formulations of both ideologies contain mutually irreconcilable elements. Underlying both systems is the modern concept of democracy based on a practically limitless middle class. As Tocqueville predicted, the largest number of people in these societies constitute "middle-income groups" with relatively few very rich and very few poor on the fringes. This does not mean that the members of this amorphous middle class do not engage in tumultuous and passionate public debates; they do, as a matter of fact, but without revolutionary fervor. These differences of opinion become increasingly superficial, and they are of concern only to certain intellectual circles which hate to witness "the end of ideologies." Yet, this milieu is eminently favorable to totalitarian tendencies and to theories about the oneness of society. Fr. John Courtney Murray identifies its chief impelling force with the ancient monistic drive: "The proposition is," he writes, "that all issues of human life—intellectual, religious, moral—are . . . to be settled by the single omnicompetent political technique of majority vote."[13]

Western and Eastern Types of Utopianism: Convergence

The movement toward utopia in the Western world has several hurdles to clear before it may find its unadulterated expression.

[13] *We Hold These Truths*, Sheed and Ward, New York, 1960, p. 208.

Traditional humanism, based on Christian and individualistic values, and the whole history of the Western world, based on free effort and enterprise, inhibit the advocates of utopia. They must explain, among other things, why collectivization should be a final objective rather than a purely temporary expedient; they must explain why power, traditionally considered a temptation and feared as such, is a good thing when concentrated, in both spiritual and temporal forms, in the hands of ideologues. In the face of such questions, the Western utopian remains rather vague when he discusses the future and prepares utopian programs. He preaches "democracy," "consensus," "socialism," "world peace," "arbitration" and a number of other high-sounding platitudes, and he regularly concludes that what the world needs is "moral regeneration." Unless he is a member of the Communist party and, therefore, outside the spiritual milieu of the West, the Western utopian prefers to address himself to planetary—and thus blurred—issues where a certain amount of intellectual irresponsibility is not only not frowned upon, but is even *de rigueur*. Thus, Salvador de Madariaga, in his desire to see the West strengthened in its struggle with communism, would establish centralizing agencies within each country and would also link all countries together with stronger bonds. He proposes that each country have a "permanent commission to watch over the working of political institutions." In the international sphere he wants a "commission to centralize, supervise and, if need be, cut off all trade with communistic countries." In addition, Madariaga recommends a bank whose resources would be the surplus capital of its member nations. The money would be used for investment abroad so that nations in need of capital could borrow without compromising themselves. The bank would also make air travel an international effort, would form a panel of technicians available to free-world countries, and "act as a regulator of all free operations in which capital and labor would not belong to the same flag." Furthermore, the "free nations . . . might try to integrate their sovereign wills; to set up adequate institutions in order to safeguard against the breaking of the peace by unruly wills; and to administer current affairs . . . to forestall conflicts. They might pool research, general staff, manufacture of armaments and organization."[14]

Madariaga, although a distinguished Liberal, shows himself as an unreserved enthusiast for integrating and organizing all aspects of life. Not a socialist economist like Beveridge or Galbraith, nor a socialist philosopher like Bertrand Russell, George Bernard Shaw or H. G. Wells, nor a socialist political scientist like Harold Lasky, yet Madariaga would probably say in self-defense that the gigantic problems of our times leave him no other alternative to propose. The complete about-face by the Liberal in the matter of State functions and powers of the State is reflected in Madariaga, the liberal intellectual who adopts with typical ease, almost automatically, the utopian stance even as he combats utopianism and the utopian regime of communism.

Communist ideologues in Communist countries naturally have none of the dilemmas and inhibitions of Western utopians. Officially, at least, all traditions—Christian, humanistic, and individualistic—have been abolished; history itself has been rewritten so that reference to the old traditional systems would be both dangerous and "unscientific." Nor does the Communist ideologue speak as frequently as one might suppose of the universal State and planetary consensus, so dear to the Western utopian. Although the Communist's utopianism is equally as unrealistic as that of the Western brand, it is, at the same time, less diffuse. Its goal is the definitive establishment of the truly communistic society within the framework of the National State. Further than that the Communist utopian does not think or, more probably, does not dare think lest he be accused by his hierarchic superiors of "left-deviationist internationalism." He concentrates, therefore, with spontaneous or

[14] All quotations have been taken from *The Blowing Up of the Parthenon,* Frederick A. Praeger, Publishers, New York, 1960.

imposed enthusiasm on the building of the utopian Communist society. At the Twenty-second Congress of the Russian Communist Party, the second chapter of the Party program bore the eloquent title of "Communism, Shining Future of All Mankind." It offered this definition of communism: "Communism is a special regime without classes, where only the nation owns the means of production and where all members of society are equal. In addition to the general development of all people, the forces of production also grow as a result of the constant progress of science and technology. Collective riches abound, and this great principle materializes: from each according to his abilities and to each according to his needs."

In the light of what we know about the stagnation of Communist economies and about the misery and servitude of the people in Communist countries, this stated definition of communism appears to be utopian indeed. We are not preoccupied here, however, with Communist realizations so much as with promises based on utopian fantasmagorias. In the Soviet magazine, *Novy Mir* (July, 1960) the economist Strumilin, member of the Academy, published a study of the "communes" of the future where all men will be happy. He begins his article by noting that those who wrote on the subject, a century and more ago, were utopians, whereas today the scientific study of general conditions permits a reasonable forecast of the future. Strumilin then speaks of "unlimited abundance" within the self-managed associations, themselves federated on the basis of "democratic centralism."[15] Material provisions for the communes are described in the finest traditional utopian style. Strumilin proposes a housing project for about 2,500 tenants. The people live

[15] The author remarks, as had Lenin, that before Soviet men win the noble reward of living in communes, they must first deserve it by "working without compensation for the general interest of society." But, he continues, "not even today or tomorrow" can we hope to see communes springing up in the country: another waiting period of about twenty-five years is necessary. In the meantime a new generation will grow up which will have lost the sense of personal property.

in three-story buildings. On the ground floor, stores and services are located; on the first floor, children and old people; on the second, households of two or three rooms; on the third floor, unmarried people. The plant where these tenants work will be nearby. The entire complex will not be too large. From the center to the peripheries will be only a ten-minute walk. Therefore, there will be no cars, buses, tramways, subways, not even elevators in the buildings. Accidents in this way will be eliminated, notes the grave Academician.

The commune, Strumilin goes on, will be a place of joyful living. Its members will even be allowed to eat their meals at home rather than in communal dining halls. Every facility for acquiring culture will be at their disposal.

What are the men of the truly communistic society like? Their chief characteristics are a completely secularized morality and the reconciliation, in their person, of all the "contradictions" that have plagued unenlightened, unemancipated man. In the Soviet Union officials constantly stress the similarity of their concept with the American concept of the separation of Church and State. It makes utopian sense to make religion-less man the first objective, because such a man is more easily manipulated. Religion must be extirpated not only because the churches are considered inimical, but also because any kind of spiritual authority outside the Party contradicts the fundamental *monism* of utopians, Communist or otherwise. Man's total allegiance must be indivisible, they argue, everything must flow from and be directed toward the Collectivity. When the Church, the most prominent source of division, is eliminated, then will man coincide with himself because he has resolved the traditional tension between manual and intellectual activity, between town and countryside, between individual and collective interests, and so on. Communists must achieve the independence of their socialist secularization program, urges M. Kozakiewicz in the Polish magazine, *Nova Kultura* (1960), and the elimination of Church influence is the first step. Once that has been done, the people's thoughts and attitudes can be developed along rationalistic lines so that the new morality will be based not on Revelation, but on the knowledge of the necessities and the mechanism of social life.

Coalesced Mankind

This question arises: Can man survive as man, that is, an individual with a conscience, when he is deprived of God and of extra-social spiritual authority? If only matter and its evolutionary forms exist, then man, too, is only matter, however complex and superior to other forms he may be. If he is not a reflection of the divine being, then he is in no sense sacred and final, and new forms of evolution may supersede him. In recognition of this, the search for such new forms has always been the ultimate quest of utopians. However, both Western and the Communist utopians have concluded their search and have found the same solution. Whether explained through Teilhard de Chardin or the Russian and Chinese communists, the solution is this: Man as we have known him is now being overcome by the new evolutionary form. This is not a new species, but *coalesced mankind*. At present we know it only as the collectivized man, still in individual units; but by further collectivizing these units, we merely activate and possibly accelerate the outcome, itself a historical, biological and perhaps cosmic necessity.

Both Teilhard de Chardin and the Communists speak of an indefinite evolution; one speaks of new extensions of the Noosphere; the others speak of an ever more radiant happiness for mankind. Yet, the imagination of the one and the efforts of the others go only as far as "totalized" or totalitarian society; everything else is figure of style or outright fuzziness. Despiritualized man, living in total society, is regarded as but one unit of the working force, relatively valueless in himself. Commenting on life in Communist China, Lucien Bodard observes that a man has no meaning except as a particle of the collectivity, which is the only reality in the universe. The individual man is conceived only as part of the mass, as a working unit in the service of production, an almost total zero.[16]

16 Cf. *La Chine du cauchemar*, Gallimard, Paris, 1961, p. 276.

CONCLUSION

AT THE end of a book devoted to criticism of the utopian pattern of thought, it is advisable to put the whole problem of utopianism once more into perspective. Two questions must be answered: Is utopianism both irrational and immoral? What place does utopianism occupy in the total economy of human thinking?

It is important to qualify our condemnation of utopianism if only because utopian thinkers have always accused the realists of being satisfied with "things as they are," of being retrogrades, of actually blocking progress by excluding the possibility of change, particularly of radical change. In our own age, when Marxism and Freudianism have a virtual monopoly on formulating criteria for judging people and events, the utopian suspects that his opponent's arguments either represent economic interests in disguise or they stem from subconscious resistance to change and novelty, or both.

Utopianism, a Permanent Thought-Pattern

We refuse to fall into the trap of reversing the utopian charges. Our position is that utopian thinking is not determined by class interests or by subconscious motivations. Intelligent discussion must

225

assume rational criteria on both sides. To call into question the rationality or motivation of the utopian would serve to render our own position futile, gratuitous and ultimately irrational. Our position throughout has been that utopianism is one view of the world shared by many people, a view which, in all likelihood, has been as steadfastly held as other trends and doctrines in the history of mankind. The fact that utopianism has appeared in every point of time and place and has reflected real events in the language of the time and place shows that the utopians are neither erring children nor are they moved by malice. In short, we may say that the clouds of utopianism will never be definitively dispersed by even the brightest sunrays of realistic thinking; by the same token, we may say also that utopianism will never gain absolute dominance. Realism and utopianism are two different ways of appraising the human condition, and they will remain in conflict until the end of time.

Does this mean that utopianism and realism have equal validity, that, as they say in academic circles, they are mere "value-judgments," neither of which may claim the privilege of being true? No. On the contrary, we think that utopianism has been shown to be not only wrong in the light of rational arguments and by the experience of life, but that it is also a demonstrably moral evil. Yet, just as erroneous judgments and evil actions cannot be eliminated from this forever imperfect world, so utopianism will always be with us as a type of human thought which must be relentlessly opposed.

Hopefully, the preceding pages have made clear that utopianism is based on errors of judgment. But why call it evil? After all, in the popular mind the utopian is regarded as an idealist who is dissatisfied with conditions in this Valley of Tears and wants to overcome the powers that be and to bring happiness on earth. Viewed in this light, the utopian is a poet, a prophet, a benefactor of the human race, the very salt of the earth.

Immorality of Utopianism

The facts in the case are otherwise. At utopia's roots there is defiance of God, pride unlimited, a yearning for enormous power and the assumption of divine attributes with a view to manipulating and shaping mankind's fate. The utopian is not content with pressing men into a mould of his own manufacture; he is not a mere despot, dictator or totalitarian leader holding all temporal and spiritual power. His real vice is, first, the desire to dismantle human individuality through the dissolution of individual conscience and consciousness, and then to replace these with the collectivity and coalesced consciousness. In a raving moment, the story goes, Caligula wished that mankind had only one head so that he might chop it off with one blow. So, too, the utopian: he wants to deal with one entity so as to simplify his own task of transforming indomitable human nature into a slave.

What the utopian conceives of as the future, fabulous as it may seem, is, in reality, a nightmare. It could not be otherwise because the utopian, in his speculation, ignores human nature, the rhythm of change, the fact that change involves not only gain but loss as well, the reality of time and the essential freedom of the soul. It is noteworthy that while, at least in the world-view of our western religions, Almighty God created man with a free will, the utopian makes the human condition so rigid that freedom is excluded from utopia. He replaces the concept of divine providence with unchangeable determinism. Yet even this does not deter him from displaying an astonishing degree of irresponsibility. Granted the man's enormous popularity, even his cult, in various circles, to this writer, at least, the frivolousness of Chardin as he juggles with "mankind," "socialization" and "millions of years" is a frightening spectacle. For example, when Teilhard wonders to what enormous distance will men find themselves transported several hundreds of million years from now if they continue in the socialization process to move toward greater consciousness, this writer can only plead baffled. No doubt, Teilhard would reply that the world is expanding in every direction and that the impossible may happen at the next turn. "How do you know it will not?" he would finally ask.

The absurdity of Teilhard's position here becomes even more evident when compared with the similar, but not utopian, views of Henri Bergson to whom Teilhard's disciples like to refer in quest of philosophical kinship for their idol. Philosophy (and science) is expected to give a satisfactory account of our experiences and observations, and this is precisely what Bergson does when he states that mankind is the supreme species, not because the *élan vital* has exhausted itself by bringing it forth, but because the *élan vital* finds in mankind the future stage of its further creative activity. No more species are to be created, Bergson argues, because in mankind the creative power continues through the channel of individuals. Like Teilhard, Bergson believed in evolution; in Bergson's view, however, not mankind but the creative individual is evolution's summit. It is through the individual, he held, that *élan vital* continues to manifest its thirst for creation.[1]

Nightmarish Re-shaping of Life

The utopian needs the Teilhardian imaginary perspectives—exaggerated beyond all realism and recognition—in order to create a framework for his absurd and grotesque prophecies. His prophecies, however, are not the product of purely arbitrary imagination, but proceed from the twofold supposition that man is a divine entity of infinite power and possibilities, and that paradise alone is worthy of him. It is a serious mistake to think that utopian liter-

[1] Cf. H. Gouhier, *Bergson et le Christ des Evangiles*, A. Fayard, Paris, 1961, p. 106.

ature is nothing more dangerous than scaling the heights of lyricism, for the cold fact is that there lurks behind each passage a terrifyingly inhuman situation in which naked force is combined with the most subtle indoctrination techniques. In such cases, utopia is revealed not as "a place which is not," but as a place of desolation and death. Here are some examples:

Writes Theodor Hertzka in *Freeland*:[2]

The departments of justice, police, military and finance, which in other countries swallow up nine-tenths of the total budget, cost nothing in Freeland. We had no judges, no police organization, our taxes flowed in spontaneously, and soldiers we know not. Yet, there was no theft, no robbery, no murders among us. As to the lack of a magistracy we did not even consider a civil or a criminal code necessary. The committee contented itself with laying all its measures before public meetings and asking for the assent of the members, which was unanimously given.

Writes Chauncey Thomas in *The Crystal Button*:[3]

Money-making is no longer the chief goal of effort, and hence many unworthy ambitions have been stifled. Places of power and trust are now filled by strong and trustworthy men; the path to all high places is such that none other can attain them.

Writes Cabet in *Icaria*:[4]

"You see," said Dinaros, "that with a single stroke, communalism suppresses and prevents thefts and thieves, crimes

[2] *The Quest for Utopia*, edited by Negley and Patrick, Doubleday & Co., Inc., Garden City, New York, 1962.
[3] *Ibid.*
[4] *Ibid.*

and criminals, so that we no longer need courts or prisons or punishments."

Writes Trotsky in *Literature and Revolution*:[5]

> In a society which will have thrown off the pinching and stultifying worry about one's daily bread, in which community restaurants will prepare good, wholesome and tasteful food for all to choose, in which communal laundries will wash clean everyone's good linen, in which children, all the children, will be well fed and strong and gay, and in which they will absorb the fundamental elements of science and art as they absorb albumen and air and the warmth of the sun, in a society in which electricity and the radio will not be the crafts they are today, but will come from inexhaustible sources of super-power at the call of a central button, in which there will be no "useless mouths," in which the liberated egotism of man—a mighty force—will be directed wholly towards the understanding, the transformation and the betterment of the universe—in such a society the dynamic development of culture will be incomparable with anything that went on in the past.

Human life, as pictured in the foregoing accounts, is out of focus, out of existential context, wholly unrecognizable. When the utopian writers deal with work, health, leisure, life expectancy, war, crimes, culture, administration, finance, judges and so on, it is as if their words were uttered by an automaton with no conception of real life. The reader has the uncomfortable feeling of walking in a dreamland of abstractions, surrounded by lifeless objects; he manages to identify them in a vague way, but, on closer inspection, he sees that they do not really conform to anything familiar in shape, color, volume or sound.

5 Published by Russell & Russell, New York (no date given).

Mechanization of Change

Finally, there is the question of freedom and choice. The utopian poses as a seer when he speaks confidently of the radical change which will restore mankind to its true dignity and of the future which will be incommensurable with the past. The evolutionary utopian even proclaims a doctrine of change which teaches that man must keep in permanent readiness and immerse himself in a climate of perpetual revolution. Such evolutionary doctrines, whether of Marx or of Teilhard, obviously preach not freedom, openness and progress, but a frozen rigidity both as to the desirable ideal and the mechanism of adaptation which leads to it. The truly frightening aspect of utopia is that there is nothing beyond it, for in utopia mankind comes to a halt, its every desire satisfied, its every instinct domesticated, its every ambition collectivized; there is neither attempt nor aspiration to think any longer, to explore new possibilities, to articulate grievances as a new starting point toward something uncharted. Utopia, then, becomes sudden immobilization, the final *congelation* of humanity at an arbitrarily chosen moment.

In such a future as this, the utopian sees the end of the horror of history, and human freedom which creates unforeseen situations will be but a vestige of an unhappy past because now man will live according to a blueprint. The unforeseeable is impossible in utopia, and its planners' deadly serious work may be fearlessly pursued. Today's utopian not ony determines the objectives of future ages, but he works on the assumption that the mechanism of change, between now and then, will conform to his present conception of it and bring his prefabricated future into reality.

Prediction and Utopia: A Distinction

The second question asked at the beginning of this chapter is this: What place does utopianism occupy in the total economy of human thought?

Utopian literature and utopianism must, first of all, be clearly distinguished. Obviously, utopian literature is the broader category and includes utopianism. It must be immediately conceded that many utopian writers offer realistic analysis and solutions to certain human problems because their speculation is based upon concrete contemporary conditions. More often than not, such portions of utopian literature deal with technical or organizational matters, and the writers clearly expose both imperfect techniques and inefficient social organizations of their own time. In many instances, utopian writers have constructively influenced later developments. Negley and Patrick, editors of *The Quest for Utopia*, are perfectly right when they point out, in speaking of nineteenth-century utopians, that "in a period of almost unrestrained individualism . . . utopists were anticipating the welfare state, the nationalization of industries, socialized medicine and health programs, unemployment insurance, old-age pensions . . . fantastically radical then, but which in 1950 have become a part of everyman's political vocabulary" (p. 15).

The range of utopian "inventions" is impressive. Thomas More spoke of artificial brooding-hens, Bacon described the benefits derived by the people of Benzalem from the use of synthetic materials and from canned food. Both Campanella and Cyrano foresaw the current preoccupation with an orderly and balanced diet. In the *City of the Sun* a physician supervised the food supply, while among the Selenians a specialist in physiognomy determined from the patient's complexion whether his meals were healthful or not. The versatile Cyrano also described a State-sponsored system of family allowances whereby, the moment a child is born, a yearly sum is provided from the State treasury for the child's education. The Selenians also built transportable homes which were manufactured from light wood and placed on wheels, so that the owners could choose between settling in a pleasant valley or on the shores of a lake. And—the ultimate refinement!—the indolent Selenians substituted phonograph records for printed books.

Although Saint-Simon wrote no utopian work as such, he was the father, or at least the imaginative formulator, of modern ideas of social and industrial organization. More than a hundred years before James Burnham, Saint-Simon had demanded supreme political power for the party of industrialists and scientists because he foresaw legislation which would be detrimental to private ownership and favorable to centralization of economic activity in the hands of industry's barons.

Robert Owen, the British social reformer, urged a plan to build small, meticulously planned cooperatives for about 1,200 members. Everything, down to the smallest detail, was to be scrupulously regulated—the size of the buildings, their shape and their arrangement. Central heating, collective eating places and dormitories for children, all included in Owen's plan, are twentieth-century realities. Some of his ideas have been incorporated in the kibbutzim of Israel, in the agrovilles so dear to former Premier Kruschchev of the Soviet Union and especially in various concepts of urbanization carried out in our days.

Cabet was another utopian who similarly sought to provide ease and comfort in a way that seemed fantastic to his contemporaries. Yet, today, some of his ideas are part of our everyday living. The apartment buildings in Icaria have mechanical load-carriers, washing machines, and various gadgets for helping women in their daily tasks; furniture angles have been rounded so that children will not be injured; flies and bedbugs have been eliminated; the women go to the hospital when childbirth approaches.

In one of his typically short dialogues, Max Stirner predicted the coming of the general strike, as did also Georges Sorel. On the matter of work and leisure, Marx makes the point that the division of labor is responsible for extreme and stultifying specialization. In his Communist society, however, the distinction disappears between intellectual and manual labor, and each individual can become accomplished in whatever branch he chooses; he can hunt in the morning, fish in the afternoon, rear cattle in the evening, and enjoy stimulating discussion after dinner. But much more sober is Kropotkin's diagnosis, for he wisely saw the answer to the work-leisure problem as the reduction of working hours and not the abolition of specialization without which industrial productivity would slow down. "When one has done in the field or the factory," he urged, "the work that he is under obligation to do for society, he can devote the other half of his day, his week or his year to the satisfaction of artistic or scientific wants."

Constant Elements in Utopian Thought

Literature in which realistic elements are found—predicted events which have later come to pass—may not be called utopian literature in the strict sense. Hence, it is premature to say that what now appears to be imagination-run wild can never materialize. But is it true that utopian literature is an imaginative literature, pregnant with possibilities and meant simply to stimulate speculation about individual social efficiency and happiness?

One effort throughout this book has been to show that utopianism is not merely a way of experimenting with social possibilities, as when a child arranges his tin soldiers in various formations. Utopianism is a system of thought, a philosophy with well established views of God, man, nature and community. The history of utopian thought in religious heresies, various Gnostic doctrines, Marxism, spiritual evolutionism and the like proves that utopianism is a perennial *type of thinking* as ineradicable as realistic philosophy itself. Recurrent though it is, expressions of utopianism have enjoyed an almost indefinite variety on the theme, although the variations follow an invariable pattern. "The logical operations of Intellect *qua* Reason," writes Eric Voegelin in "Debate and Existence," "will arrive at widely different results if Reason has been cut loose from the *conditio humana*." And variety is to be expected since all utopian speculations operate on the assumption that the "spirit" is sovereign as a source of knowledge and illumination. Irenæus, one of the Church fathers, remarked in his work against the heretics that each of them invent something new every day. Be this as it may, it is far more important to understand philosophical, ethical and historical motivations of utopianism.

Philosophical Motivation

Simply stated, the *philosophical motivation* of utopianism lies in the natural temptation of the mind as it faces the problem of existence, to consider the entire universe as one substance, diversified in space and time by various immanent forces—evolution for example—but nevertheless one substance, universal, self-creating and self-sufficient. God is acceptable to this monistic frame of mind only if God is not something outside of and superior to the universe, but one with it. The presence among men of impurity and evil, however, is a constant reminder to the monist (pantheist) that the world substance is not yet fully spiritualized and divinized. In order to bridge the contradiction between a divine universe and the existence of evil, evolution, or self-perfecting, must be added to the utopian's monism. Through evolution the world substance becomes progressively pure, homogeneous and perfect until the terminal point is reached: the spiritualized whole.

As the world approaches divinization, it must rid itself of all imperfect material. Although monism posits the existence of one substance only, it must nevertheless explain the slowness and difficulty of the self-perfecting process by admitting that the world substance is only *potentially* one. The impure element is gradually eliminated, or, rather, it becomes suffused with spirit. The principal effort of all utopians is directed, therefore, toward the dissociation of such *pure* (good) and *impure* (evil) elements interlocked in this imperfect world as soul and body, peace and war, unity and multiplicity, virtue and vice, progress and reaction, love and selfishness.[6]

The Historical Motivation

Utopianism's *historical motivation* was noted in our examination of the cyclical theory of history. Obvious in that theory and its modern adaptations was the utopian desire to deal only with the known and predictable, whether in the form of recurrent cycles which repeatedly bring with them the already familiar or in the form of a pre-established design for mankind. In either case, the incalculable individual element is reduced to a minimum: if the outcome is known, then this or that individual action, rooted in freedom, may be safely ignored as irrelevant. And, of course, it is also possible to penalize the individual agent for disturbing the only valid collective pattern. One may say about the utopian's general outlook on history what Eric Voegelin has observed concerning the Gnostic movements of our time, that they attempt to transform the uncertainties and ambiguities of the expression of existence into the certainty of one-dimensional intramundane experience.

Regarding the *ethical motivation* of utopianism, it helps to recall that ethics deals with the merits or demerits of human intentions and actions, that it is organically linked with man's freedom. Granted, man is far from possessing complete freedom; he lacks,

---

[6] On the contrary, as Jean Guitton writes, "the Church was never a party of the Pure. She sought not so much perfect purity as purification. She founded, in turn, institutions permitting the recovery of purity lost: confession, penitence, instruction . . ." Cf. Jean Guitton, *Le Christ écartelé*, Librairie Académique Perrin, Paris, 1963, p. 176.

therefore, full responsibility for his acts and even for his intentions. Aside from bodily, psychological and intellectual limitations, man is limited also in the realm of being. He is incapable of fully conceptualizing and grasping even his own finite existence, to say nothing of all the spheres opened up to him by his actions. And it is here precisely that the utopian falls into illusion and speaks of mankind rather than of individual men. He believes that by building a "system" and making it "permanent" he compensates for man's finiteness in time and space, for he feels that he has endowed the collectivity with the super-intelligence and super-morality necessarily lacking in individuals. But in this very process the utopian succeeds only in depriving the individual of his limited freedom and, therefore, of the value of his action.

Permanence of the Utopian Temptation

Behind all this there is obviously the burning ambition and explosive hopes of the zealot, and behind his ambition and hope is his conviction that only the pure have knowledge and that knowedge is power. It was precisely against such temptation that man was warned under the Tree of Life, but the utopian wants to restore the original purity, the knowledge and the power as an act of vengeance against that God who drove men from Paradise. The history of utopianism is the story of the Tower of Babel which all of mankind built to reach as high as heaven.

The temptation to which utopians succumb is as permanent as our imperfect condition rooted in orginal sin. One might even say that utopianism is the original temptation. Like every temptation, utopianism must be fought, but to believe that it will be overcome forever is of the very folly of utopianism itself. The unreasonable pessimism about the individual and the equally unreasonable optimism about the collectivity betray the utopian's contempt for creation, for the world and for nature as they are. The Gnostics expressed this contempt through an elaborate mythology in which Buddhist, Indian, Egyptian and Semitic elements were mixed with Greek and Judeo-Christian speculation. They taught that the real God is infinitely distant and did not participate in creation; creation was the work of the *demiurgos*, hence all the evil. The conclusion was unescapable that the original sin is not situated within creation, but that creation is itself the result of the pre-cosmic fall. Whose fall? By all evidence, the fall of God.

The restoration of knowedge and of universal purity is, therefore, the task of man who acquires, in Gnostic thought, a definitive superiority over God, not only over the creator-god (*demiurgos*), but over the God beyond the creator-god (*deus absconditus*). For it is man who possesses, in the depths of his psychic essence, the spark of knowledge which is lacking in God, having been relinquished by Him since the moment of creation. Knowledge has been dispersed, each individual possessing a particle of it. Only when all men act together may the restoration of divine plenitude be achieved; only then will the act of creation be reversed; only then will the Whole return to its original stillness. "Salvation," writes Hans Jonas,[7] "involves a process of gathering in, of re-collection of what has been dispersed, and salvation aims at the restoration of the original unity. This self-gathering is regarded as proceeding, *pari passu*, with the progress of knowledge, and its completion as a condition for the ultimate release from the world."

Utopian pessimism, then, has its basis in the utopian's hatred of the world as it is. Man can assert his mastery over nature only if he eliminates God as creator or, at least, discredits creation. In either case, God is pushed so far out of the universe that his relationship to man and his admonitions have no effectiveness.[8] The

---

[7] *The Gnostic Religion* (second edition), Beacon Press, Boston, 1958, pp. 59–60.

[8] The Archons (creators and gaolers of this world in the Gnostic doctrine) have the power to prevent souls seeking, after death, to reach God. Thus God's power in rescuing souls and saving them is denied.

second step is marked by man's liberation in order to remodel creation which, in its present form, is either totally evil or unnecessarily but gravely imperfect. So far the individual speculates and acts alone; he wills his own emancipation because he possesses a particle of divine or quasi-divine perfection. The third phase, however, is the coalescence of all individuals who must re-form the lost unity. Since this unity is again of divine character, it tolerates no inner division; indeed, it must be a cohesive thing *par excellence* both to suggest a flawless whole and to resume the act of new creation with infinite dynamism. A fourth phase, or, rather, a by-product of the third, is that man recreates God by restoring his lost unity and perfection. This is how we may explain the utopian insistence—at times whispered and implied, at other times loud and aggressive—that God will emerge with the establishment of a peaceful and harmonious human society.

Why do we say that this is a pessimistic thought-pattern? Does it not exalt man, raise his expectations, instil in him confidence to deal with nature and society with ever-increasing competence and vigor? Far from it, as has been shown throughout this book. It seems important, however, to add at this point that two sinister consequences will follow from any application of utopian thought.

The first is that man-become-creator manufactures an impersonal system because nature no longer stands by with its elasticity, advice and its recognizable and manageable forms. This "second nature," product of our power, cannot be an object of trust, only an object of conquest; and relationship with it cannot be stimulating competition, only grim determination to overwhelm it. We said in an earlier chapter that the contemporary utopian expects through technology and its baffling inventions to influence decisively the restructuring of mankind after he has proved technology's tremendous power of transforming the outside world and the conditions of life. But more than technology is involved in the "second creation"; the latter is placed under the sign of science because,

with the removal of God from utopian man's concern, only
science remains to reassure us, to protect us against its own
fantastic realizations, to fill an otherwise empty universe with the
noise of its agitation.

The second consequence is that the power system that man
develops as a result of his utopian aspirations will no longer have
divine sanctions; like the "new" nature, "new" society, too, will be
impersonal, without standards and codes rooted in a transcendent
yet benevolent universe. The latter will bear no resemblance to
the Greek cosmos, but to the Sartrian absurd, cold, and, at best,
indifferent spaces; similarly, society will be a network of naked
power in which perfected systems of self-defense grimly face other
systems of self-defense. In other words, our vision of the universe
inevitably influences our vision of society and, hence, our organization of society. If the universe is hostile to us, we conceive of
society, our little universe, as also hostile. Vain efforts are made
at present to reassure contemporary man about the benevolence
which the collectivity offers him. He is told that he can become,
with a little good will and enthusiasm, a world citizen in the
political sphere and a man with deep concern for all in the moral
sphere. Yet the truth is that the philosophical and spiritual foundations are lacking and trust is lost not only in the essential goodness
of creation, but also in creation itself. The individual who is
spiritually a non-participant cannot be but an aimlessly drifting
atom in the political realm. No wonder that utopia remains his
only shelter: but is utopia not a shelter for anonymous individuals,
for a lawless and sorry herd?

EPILOGUE

WHEN THIS BOOK was first published—in America; then French, Spanish, and Italian translations followed—many, not all, Catholic critics liked its joint treatment of utopian thought and heresy. The "secular" critics also praised this new light cast on the subject, and those who disagreed with the main thesis objected to my negative view of utopianism. In summary, they wrote: utopian thinking is an organic part of western man's projection of a future. It nourishes and widens political imagination.

True, but there are various modes of projection, some of them block the future in favor of a here-and-now terminal point, as it is argued on these pages. The future is essentially incalculable, utopia would be a *frozen present*, if ever carried out. The collapse of one utopian product is taking place before our eyes at the time I write this Epilogue. This collapse is the vindication of human nature which seems not to tolerate for too long—in the case of this century, two, three, or four generations—an artificial system, an ideological Procrustes bed, mutilating man's

241

earthly ambitions, intellectual curiosity, and sacred dimensions. It is the justification of our view of utopias, as well as a splendid historical irony that the masters of totalitarian empires miscalculated along the whole length of the ideological front: they believed that collectivistic slogans can be a substitute for bread (or rice), and that loyalty to nation and religious faith can be liquidated by propaganda and terror. Their original—utopian—error costs them their power, which in the given case is a greater sacrifice than life since life's meaning was for them power, an equal power to God's.

This book, however, evaluates the cost of other utopian illusions too. More exactly, of another ideology which has gained a great, if not exclusive prominence since the book was first published (1967). We may call it "technological ideology," although other labels come also easily to mind. Its origin and widest expansion are rooted in the western mentality, and its main danger is that the western world, in its self-bestowed purity, indeed its angelism, does not see itself as a fertile terrain for ideologies, that is for utopian systems. Thus the dogmas distilled by *technology* become the more aggressive as western man regards himself incapable of aggressiveness through the construction of utopian designs. Yet, perhaps since the astronauts went to the Moon and beyond, we have built a new Tower of Babel—now reaching to galactic heights—and have tried to remodel human aspirations in favor of mechanical solutions. I find some satisfaction in the fact that the chapter on "Theocracy" (pp. 177-203) is immediately followed by the (last) chapter centered on a discussion of "Technology" (pp. 207 and following). The juxtaposition becomes symbolic of the nature of the new utopianism in the sense that the technological hubris too elaborates a new theocracy: of Technocrats, World Bureaucrats, and other exalted Salesmen of Progress.[1] The frequent mention nowadays of the "end of ideologies" appears therefore to be false. One branch of the common utopian stem may indeed be withering, the ruthless tyranny of brutal gulagization; another has, however, survived, in fact it is strengthened by the rival's defeat. This book emphasized it but it bears a new emphasis: we deal, in the case of technology, with off-shoots of the same utopian temptation, the same revolt against God, whether of Lucifer, the Grand Inquisitor, Prometheus, Dr. Faustus—or the names and systems mentioned on the previous pages. The danger is greater because the latest off-shoot, *technological utopianism*, is believed to be ideologically neutral, sollicitous only for our material wellbeing and achievements, respectful of the inner man. Yet, by manipulating the object-world around us, by turning it into a mechanically functioning continuum, it achieves two of its implicit objectives. It reaches our inner being through the steadily accumulating and therefore obnoxious object world (goods, images, images of images and of objects) until the equilibrium is broken between nature and artifact: and through this monstrous accumulation it removes from our scope the sacredness of things, the areas of divine intervention.[2] In the end (western) man becomes an *object* and an *image*, increasingly artificial, uniform, homogenized, automatized, mass-produced. Both in his

---

[1] See my article, "Is Technology Ideological?" in *The Political Science Reviewer*, vol. XVIII, Fall 1988, pp. 285-304.

[2] See my *Twin Powers, Politics and the Sacred*, William B. Eerdmans Publishing Company, Grand Rapids, Mich., 1988.

self-evaluation and in the treatment he receives from the theocrats of technology. The goal of utopias is thereby reached: the evacuation of inner life, the dissolution of the soul.

Utopianism is a permanent temptation, whether the system is set up and operated by apparatchiks or by technocrats. In the last two decades the latter's impact grew steadily, perhaps because ideologies had prepared the terrain for the *transparent man* whose vacuousness no longer presents obstacles to the scrutinizers and the manipulators. In a way, man lives now outside himself, as if he were all in surfaces, with no gravitational center. He seems to be an extension of machines, his habitat, office, and leisure area have turned into one continuous technostructure. He likes to play at operating these machines; and does not notice that he has become their plaything, in truth their soulless accomplice.

INDEX OF NAMES